a passion for life

Real life stories about faith

D.J.Carswell

A Passion for Life

Published by 10Publishing, a division of 10ofthose.com

9D Centurion Court, Farington, Leyland, PR25 3UQ, England

Email: info@10ofthose.com Website: www.10ofthose.com

ISBN: 978-1-909611-33-7

Designed by Mike Thorpe / www.design-chapel.com

Printed and bound by CPI Group (UK) Ltd, Croydon, England, CR0 4YY

Acknowledgements

I am very grateful to friends and family for their encouragement, including Jeanette Thorn and Hannah Peace for their excellent secretarial help, and to my editor, Julia Hatherall.

Special thanks to Jonathan and Nick at 10Publishing, plus their incredible team, for their hard work, enthusiasm and dedication to God.

Finally, I would like to thank all the contributors for allowing their stories to be told; men and women who all have a passion for life.

Contents

Introduction

Passion for Life is a collection of biographies of people who have a passion not only for this life but also for the one to come, because of something that has happened to them. These people have allowed us a glimpse of their personal lives, often at things they are ashamed of, or personal grief or suffering, as well as their triumphs, accomplishments and happiness. Their backgrounds, race, age and education are completely different from each other. Sometimes questions of faith are asked in their lives:

Am I too bad for God?
Am I good enough?
Why is there suffering?
Do all roads lead to God?
Is there a God anyway?

Maybe you and I have also thought along these lines.

In each mini biography, though, you will discover hope and a passion for life now, and a certainty of abundant life ahead. You don't have to start at the beginning of the book – just dip in to whichever chapter you want and in any order.

In the last chapter we discover the 'nuts and bolts' of faith – this is not a list of dos and don'ts but an explanation of how much God loves us and what it cost Him in order for us to know a different life that will never end.

So settle back and turn the page ...

Vijay Menon

THE ENGINEER

It was the early morning of 21 August 1930. In one of the bedrooms of Kundavalappil House there was an air of barely suppressed excitement. One of a small group of women held a motionless body suspended from her arm. A couple of vigorous slaps to its rear galvanised the silent form into uttering protesting cries, which were answered by the loud squawking of a crow in a jackfruit tree outside the window. Yet one more human statistic had been added to India's teeming millions; Vijay Menon had arrived on planet earth.

If Vijay had been given the choice, he could hardly have chosen a more delightful spot in which to be born. Tourists and inhabitants alike describe Kerala as paradise. The coast consists of beautiful sandy beaches that are backed by blue lagoons interspersed with dunes, which in turn are dotted with coconut palms. His birthplace was about 15 miles inland. This idyllic rural locality was to be his home for only ten months. After this, unusually, he was brought up in his father's home in a nearby town while his mother remained at Puzhakkal. (The Indian tradition is that after a wedding the bride usually returns to her mother's home and the husband likewise to his mother's home, but he will visit his wife at night if his work is in that locality.)

Vijay was looked after by one of his father's sisters. The household consisted of his father, his sisters and nieces, several women servants and himself. Almost the entire family depended for their existence on his father's earnings. This was due to a brother-in-law dying and, as was the custom, his family taking his money, thereby leaving nothing for the wife and children. In consequence, Vijay's father had to work extremely hard, rising at 5 a.m. to go to work as a clerk, coming home later to catch a hasty meal and then going to another job until nine thirty at night. Although he was so busy, he always had time for morning and evening devotions in a special room that was kept as a shrine.

Almost the entire family depended for their existence on his father's earnings.

This was a Hindu family. The intensity of his father's beliefs and conduct undoubtedly had a great effect on Vijay's impressionable mind. Hinduism is really a compound of religion, philosophy and a highly specialised social system. Within it there is a tremendous variety of belief and conduct. Everything is continually evolving; even gods disappear only to be replaced by others. There is a constant state of flux. Westerners are often taken aback by just how many gods Hindus have – over 33,000, although there are three principle gods: Brahma, Vishnu and Siva. People may worship any god at all, and as many gods as they want.

Hinduism tends to be fatalistic: 'What will be, will be.' Their idea of salvation is vastly different from Christian beliefs. Salvation for the Hindu comes from contemplation and right thinking, and is achieved when the pinnacle of the mystic state is reached and the human soul is united with Brahman. Hindus believe that they can go a long way towards earning their salvation by strict performance of their religious duties. There is very little consciousness of personal sin against a holy god. As Vijay explains, 'The sweet reality of forgiveness forms no part of Hinduism. Its faith originates from within and depends on the devotees' ability to believe.' This is quite a contrast with Christianity!

Christianity teaches that it is totally impossible to earn salvation. There is nothing that unaided humanity can do about their sin. Men and women first have to realise the hopelessness of their position. Then God can do something for them. God, in Christ, entered the world in order to save the world. On the cross, where He was crucified, Jesus died in order to pay the penalty that was required for our sin. If we trust in the risen, living Jesus, we will be forgiven and brought to know God. While Krishna is said to come to destroy sinners, Jesus says, 'I come not to call the righteous but sinners to repentance.' Vijay knew nothing of this Christian teaching as yet, but an awareness of the Creator God was to be awakened gradually within his innermost being.

His father was anxious that he should start school as soon as possible. Vijay recalls that for the first four years he was an average pupil and that he did not learn as much as he ought, not because the subjects were beyond him but simply because he was lazy. Aged eight, he moved up to a Roman Catholic school whose headmaster ran a very strict establishment and was very free with corporal punishment.

This school was three miles away so Vijay had to walk, barefoot. He never wore any kind of shoes until he was 16 years old. Sometimes he used to wear a shirt and shorts, but often he wore the traditional 'lungi', which is a cloth-like towel some three yards long wrapped around the body.

Each day would begin at six o'clock with a bath or shower, then Vijay would go off to the temple for his devotions. Religion was as much a part of life as the washing that preceded it; indeed this personal cleansing was essentially a religious activity. On returning home Vijay would be given a cup of tea, which he says had a horrible taste but, because he was so hungry, he enjoyed. Then he did homework until nine o'clock. Breakfast always consisted of a little rice and curry, but that was all Vijay ate until he returned from school later in the day.

After school Vijay usually had a cup of tea and sometimes rice as well before studying more and then doing housework. At dusk the entire family would gather together for what they called 'puja' in the room set aside as a shrine. This was prayer performed in front of the image of a god. This was followed by the main meal of the day, rice and curry. After even more study Vijay was glad to get some well-earned sleep!

His childhood, though often serious and with very few toys, was a happy one.

His childhood, though often serious and with very few toys, was a happy one, despite not experiencing parental love and companionship as it is known in the West. His father worked so hard, to the point of exhaustion, to maintain his large extended family. His social and religious consciousness drove him to do much voluntary work. Yet there was not a closeness between father and son. Although a disciplinarian like Vijay's father, his mother did love him, but she did not see her son very often.

In later years, Vijay was able to take his school leaving exams two years early but he failed in English. How he bitterly regretted his laziness in formative years. He desperately wanted to go to university to study engineering but perhaps his ambition was not to be realised.

Up until that moment he was by tradition and family practice a Hindu, but Vijay was also very much aware of the evidence of a Creator in the world of nature. He could not help but believe in God. Now in his desperate need he prayed to that God, but this was an entirely different prayer to his normal prayers. It was the first time he turned to God in a personal way: 'Lord, help me through this situation. Lead and direct my life from now on and I promise I will follow you. I have made a mess of my life and I have failed. You are my only help now.'

'Lead and direct my life from now on and I promise I will follow you.'

A few weeks later he received news that Madras University was willing to offer him a place. Overjoyed, Vijay felt that this was an important turning point in his life. He knew the reality of God not only because of His works in creation but also because He had answered his prayer. Of course his understanding was still that of a Hindu, but looking back now Vijay feels that from that time God was gently guiding him to a personal faith in the God of the Bible.

A fascination with ships was to lead him to an apprenticeship and maritime career. Vijay eventually left India, working his way to England to be better qualified and to further his professional skills. Having done so, he intended to go back to India for a better job.

After ten years of maritime service, rising from Junior to Chief Engineer, he married Susheila, the daughter of his cousin. Having known her as a friend from his youth, he was fascinated by her charm and beauty. He knew that she was the one to be his wife. Sufficiently 'Westernised' by now to make his own request and not to wait for an 'arranged' marriage, he asked permission to marry her. Three days after his ship sailed into Bombay harbour, they were married, only to part the day after as he had to sail to New Zealand. The honeymoon was postponed to later in the year when she joined him on board his ship, which was now bound for England. The ensuing months were to prove a traumatic experience for his young bride. Arriving in England on a bitterly cold day in December, she found the climate almost unendurable.

Vijay had had three teenage ambitions: to marry a beautiful girl, to be a Lloyd's surveyor and to know God. Although by now he had his Chief Engineer's Certificate, he decided to move north to South Shields to study for his Extra Certificate. This would enable him to take up the prime job of Senior Engineer Surveyor with Lloyd's Register in London. Passing with just five marks short of winning the gold medal, Vijay applied for and subsequently took up this key job. All the long hours spent in 'burning the midnight oil', all the monotony of months passed in the hard grind of study and all the patient years of waiting now lay in the past. Accreditations came his way. He became a member of the British Nuclear Energy Society and the Royal Institute of Naval Architects; a Chartered Engineer; and also a fellow of the Institute of Marine Engineers.

Vijay had had three teenage ambitions: to marry a beautiful girl, to be a Lloyd's surveyor and to know God.

One day this highly qualified man found himself doing a spot of shopping during his lunch break. At one o'clock he happened to walk into Bishopsgate, right in the centre of the City of London. He retells what was to be the hinge that changed the whole direction of his life:

'To my surprise, I saw hundreds of city gents in their pinstripe suits all rushing through a cubbyhole at Great St Helen's. I followed them out of curiosity and landed up in a big packed hall with hundreds of men, some even sitting on the concrete steps. They ushered me in and all I could see in the corner was a big table with sandwiches, fruits, cakes and delicious food.

'So I sat down wedged between the city gents wondering 'What next?' Then I realised that I was in a church and I panicked! You wouldn't have seen me dead in a church; but I couldn't get out and had to sit down and suffer the next half an hour! Can you imagine over 500 people coming to a church in a space of just five minutes? There were managing directors, brokers, underwriters, bank managers, solicitors, accountants, clerks, engineers and others; predominately men but also some

women. Everyone had arrived to listen to a 20-minute talk from the Bible and then to eat lunch together.

'I sat down and heard for the first time that Jesus died not only for me but also for Hindus, Muslims, Buddhists, Sikhs, those who go to church and those who don't. Jesus died so that I may know God. All I had to do was to come to Him. The preacher, Revd Dick Lucas, went on to say that God had done everything necessary for anyone to find God today and know Him personally. It is not what I can do for God that is important but what God has done for me. According to the Word of God, the Bible, I could be assured of a place in heaven when I died and have eternal life if I turned to Jesus.'

In the course of a fairly short message something amazing happened to Vijay. He turned his thoughts towards Jesus and said, 'I'll have a try. I don't know any prayers, but you help me, God, and I'll try. I want to obey you. Please help me to belong to you.' Trying was his way of saying 'yes' to Jesus, which led him on to understand that it is by trusting that we have faith. So Vijay went back to his office and asked his Australian colleague how he could get a religious book to know all about Jesus. Vijay recalls:

> *'To my surprise I found out that he also went to St Helen's church every Tuesday. Although he had been sitting behind me at work for two years and had been secretly praying for me, he didn't have enough guts to ask me to go with him. But (after our conversation) he gave me a Bible with a bookmark in John's Gospel, advising me to read it from there. I am glad he did, because if I had started from the beginning in Genesis perhaps I would have soon given up.'*

From then on Vijay went every Tuesday to the meeting at St Helen's church. Within Lloyd's there was also a small group of people called the Christian Union who met regularly to read the Bible and discuss faith issues. Vijay went along because, as a thinking man, he had lots of questions and was not going to be swept into Christianity on a wave of emotions. Diligently and prayerfully he sought the truth, praying, 'Jesus, show me please if you are alive.'

'Jesus, show me please if you are alive.'

One day, while looking at some beautiful, old-fashioned English roses, Vijay thought, 'If God can create a beautiful flower from a seed, which has neither beauty nor perfume, it is not difficult for God to bring Jesus back to life. If I were to bring all the scientists of the world and give them all the equipment that they wanted, they would not be able to produce a seed from ammonia, phosphate, calcium and nitrogen which can result in a flower, but God does it.'

Vijay's earlier prayer was answered. 'My faith in God is not blind. It is based on the historical facts of the birth and resurrection of Jesus Christ and on the certainty of God's promises.' As a result Vijay was publicly baptised on his confession and belief that: Jesus Christ died for his sins on the cross, was raised from the dead and gives eternal life to all who trust in Him.

> *'Something happened to me. Jesus had come into my life; he touched every part of it; He turned it upside down. For 35 years I had tried to lead a good Hindu life – I did not smoke, I did not drink and I prayed to god every day. When I got up in the morning I would ask 'god' to help me; before I fell asleep at night I would say a short prayer; and in major decisions I always sought his guidance. Yet I never really knew the true and living God until He found*

> *me. I had an excellent job in the City, a house in suburbia, a wife, sons, enough money in the bank to meet my needs, but, although I was not the worrying type, I never enjoyed life until Jesus found me. Jesus said, 'I have come that they might have life, and have it to the full.' I have proved those words to be gloriously true.'*

Three years after Vijay did so, Susheila trusted Christ as her Lord and Saviour, as did their two sons. Vijay still lives in London, attending St Helen's Church, Bishopsgate. He is now retired, but is part of the team of volunteers who work at that church. His chirpy character is such that he is loved by everyone, and he always has heartening words of encouragement to pass on to those he meets.

Fiona Castle

THE ENTERTAINER

Morecambe and Wise were appearing at the Coventry Hippodrome. An attractive, but as yet little-known, dancer carried her bag through the stage door. Her name, Fiona, was not on the billboard or in bright lights. However, that booking was to lead not only to a long-lasting friendship with Eric and Joan Morecambe, but also to a famous showbiz marriage to the much-loved and extraordinarily talented entertainer Roy Castle.

All this was a long way from Fiona's childhood roots back in West Kirby on the Wirral. Her father was the revered local doctor who lived above 'the business' in an old, rambling Victorian house. During the war the family would disappear down into the cellar whenever there was a raid on as they were not far from the vulnerable target of Liverpool. Life was frugal for everyone including Fiona and her two sisters and brother. No one was 'spoilt' in those days!

A highlight in her week was the dancing class at her local primary school where an enterprising teacher spotted that Fiona 'had talent' and recommended that her parents follow this up. With much excitement they heeded her advice by sending Fiona, now aged nine, to a boarding school, which unfortunately happened to be 250 miles away in Surrey. Until she was 17 years old Fiona was a boarder at this ballet school. One of the things that she learned during her time there was to do the splits, and famously she can still do them although she is now in what is termed the 'third generation'!

Boarding schools of that era were quite traditional in their attitude to religion and were Anglo-Catholic. While living with her family, Fiona had been used to saying grace before meals and attending church on Sundays, as most of their neighbours did. Therefore it did not come as any surprise to her that she and the other dancers were expected to attend chapel every morning and three services on Sundays. As dancers the most exciting aspect was processing up and down the aisles, dancing and swinging the incense. It was the young girls' greatest ambition. They thought it was wonderful!

It was the young girls' greatest ambition.

As far as belief was concerned, however, Fiona mistakenly thought that by going to church, trying to live a good life and helping people she would tick all the boxes for her to get to heaven. She had been brought up thinking that God was wagging his finger at her, telling her that she wasn't good enough and that she had to do this and that in order to please God, otherwise she would go to hell. As Fiona says, 'I thought that if I didn't get everything right, I would never be good enough.' This was quite scary for her and all part of the ritual at that period of her life.

Fiona would have loved to have joined a ballet company in order to become a ballerina, but realistically she decided that she would never be good enough. Instead she embarked on what was the next best thing in those days, a career of variety shows. The trick was to get oneself booked up for the longest-running pantomime and 'summer season' so that there was little time in between to starve!

Coventry Hippodrome was popular among artists as their pantomimes ran into April. For one particular season Harry Secombe was topping the bill, followed by Morecambe and Wise. This comedy duo weren't hugely famous then as it was before their television series. Nevertheless, they were very talented and popular. Fiona joined the company, glad not only for work but also for friendship with Eric Morecambe and his wife, Joan, that was to last for many, many years. They were really good to her even though they had their own family to look after and provide for. As a 'starving dancer' Fiona would always be welcome at their home at weekends. Having given her a good 'feed', they would pack her up with any food that was left over so that she didn't starve during the rest of the week.

Recalling her times staying in their home, Fiona says, 'Whenever Eric was in company, he was absolutely brilliant. He had an amazing sense of humour and timing. He had us in hysterics all the time. Once we were all sitting round my kitchen table having lunch when the phone rang. Eric was closest to the phone so he picked it up and immediately said, "I'm sorry, you must have the wrong number. There is no phone here!" And then he put the phone down.'

Whenever Eric was in company, he was absolutely brilliant.

On another occasion they were all sitting down watching television when Roy Castle appeared on the screen. Being quite famous by now, Roy had achieved the ultimate honour of having his own television show. Fiona had already seen him perform at the London Palladium and thought him to be absolutely brilliant and so talented. On a very stupid impulse she asked Eric if he would introduce him to her the next time they worked together as she would love to meet Roy.

By then Eric and Ernie were performing at the Palladium but Fiona was also doing very well. She had landed a part in the original cast of 'The Sound of Music', having been cast as Liesel who sings, 'I am sixteen, going on seventeen'.

Thus it was that Fiona found herself travelling with Joan to the Wood Green Empire where Roy was busy with his live television show. Eric came along and took her backstage to Roy's dressing room to introduce her to him, saying, 'Roy, this is Fiona. She's madly in love with you!'

'Roy, this is Fiona. She's madly in love with you!'

Blushing to the very roots of her blonde hair, Fiona wanted to curl up and die. The other party looked equally shy and was struck dumb. Neither of them could think what to say. Later they all went out for a meal together, having quite a lovely time. The relationship, despite its unusual beginning, blossomed with marriage and four children making up a very happy family.

Roy will always be remembered for being a multi-talented entertainer, musician, comedian, singer and dancer. It was always good, clean, family entertainment, but most people remember him for his very successful television series 'Record Breakers'. Amazingly he managed to complete series after series of these shows for a staggering 22 years. For those who never saw the programmes, he would do daring, often dangerous, scary but always thrilling things. One such challenge was wing-walking on top of a plane that was flying across the English channel, with no sound system for communication between him and the pilot.

The scariest feat was the Death Slide, in which he descended from the top of Blackpool Tower to the beach by means of just a wire in a figure of eight rope. The rope had to be soaked in water for 24 hours, otherwise it would have burnt right through before the person reached the bottom!

His other antics were less dangerous but revealed such talent. Roy famously holds the record for playing 43 instruments (including a kitchen sink as well as his trumpet) in four minutes with one tune.

With a busy husband working mostly in the United States of America, Fiona decided, as soon as they were married, to give up her dancing career (although she still loved to dance whenever and wherever she heard music, much to the embarrassment of her children). Fiona was the anchor at home. She understood the demands of Roy's job as she herself had made the same career choice. Above all she enjoyed being a homemaker and a mum.

However, Fiona was also a perfectionist. As she explains, 'When you are a perfectionist, you feel you are a failure because you never match up to your own expectations of what that perfection should be. I would look around at other people who were doing the same sort of things that I was doing and I saw them doing everything far better than I did.'

Standing chatting at the school gates with other mothers, who told her all the wonderful things that they were able to do, was hard for Fiona. Besides, they also looked as though they had just stepped off the cover of Vogue magazine, with not a hair out of place. Fiona, on the other hand, according to her own image of herself, was always flying around in a terrible state and looking such a mess. She kept thinking, 'Why can't I be calm? Why can't I do everything the same way other people do?' This really got to her. As a result Fiona became depressed, not clinically, but feeling very low. She describes what this was like:

> *'We're all good at hiding our weaknesses. I would put on a big smile like a mask in front of my face. To others I would look as if I was fine, but as soon as I 'took the mask off' I was miserable. I'm ashamed to say that so much depended on how I was feeling as to how I would treat the children. They never knew what mood I would be in when I came home. (They have since talked to me about this period in my life and, bless them, they still love me and I them!)'*

Roy was very aware of all this. Being such an easy-going guy, he was happy if people around him were happy. His whole aim was to make people happy. Fiona was the one it didn't work with and he couldn't fathom why. Sadly Fiona had no one other than Roy that she could share these dark feelings with, as she didn't want to let the side down. So she kept up with the pretence, even though inside she was falling apart. She says, 'I wouldn't have blamed Roy if he had left me to go with someone else, after all he was in show business! But Roy was faithful in marriage, even on tour where he would have had loads of opportunities to be unfaithful.'

As he was so worried about her, Roy and Fiona would discuss her problem and he gave her ideas about how to cope with things. Always, though, she would come back to this sense of failure. This lasted several years until she was 35, and her children were between the ages of one and eight.

'God, if you are there, You've got to help me ...'

Fiona was still going to church each week but Roy used to tell her, 'I don't know why you bother because by the time you've got everybody ready and in the car, you are in such a foul mood it can't possibly do you any good!' Fiona says of herself, 'I was a very privileged person with a loving husband, family and home. I had everything materially, but emotionally I was falling apart. Eventually it all came to a head. I thought to myself that I can't go on like this.' What Fiona did next is to be recommended to anyone who finds themself at a crisis point in their lives.

Going to her bedroom, she shut the door and on her knees cried out to God saying, 'God, if you are there, You've got to help me ... and You've got to help me now because I have had it. I can't go on like this any longer.' That was all that she said but she meant it, even though she wasn't sure that God was even there. Roy was at home but she had closed the door to be alone.

Fiona recounts what happened next:

> *'I was so desperate. But before I had even got off my knees the phone rang so I picked it up. The person at the other end was a woman whom I had met a couple of times. I would never have expected her to phone me socially but I did know that she was a Christian. She just said that she didn't know exactly why she was phoning me but that I had been on her mind recently. Would I like to come over and have a coffee and talk together? I had to recognise that as God's answer to my cry for help.'*

Fiona dumped their youngest child into Roy's arms, saying that she was going out, and left the house. Later he told her that he thought that she had left him, literally holding the baby, and wasn't going to return!

Fiona found that because this lady knew nothing about her, her life or friends, she was able to totally confide in her. All her problems came pouring out like the rubbish being tipped from a bin lorry. And this lady was a good listener. She then asked Fiona, kindly, a challenging question: 'Fiona, you know you think that you are a Christian because you go to church? But have you ever invited Jesus to come in and take over your life?'

Fiona's immediate response was, 'No, I didn't realise you were supposed to.' She thought she had done all the things she was supposed to have done, not having noticed that need in the Book of Common Prayer; but the lady continued, 'Well, don't you feel it's about time you did?' Fiona recalls her reaction and response:

> *'I said 'yes' because I was afraid to say 'no'. I hadn't anywhere to run. What I was worried about was that if I did say 'yes', I thought that I would have to wear sandals and socks, put my hair in a bun and never wear make-up again! However, this lady was very pretty and didn't look anything like that, and besides she too had suffered from depression for many years but had taken that step which had turned her life around. When I heard that, I felt I had nothing to lose and it was worth a try.*
>
> *'I wasn't very good at praying without a prayer book apart from saying the 'God bless Mummy and Daddy' type of prayer. So with her help I*

prayed, very simply but meaning every word: 'God, please forgive me for the mess I've made of my marriage, my family and my life. I recognise the way I have tried to run my life hasn't worked, so please come into my life and take it over and see what you can do with the rest of it.' '

That was all.

Unsure of what would follow, all that Fiona can explain is that she felt peace flowing over her. She thought that maybe she would have to try even harder to be good ... but no, instead it was as if she was able to let go of all the stress and strain, anxiety, fear and worries. 'It was like healing oil had been poured over all the hurting areas of life. I knew I was different. Something incredible had happened.'

There were no tears. For the first time in years she was relaxed, knowing a great peace that didn't disappear. Reality kicked in straight away, as she had to drive home. Not knowing how all this would work out with the family, Fiona believes that God, in His wisdom, laid it on her heart not to tell Roy what had happened straight

For the first time in years she was relaxed, knowing a great peace.

away. Instead she was going to live out what had happened, not by telling him she was different but by being different. Otherwise maybe her comedian husband would have run a mile thinking she had religious mania as well!

About a month later Roy asked Fiona where she had gone that other morning in such a dramatic manner. He said, 'It was as if somebody had painted our house in two seconds flat and had gone out with the door black and blue, only to come back in and suddenly it was light, bright and sunny!' And this change did last. Fiona grew as a Christian and her faith developed.

Roy Castle was not a smoker but had worked in smoke-filled atmospheres as part of his work. He and Fiona had returned from a working trip to Australia but somehow he couldn't get over the jet lag. One night Fiona thought he was having a heart attack so called an ambulance as he was obviously desperately ill. It was not a heart attack; instead a very extreme virus appeared to have taken away all the salts in his blood stream. As a result his immune system was lowered, allowing latent cancer cells to start growing in his lungs. A couple of months later

One night Fiona thought he was having a heart attack.

the doctors confirmed the diagnosis of lung cancer. Fiona explains more:

> *'In those days nobody believed that passive smoking was dangerous, so he was probably a pioneer when the scientists were starting to understand the dangers of breathing in other people's smoke. We were at home doing some voiceovers for a charity film when Roy told us what the doctors had said. 'Well, I've got lung cancer and it's the fastest growing kind. Without treatment I have three months to live and with treatment I have six months. It is inoperable. Okay let's get on with the recording.' '*

Fiona, of course, was shocked. Not knowing what to do, she prayed asking God, 'What was He doing?'; 'What was happening?' It was almost as if she heard an audible voice in the room saying, 'Stand back and see what I am going to do through this.'

Suddenly she realised that God hadn't abandoned them; He still loved them. He knew what was happening. All He was asking was that they would allow Him to work through the circumstances they found themselves in at this particular time.

Fiona and Roy weren't interested in publicity. In

Fiona's words, 'Roy was not a celebrity as people are today. He had had a wonderful career where he enjoyed being able to do something at which he was immensely talented.' The press had always left them alone ... until two weeks into his treatment. Having heard that Roy had cancer, media folk were straight on the phone while reporters and photographers were outside the house wanting interviews. When the last ones had gone, Roy turned to Fiona and said:

> *'I don't know what they have put in the newspapers but I told them all about Jesus! I've never been keen on telling people for the sake of it that I am a Christian but I now have a platform. I've always tried to live it out in the way I've lived my life, but if my faith had not been real, it would have gone out of the window with the cancer. It is more real now than it has ever been. The press can say what they like.'*

Maybe they did, but Fiona feels that the press were 'absolutely wonderful throughout'.

Roy actually lived, with treatment, for another two and a half years, which was a bonus for them both. As Fiona puts it, 'You make the most of life when you think you might not have many more days.' Nevertheless Roy died on 4 September 1994 at his Buckinghamshire home. He was just 62 years old.

Fiona's life was non-stop from then on to the funeral and beyond as the press followed the story. There is no blueprint for grieving. Every person handles it differently. Although Fiona was grieving the loss of the one person she loved most in the whole world, it was as if God had graciously given her the gift of joy like a well bubbling up within her, because He knew she needed it to help her cope with all that was going on. Obviously she was not happy, but happiness is not the same as having the joy within that only God can give in such times of sorrow and anguish.

Life has a habit of catching us off guard when we are at our most vulnerable.

Life has a habit of catching us off guard when we are at our most vulnerable. For Fiona this was when she took her first plane trip alone and as a widow. On her return, on seeing people waiting for the 'arrivals', she realised that 'Roy was not there to greet me, hug me or take me home. I sobbed and sobbed.'

As the months passed by, God spoke into her heart,

gently reminding her that she was to get on with the rest of her life. There was much He wanted her to do. 'Then I came to recognise the difference between tears of grief and tears of self-pity. I allowed myself tears of grief. I still do sometimes. But as a former pastor of mine once wrote, "There comes a time when we have to give ourselves permission to stop grieving."'

Roy had bravely encouraged her during his illness by saying, 'Other people get problems, why should I be exempt? We must never complain, Fiona, we've had such an amazing life together. We must always be grateful.' And she is.

Fiona has written many books and often speaks at public meetings or functions about her life and faith. If you would like to know more about these and also receive a free DVD or booklet about what it means to trust in Jesus Christ, please contact www.10ofthose.com.

Jamie Jones-Buchanan

THE PROFESSIONAL RUGBY PLAYER

To hold aloft a huge, shining silver trophy, in front of thousands of fans, must be the dream of a lifetime for many sport lovers. For most of us it is only a dream, but for JJB it has been reality – not once, but six times.

Jamie Jones-Buchanan, the successful and very popular Rugby League player with Leeds Rhinos, has helped his team win six Grand Finals. He has represented England and Great Britain, and recently played his 300th game for his famous club. But even having reached such heights of success, he still felt that there was more to life.

Instantly recognisable on the pitch and posters, mainly because of his facial hair, Jamie cuts a formidable figure – and with muscles most men and boys would die for! His beard was much fuller once, but Jamie explains why it is more trim now:

'It was very bushy but, to be honest, I got fed up of being called a terrorist. It was in 2007 that the team decided that everyone was going to grow facial hair until we had won five games on the trot. About seven or eight games in to this agreement, we were struggling a little bit. The others decided that they didn't want their beards and moustaches anymore and started shaving them off. I thought that as I have got a face for radio anyway, I was not bothered whether I let it grow or not, so I made a point and let it grow regardless of whether we won or lost. By the end of the season it was huge, absolutely massive! My youngest son kept pulling it, and when I was cooking it would nearly catch on fire sometimes. People started saying, 'What are you doing with it right out here?' Yet by growing this beard I raised money for my amateur club, before eventually shaving it off at the 2007 homecoming after the Grand Final. I had some 'lamb chops' in 2010 but after that I thought that as I'm getting old, a

By growing this beard I raised money for my amateur club.

beard is getting tough to maintain, so I keep it nice and short and trim and just get on with playing.'

The Challenge Cup certainly lives up to its name for Leeds Rhinos. They last won it in 1999. The Challenge Cup is a knockout cup competition for Rugby League clubs organised by the Rugby Football League. Jamie needs no reminding that it is a big one on the hit list of the fans:

'It just never seems to be our year. This time Huddersfield knocked us out. Having lost a few games, plus picking up a few injuries to some of our top guys on the way, it has been tough. It's looked pretty bleak but we've been there before. The last two years we finished fifth in the league and everybody wrote us off in 2011. Nobody had won it from fifth position before. But we muddle together. A lot of the lads have grown up together, coming through the academy. The nucleus of the side is very close-knit, very much like a family; we pull together. And we did become the first team to win it from fifth. 'A fluke, an accident,' everyone said. 'You can't do it again.' But we did, the year after.

'This year our coach said that he has had

enough of finishing in fifth! He wants us in the top two, so keep watching us to see if we do. We're trying our best.

'The problem with Leeds is that, as it is such a big club, there are high expectations every year, which puts more pressure on the players. They have only to lose a few games for some of the fans to get agitated. Off the pitch and back in the dressing room it can be very tough, especially after losing a big match. Everybody's head is down, reflecting on the game and what we could have done better. The captain will speak, and sometimes the coach. The Chief Executive usually walks in too.'

In the world of Rugby League, Leeds Rhinos is a prestigious team. For the uninitiated, the game of rugby has two codes, league and union, with the former firmly in favour with the northern counties of England. Maybe you have heard of the old saying that: 'Rugby League is a gentleman's game played by thugs, and Rugby Union is a thug's game played by gentlemen'?

Rugby League has a good reputation for being family friendly, with Leeds having a particularly good, 'hands-on' approach to community life in the city.

But how did Jamie get to be called up to the team in the first place, especially when the competition to do so is enormous?

Jamie loves to tell everyone that he grew up in 'the Big Apple': Bramley, Leeds – not New York, USA! He was very much a 'local lad', an average kid, going to a local school and loving sport. As he was born in August, he was the youngest in his year.

When he now goes coaching in schools, Jamie finds that young kids who are born at the latter end of the year tend to be a bit smaller and a little bit more fragile than the others. They don't get recognised as quickly as being athletic, so a lot of them get put off at a young age. It is called the 'relative age effect'. So Jamie always tries to encourage them. He realises that their comparative weakness is not because they are not good at sport; it's just that they are not as broad as kids born at the other end of the year.

Jamie loves to tell everyone that he grew up in 'the Big Apple': Bramley, Leeds.

However, Jamie himself was quite big. He jokes, 'I was one of those tanks.' Outside his house was a big patch of grass where the boys all played rugby. He didn't know anything about it at the time but they used to give each other names when they played. As he didn't know any rugby players, his mates would choose either Ellery Hanley or Martin Offiah for him. He thought this was because he was a good player. Yet when he played football, his name was John Barnes, the ex-Liverpool and England player. Then he realised why.

When Jamie was at school, Brian Sowden, who was coach at Stanningley, saw Jamie there and said that he seemed like a decent player and that he was to bring his boots on Saturday. Jamie did and he never looked back. It also kept him off the streets, although he had never been arrested or done anything illegal.

Everyone in the team was a hero to Jamie.

Now Jamie was in a rugby team. He had camaraderie, friends and a team environment. It felt like he belonged. He was fortunate to play as a schoolboy for Yorkshire, and it was there that the scouts used to come to spot potential talent for the city team of Leeds Rhinos. After their games, his friends and he would go on to Headingley to stand in the stadium to support Leeds. Everyone in the team was a hero to Jamie, and were people he looked up to. He, with his friends, used to watch and admire them, but they were a team who always came in second, which was unfortunate.

When he was 15 years old, he was signed on for Leeds Rhinos. His debut was in 1999, aged 17. When they won the first Grand Final in 2004, it was really special – as a supporter, as a player and as somebody who grew up in Leeds – to be part of the first winning champion team for 35 years.

> *'It felt tough, very nerve-racking, running on to the pitch for the first time as 15,000 people were watching you. Most of them were local, your friends and family plus people from Bramley – all people you didn't want to let down. You just wanted to do your best for them and for yourself.*
>
> *'It was hard work. Like going a hundred miles an hour! The lads we played against were twice the size of me. I'm a forward, but I am big enough to sort of handle myself a little bit as well as being quick enough to run away from the big fellows. So I have the best of both worlds. But to be honest, it was a fantastic feeling running out. And still is.'*

Life as a professional rugby player is definitely not for the faint-hearted. Kick-off for matches is usually about 8 p.m. Afterwards there will be a presentation in the sponsors' lounge. Then it is off to one of the local health clubs to go swimming at midnight to get rid of the bumps and bruises. After that there are two days off, followed by training the next day, and then maybe another day off before training again the next day.

The training sessions start properly at 8.30 a.m. There will be jump tests, stretch tests plus physio examinations to make sure that no one is struggling with an injury or getting tight. If they are, they get pulled back out of training. Everyone does a lot with weights and combat wrestling, because obviously Rugby League is very much a contact sport. Then they will go upstairs to view a video of the previous game, to look at the things they did well and the things that they didn't do well. After this there is more training and more weights, they look at the next team they are going to play, then they do weights again. Afterwards there is training and practice outside, going through the game plan that they are going to execute that weekend against their opposing team.

It is gruelling, tough work, especially when you get to Jamie's age and join the ranks of the over 30s. He says, 'I don't feel much until Tuesdays these days! There are plenty of aches, pains and bruises. It gets tougher as you get older, but they do look after you. There is a brilliant medical team to make sure that things are done properly – and of course there are the ice baths!'

One player was to become a special friend of Jamie's. Some years ago the Rhinos employed an overseas player from New Zealand, a famous All Black, called Ali Lauitiiti. Jamie explains why Ali had such an important effect on his life:

> *'Ali wasn't an aggressive guy apart from when he played on the field, but then he always played according to the rules. His true character was that of a very kind and gentle person who stayed calm. There he was, a long way from home, in the midst of a group of boisterous, cantankerous rugby players who were used to living their lives, going out drinking and things. But he would share with them about his faith as a Christian and would avoid the late nights and occasional celebratory drinking. He wasn't shy about his faith, or that he went to church. Just in a very natural way, he separated himself from wild excesses, and it was obvious it was because of his faith.*

Ali would share with them about his faith as a Christian.

'This was an opportunity for me to ask him some questions. I always felt that there was 'something' out there and I was desperate to know. I only went to church as a kid for weddings and christenings. I didn't grow up with any sort of religious or faith background, but I had a loving childhood. My mum and dad separated when I was very young – about two years old. She went on to marry my stepdad, Chris, who was in the navy and brought me up. They had a daughter, my sister Samantha, but later divorced. My mum then met Steve, who is the dad of my brother Shane, who is 16 years younger than me. Shane is a good rugby player too. My biological dad went on to have 11 children, some of them having different mums. I didn't have anything to do with my dad's other children because I didn't see him that often, but three of them – Austin, Jodie and Brooke – have gone on to play rugby professionally. Jodie is doing very well at the moment at Salford. The first time I met Jodie was when he turned up at Leeds in the academy. I knew of him and we instantly

When I was younger, I used to always think about God.

realised who each other was; we said hello and hugged.

'My Nana (Mum's Mum) used to pray a lot. When she would baby-sit for us kids, she always prayed with us before bedtime. When I was younger, I used to always think about God. I had this feeling that there must be something out there. There must be an overhead power. I remember I used to go to sleep at night feeling numb and scared of dying.

'I did have a little red Gideon's Bible. I read a bit of it and tried to understand it. If you had asked me at the age of 15 if I was a Christian, I would probably have said 'yes', but I wouldn't have known what that really meant at that time.

'When I met Ali at the Rhinos, I quizzed him about his faith. I was just longing to know what that 'something' out there was. I knew that there were things in my life that needed to change. It was great to have a colleague there, somebody whom I trusted and somebody who would become a friend. When I asked him about his faith, he invited me to his church, City Evangelical Church in Beeston, Leeds –

near Elland Road, home of the football stadium. I wasn't too sure about going. I thought that it would be full of people like Ned Flanders in The Simpsons, and people wearing nice little jumpers and saying funny things! I thought that I would have to dress up a bit and put on my 'Sunday best'. I thought it would altogether be a bit strange. How wrong I was!

'It was fantastic. It was casual and down to earth. I met the pastor of the church, Mike Wildsmith, who has become a brilliant friend. I went along to something called Christianity Explored, where we would grab a bite to eat and then look at what the Bible said about Jesus – who He was, why He came and what that meant for me. I started to realise that the more I learned about Jesus in the Bible, the more I knew that it was the truth. It was just as if a light had been switched on and I could see what it was all about. It makes the hairs stand up on the back of the neck when you start to realise this. How could I have missed it? It became so obvious and I wanted to tell everyone about Jesus. It is important.

It was just as if a light had been switched on.

And I knew that I had to let go of the old me and start growing in my faith, becoming more like Jesus.'

With his background, Jamie didn't really know how to pray. Perhaps, he wondered, he needed to do it in church, kneeling at a pew, but he found that it wasn't like that at all. Just where he was at that time, Jamie bowed his head and simply asked God to forgive him and become the Lord of his life. When he went home, he wondered if this had truly happened and asked God to give him strength, knowing life isn't always easy. The Bible says, 'Therefore, if anyone is in Christ, he is a new creation; the old has gone, the new has come!'

His prayer was answered, and he found he understood why Ali was like he was. The Bible was not a closed book anymore. He found he loved to read it and he discovered how helpful it was. There were choice verses in the Bible that became very special to him, such as the famous one: 'For God so loved the world that he gave his one and only Son that whoever believes in him shall not perish but have eternal life.'

Nowadays, Jamie publicly shares all that has happened in his life and how others can come to faith in Christ themselves. 'I had a girlfriend at that time. We decided to get married. On my wedding ring, engraved on the inside, are the words 'in Christ' to remind me that my marriage on earth is the most important thing to me and I want God to be at the centre of it and my life.'

He will publicly say that a lot of sporting personalities have achieved everything and yet feel so empty. He believes it's because they've not got God to fill that emptiness in their heart.

He is often asked whether he prays before a match, and if so does he pray to win? He replies, 'What is important is that I go out there to try my hardest and to do it for God's glory.' Whether he wins or loses, he learns lessons on the back of that – even in defeat and adversity. He stresses that winning is only for a season and then you have to do it all over again. Winning doesn't last forever. He concludes by saying, 'Perhaps I will eventually go into coaching when my playing career is over, but right now I have four young boys of my own at home to coach!'

Leeds Rhinos made it into the semi-finals again, but did not go on to win the coveted Grand Slam trophy. As they prepare for the new season, you can be sure that there is even greater determination in the team to be winners next time.

If you would like to try out a Christianity Explored course near where you live or work, then please email moreinfo@10ofthose.com or write to: A Passion for Life, c/o 9D Centurion Court, Leyland, PR25 3UQ, England.

'Cossy' (Steve Cossack)

THE CARETAKER

Football and the Beatles have made Liverpool famous throughout the world. Liverpudlians, otherwise known as 'Scousers', have a keen sense of humour and are known for their big-heartedness, fierce loyalty and passion.

Steve Cossack, or 'Cossy', discovered that his beloved city was also a divided one in many ways. Born into a loving family in Toxteth, he would grow up discovering that as well as having leafy parks and the grandeur of Georgian buildings boasting of former glory, his area was one of the most culturally diverse in the city.

Cossy's own life was evidence of another divide, that between Catholics and Protestants. He explains:

> *'Liverpool is a city divided – not just by its footy clubs, Liverpool FC and Everton, so red and blue, but also by its religion, into green*

and orange. Historically Irish immigrants moved to the city with a lot of Catholic influence. It has even been said by some, tongue in cheek, that Liverpool is the capital of Ireland! Inevitably, over time, families became mixed with divisions over religion. Mine was typical – split right down the middle. When my father told my Nan that he was going to marry a Protestant girl, she refused to speak to him for a number of years. However, years later after her death while we were going through her personal papers, we discovered ironically and to our amusement that she got married to a Polish Jew in a Protestant church, and when she was three months pregnant. Wonderful morals!'

Cossy's father was a docker and his mother a seamstress. He felt that his was just a normal, working-class family that never had much money, but neither did they see hungry days and they all had shoes on their feet. Cossy was always made to go to Sunday School, not because his parents were particularly moral but rather because it got him out of the house for two hours on a Sunday afternoon so that his father could go and have a couple of pints and then come back to Sunday lunch with the rest of the family.

On weekdays, when Cossy should have been at school, he used to get registered there then 'bunk off'. As to his credentials, he was voted the guy most likely to have a prison sentence, which, eventually, is just what happened. Although school was in a 'mean' area of dockland, nevertheless he did quite like it. Children grew up quickly. As Cossy summarises, 'Your fists got hard, your wits got keen and you learnt to survive.' Cossy was no Mohammed Ali, but he could handle himself well. He was known as someone who never took a liberty, but woe betide you if you ever tried to take a liberty with him.

Desperate, his parents tried to restrain his behaviour, but he freely admits that he drove his poor mother to distraction. As so many did in the Dingle, an inner-city area of Liverpool, Cossy's activities descended from petty theft to grand larceny. To this day, and with shame, he still remembers the first time he stole. It was from his sister's leprosy box in which she used to collect for charity.

Leaving school behind at the age of 15, Cossy started out in the butchery trade. But before long Cossie was off to sea. Soon he learnt that there are ways to earn money other than by honest labour. Cossy explains, 'By the age of 26 I had had enough of this four-letter word they call W-O-R-K, and I decided to retire.' He had 'a wonderful little scam' going that enabled him to have a villa in Spain plus a brand new boat and car. He was a 'good crook' with everything going for him.

One thing he never forgot from his Sunday School days was when his teacher – an old, Irish lady (at least she always seemed old to him because of her white hair) – said to him, 'Steven, one day everyone of us will stand before God and give an account of ourselves.' Cossy's childhood reaction was that he didn't want to hear about a God whom he regarded as a non-entity, and 'didn't come into the equation'.

Although life seemed good, his wealthy lifestyle was to be cut short because, as Cossy puts it, 'I had my collar felt. I spent a number of years in Walton prison. Easy! You can do prison standing on your head. It's not a hard life – but it is hard for family on the outside; trying to provide for themselves while surviving on little money is no easy task, while I had three good meals a day!'

'I had my collar felt. I spent a number of years in Walton prison.'

When Cossy was serving time they had what was called 'the 23-hour bang up'. Prisoners only got out of their cell for one hour a day, if they were fortunate, when it wasn't raining and 'the screw' was in the mood to let them out. There was no television, no room for nonsense and no association with others; instead, you were just 'banged into' your cell. But the prisoners were allowed books to read.

Cossy would tell you that it is his belief that prison is the greatest school for criminals, giving the greatest education to prisoners, because it teaches inmates how to thieve better and how to do horrible things 'better'. He is not an advocate of the effectiveness of prison.

Being caught and sentenced had no positive effect on Cossy. A total absence of any sense of guilt or regret revealed that he had totally silenced his conscience. As far as he was concerned, his type of crime was victim-less, so it was all the better if he could just get away with it. When in prison, though he didn't dwell on this much, he realised that if all there is to life is what we see, then everything is futile and all our experiences are just a waste. Thinking that the answer to life's big questions lay in philosophy, Cossy began reading the writings of philosophers including Nietzsche, who was his favourite, and Plato.

When he was released, and with no ideas of reform in his head, Cossy headed back to Spain, the sun, his villa and his wife. Plans were being made for just one more 'big hit'. He was in a group stake, which, if it were a hit, would have netted a vast fortune between the three of them. On a return visit to Liverpool, everything was set up and ready to go, but then he met Bill.

Bill was a mate from football and school. He and Cossy went back a long way. When they met again, there was the usual catching up: 'How's it going?'; 'Are you married?'; 'Do you have kids?' Then Bill asked, 'What are you doing now, son?' Cossy boasted that he was just about to retire at the age of 26.

Bill replied, 'I'm made up for you' (which is local slang for 'I'm pleased for you'). 'What then?'

So Cossy responded, 'I've heard that the average family has 2.4 children, so I'm going to make 2.4 children and settle down.'

Bill said, 'I'm really pleased for you. What then?'

Cossy answered, 'Well, you know they are going to want for nothing. They will have private education and the best of everything. Wait until you see my mansion, Bill. Wait until you see my boat, Bill. Wait until you see my car, Bill – it's unbelievable!' (And it was!)

'Great', Bill said. 'I'm so pleased for you. What then?'

'Well, to be honest, I'm going to watch my kids grow up. I believe the best thing since sliced bread is grandkids. Grandkids are God's reward for not killing your own!'

Bill just responded with, 'You know what, lad, I'm so pleased for you, I'm over the moon for you, I'm really made up. What then?'

By now Cossy was beginning to feel a bit uncomfortable because he had worked out what was coming. He said to Bill, 'I'm going to get older, aren't I?'

'I believe the best thing since sliced bread is grandkids.'

Bill gently replied, 'What then?'

'I'm going to die, aren't I, stupid? We all die. One out of one dies. I am going to die. I am not going to be the one who breaks the mould.'

Bill came back, 'And what then?'

Suddenly the words of the Sunday School teacher from years before came to the front of his mind.

He felt as though somebody had smacked him in the mouth like the hardest hit in the solar plexus you've ever had. He felt sick when he realised that his teacher was right, that he was going to stand before God and give an account of what he had done with his life.

For the next six months Cossy recalls how his mind was in turmoil. His thoughts were everywhere. He couldn't let it rest. It was as if he had been a victim of grievous bodily harm of the brain! He would go to bed with big questions going round and round in his mind. He longed for the thoughts to just go away so he could sleep but, as he puts it, his head felt 'cabbaged, with six months of mental GBH'.

One night he came to the point in his life when he concluded that if Jesus Christ is worth anything, then He is worth everything. He decided there and then that he had to give up his self-centred life. He had to pack in the way he lived and, more than that, he would give back every single thing that he had taken from others. That was hard and costly for Cossy. After having had a massive disposable weekly income, enabling him to gamble at the roulette wheel many, many times a week, he was now in the position where he couldn't even afford a pair of shoes.

There was one thing that he still had that was very precious to him – his family. To him, his mum, his wife Cath, and his family were deeply loved. It was a big step for Cossy to announce to them that he had become a Christian. He feared that his wife would think he had flipped and she would clear the house, leaving his possessions in a bin bag on the front door step. He had been bin-bagged before, and didn't want it to happen again.

Eventually one night he told Cath everything: 'For some time now I've been bothered. I've realised my life's got to change, and I've given my life to Jesus Christ.' Cossy thought that there would be a screaming kick-off, as there usually was, especially when she had had a few drinks. To his surprise, all was quiet. That night he slept in the other room, putting the bed near the door, fearing his wife might come in and stab him in his sleep! But all was quiet. That was on the Sunday night.

Come Wednesday, as they sat down to tea, Cath said, 'I want to talk to you.' 'Uh oh!' Cossy thought, imagining she was about to leave. He figured though that if Jesus is worth anything, He is worth everything, and that if she didn't want to stay with him, so be it. He knew he had to do what was right even if it meant losing his beloved Cath. He felt he had lost everything else, so why worry?

To his utter amazement, Cath turned to him and confessed that for the last six months she had been tossing and turning under a deep sense of her own sinfulness and that Jesus Christ had been speaking to her. She had wanted to become a Christian but was scared of losing Cossy. That very week, though, she had decided that if Jesus was worth anything, He was worth everything. She had become a Christian two days after him. Which of them was the most surprised?

Liverpool Football Club has a chaplain, Cossy's old mate Bill, whose primary job is as the pastor of Bridge Chapel in Garston Bridge, Liverpool. When Cossy and Cath turned up for church, Bill's reaction was, 'O Lord, no, not him, not her, not now, not tonight. Please not him.' This was because Cossy used to wind him up terribly. But Cossy remembers the sermon clearly – while Bill later said it was one of his worst, Cossie thinks it was one of his best.

Bill preached on how Pharoah had hardened his heart against God when Moses had approached him to ask that he let the Israelites leave the land of Egypt. Eventually God Himself hardened Pharoah's heart. That was the point when God's offer of mercy was withdrawn. Then Bill, still preaching, said that there is a point when God's offer of salvation will be withdrawn. No one knows when that will be, but the Bible teaches that now is the appointed hour, now is the day of salvation, now is the time to be saved. So don't put off trusting Jesus. There is no guarantee about tomorrow. Yesterday is gone, all you have is now. Respond now, because God may say that He's offered salvation so many times but now the offer is over.

Cossy and Cath knew they had responded to God, and were resting in the fact that He loved them, had given His Son Jesus to die for their sin and had given them a new life in Him. Now they could sleep at night!

Friends were still important to Cossy, but now he experienced a deep concern that they too should come to know Jesus and the 'riches' that there are in Him rather than the material wealth that had been their all-consuming dream. Tommy was a good friend, who just happened to be the first major drug importer in the UK. He was the type of guy who would walk into a pub with a stash of cash in a briefcase and offer to buy the place. Cossy decided that he would visit Tommy and tell him what had happened. Tommy offered him a Winston Churchill cigar and opened a bottle of Bollinger.

As they sat sipping champagne together, Cossy said, 'Right, son, I've come to tell you that I've become a Christian.'

Tommy replied, 'Oh, that's great. Have another glass of champagne!'

Cossy continued, 'I've come to tell you that this is the last time we'll be having a cigar and sipping champagne together. I've become a Christian and I can't do the things we used to do. You've got my word, though, that what I know about you I will take to my grave. I promise you.'

Tommy would never kowtow to anyone.

Cossy's friend shook his head and said, 'Well, I believe you on that 'cos I know you are a man of your word. My boy, you are a sad loss to us.' He left it at that.

Tommy was facing a big prison sentence, which was increased because he wouldn't give information about his deals with the dealers. Tommy would never kowtow to anyone. However, as he had a good barrister, he was out on bail. During this time he and Cossy met up again. People knew that Cossy had gone from having 'stupid money' to living on the dole. Tommy enquired, 'How's this Christianity lark going with you? Tell me one thing, tell me the truth, and don't lie to me, how do you sleep at night?'

Cossy replied, 'For the first time in my life, I sleep just like a baby.'

'How I envy you,' Tommy sighed.

Tommy eventually embraced Jesus Christ as his Lord and Saviour in the 19th year of his incarceration. Later that same year he was released from prison and eventually he was also released from this earth having died from cancer. As far as British justice is concerned, he had served his time. Yet regarding eternity, all Tommy's judgement had been paid by Jesus on the cross, and he has gone to be with His Lord whom he had come to know and love.

Meanwhile, Cossy's old mate, Pastor Bill, had recruited him to become the caretaker and cook at the Bridge Chapel, which by now was quite a busy centre in the local community. Accommodation was also provided, which was an added bonus. Cossy soon became a well-known and much-loved character in the church.

Recently minor surgery was needed on one of Cossy's knees. He should have been in and out of hospital in a couple of days, but things went wrong. He caught the MRSA bug, nearly died and spent nine months hospitalised. From being an able-bodied football player, now he travels on a mobility scooter; quite a contrast from the flash cars he once drove.

One thing that worries Cossy is that there are some people who think they are good and therefore don't need forgiveness. While readily admitting that Cossy needed to be saved, they feel that they themselves are all right! He responds by asking:

> *'Don't middle-class people sin? Doesn't everyone sin? Yes, I was a bad lad, but all our hearts are sinful, and we are all going to die. You can't live and not see the grave. There are only two certain things: death and taxes. I may have been good at avoiding the taxes, but I couldn't avoid the other one. The beauty is that Jesus Christ has paid the price for us on the cross. Sins can be forgiven. Will it be easy? No, it was the hardest thing for me to do, but it has been the most rewarding too. I'm just a 'Dingle scally', but I will speak for my Saviour because He has done that much for me.'*

Peter Dungey

THE IMMORAL PRIEST

For he has rescued us from the dominion of darkness and brought us into the kingdom of the Son He loves. *(The Bible)*

Peter's story is not a pretty one nor is it an easy one for him to share. It contains much human wickedness, his and others. It is, though, the story of the making of the man he was to become.

If you had met him some years ago, he might have presented himself to you as Monsignor Peter, who was also Vicar Foran and a member of the 23rd level of the Knights Templar, plus a gay champion of the homosexual fraternity in Manchester's gay village and the proud head of that city's annual gay parade. Adorned in the vestments becoming to his rank and status, he was, in his words, 'the godless leader of his own godless flock'.

In the beginning life at home had seemed a little simpler. He was the most dearly loved son of adoring parents and had a loving sister too. What could possibly go wrong?

At the crucial age of eleven his parents' marriage split apart. Unceremoniously he was dispatched to the care of a far distant Catholic boarding school. Separated from his parents and sister, he had little idea that he would never see them again. His reception at this august establishment was made memorable by the attendance of one of the older priests, a man who, at his first opportunity, began to systematically rape him.

As shocking as this debasing treatment was, it did not compare to the physical and emotional cruelties he suffered there. To avoid the viciousness and malicious attentions, he would often shield himself in the security of a cupboard he had found. Peter explains, 'The point of this pathetic sanctuary was that once I was inside, it could not be opened and I could not be beaten. However, the only thing this ever succeeded in doing was to bring even further wrath down upon my head, when I did eventually make my exit.'

Things were so bad that Peter ran away, but he was soon discovered hiding in a forest. On his return to the establishment, the 'headmistress' subjected him to a severe beating and the removal of all his clothing for a period of a fortnight. She had correctly calculated that his punishment was more than enough to dissuade him from ever doing that again. (If this report may seem a little too extreme to be completely reliable, Peter is keen to state that the establishment has since been the focus of an abuse enquiry.)

When Peter reached the age of 16, funding for his accommodation ceased, enabling him to legitimately leave the place for good. Unfortunately, instead of preparing him for life as an adult and a career to on which to embark, and because of the abuse he had sustained, Peter went to live in Soho, London, as a rent boy.

Among the most famous and feared gangsters in London were the Kray bothers. During that time he became involved with the homosexual, crime boss Ronnie Kray. He had a wildly psychotic nature, was given to extremes of violence, and infamously was arrested and sentenced for murder. Peter was the young man the police found in his bed on the night he was arrested. Peter wants to stress that he repeats this episode not to glorify the extremes of the life he was then living, but to illustrate the depths of his own degeneracy.

'It begin to dawn on me that I was on the long road to nowhere.'

As he grew older, his looks naturally aged, thus losing the fresh-faced appearance of youthfulness. As a consequence, his appeal to those men diminished, so it became time for him to look for another trade.

He became a criminal. His particular talent was violence. Peter explains, 'I gained an unhealthy satisfaction from working for the many criminal gangs operating in London. I excelled as a protection racket enforcer, earning for myself the name "Pickaxe Pete" (because of my preference for that particular tool of the trade).'

This behaviour of his did not go unnoticed by the Metropolitan Police. They kept sending him down as a regular guest of Her Majesty's Prison Service. Each additional conviction lengthened his 'form card', which in turn resulted in an increasingly longer prison sentence. As Peter adds, 'Only after several incarcerations did it begin to dawn on me that I was on the long road to nowhere.'

During what turned out to be his final spell in prison, he was challenged by a prison visitor to study the Bible more by enrolling on a correspondence course with a Bible college. To Peter's astonishment, he actually passed. Not only did he pass, but he did so with the highest pass level ever recorded for a beginner. Instead of standing back, simply gasping with amazement, the same prison visitor asked if he understood what the exam was about. Peter continues:

> *'I had just passed with the highest mark recorded ... and he was asking me if I knew what the exam was about! Of course I did. But the fact of the matter was I couldn't answer his question. All I could reply was to lamely say, 'It was about the Bible, wannit?' He asked again. Finally he ended our conversation by telling me what I didn't know. 'It was about Jesus, Peter.' I learned something that day.'*

Each time a new door opened in his life, it usually led to more trouble. But when his three years in Parkhurst Prison on the Isle of Wight were up, the door opened to an entirely different perspective. This time he was leaving with a qualification! 'For the very first time in my life, I felt that I finally had a goal and an aim. And not just any old qualification; I had a 98 per cent mega-pass to a better life!' Peter exclaims.

Inspired by the heights of his newly discovered religious talents, Peter joined the Roman Catholic Church. He enrolled at a Catholic seminary and began to train for the priesthood. It was quite a smart way to avoid the usual merry-go-round back to prison, he thought. He adds, 'I had no illusions about my reasons for being there. It was certainly not to cover myself with sackcloth and ashes and to piously plead for a glimpse of the face of God. Nope, I was there to advance myself!'

His past experiences with monks and priests had taught him all he needed to know about the calibre of brother he would find in that place, and he admits that he knew that he would not be disappointed. Peter soon discovered that a number of priests in training were just as troubled and corrupt as he was. They had come to the ascetic cloistered halls, seeking monastic sanctuary from the normal world. They had found it in the fellowship of their own kind. But whereas they had come to hide themselves away, he was looking for much more than that.

After attaining the level of 'Monsignor' in his higher education, he had the opportunity to join the Knights Templar. It was only a matter of time before he rose to the position of Vicar Foran and became a member of the 23rd level of the Masonic organisation. 'The unusual speed of my ascendance through their hierarchy was due in no small part, I believe, to my early training at the hands of those

Catholic priests long ago,' Peter admits.

As his career as a priest developed, every year he would happily lead his flock in the city of Manchester's gay parade, dispensing sprinkles of holy water to all and sundry. As far as he was concerned, he had made it. The once crushed and broken-hearted little boy, who had endured constant and soul-destroying abuse at the hands of perverted elderly priests, thought that he had not only survived but triumphed. As he summarises, 'I had recognition and position. I had many good friends. I felt I had made it. Despite everything this life could possibly throw at me, I felt that I had emerged a winner!'

This perceived 'pinnacle' had been achieved through falsehood and corruption and in complete spiritual darkness. He had no personal relationship with God. He was a lost soul. Then his greatest friend died.

Father Liam possessed an exceptionally caring heart. Peter loved him as one would love a father or a good brother. Father Liam gave him a quality of genuine affection that never failed, unlike his homosexual predecessors. He was Peter's one real, sustaining friend. With his unexpected death Peter felt he had lost everything. He was beside himself and became completely lost to sorrow. Once again he was reduced to the desperation he had spent his whole life trying to escape.

Quite inconsolable in the gloom of that state, Peter wandered into a Christian bookshop one day. It probably wouldn't have looked unusual for a priest to be looking at Christian books. Peter was drawn to the bargain bin, but actually God's hand was on this. Inside it he discovered a very cheap book costing the knockdown price of 25p, but it turned out to be the biggest bargain he had ever come across in his life. He read it from cover to cover. He devoured it. He saw something in those pages he had never realised could exist. He saw a man as desperate and as unhappy as himself. This man had been sentenced to over 12 years behind the bars of an Irish jail; he was enduring a living death.

He saw a man as desperate and as unhappy as himself.

Peter says, 'I read in his book how he cried out in sheer desperation, to the Living God; I could see him in that prison cell, facing those lonely years behind bars, and in utter torment crying out, "Jesus! I can't take this anymore, save me." And reading on, I discovered the amazing result of that terrible cry for help – how this man was changed that very same night!'

In the bleakness of his wretched prison cell, that man experienced the supernatural joy of actually being visited by Almighty God. Peter read of how he felt the love of God both reach out and forgive him for his past life of desperate shame, and also touch his soul with the tender love of Christ, thus filling him with hope for the future. Peter was challenged by what he read. 'Where are you, God?' was the cry from his heart. 'Help me!'

Deep within Peter was overwhelmed with the desire to meet this person, David Hamilton, who was now pastor of a church that, coincidentally, was only about fifteen minutes away from Peter's home. Unfortunately, the day that Peter visited it, the pastor was away on holiday. Nevertheless, still dressing with a dog collar, Peter found a seat at the back and listened intently to the preacher. What he was saying about Jesus was certainly hitting Peter like bullets right on target. 'For God so loved the world that he gave his one and only Son, that whoever believes in him shall not perish but have eternal life' are words from the Bible that Peter was going to come to understand. But first there was the question Peter posed to himself and to God: 'Where do I go from here?'

Known for his hospitality, another man in the church generously invited him to come to his house for lunch, which Peter gladly accepted. This was the beginning of a genuine friendship, based around meals and studying the Bible with much discussion, as Peter discovered who Jesus was, why He died on the cross and why He rose from the dead.

So far in his life Peter had committed crimes, been an immoral priest and also contracted AIDS, which he describes as being handed a life sentence. But then he heard that God loved him. All the sin and filth in Peter's life deserved punishment, but God sent Jesus to bear it instead. Broken and ashamed before God, Peter thanked God for taking the punishment he deserved and recognised Jesus as Lord and Saviour of his life.

On 22 August Peter Dungey denounced his former wicked ways, with tears of penitence and relief, as he discovered the freedom in Christ when a sinner truly repents. As he puts it, 'I felt clean and free. The Bible says, "So if the Son sets you free, you will be free indeed."'

Peter was about to receive another piece of good news, not from God exactly, but from the hospital that he attended for regular blood tests on account of him being HIV positive. The latest test was causing everyone concern so it had to be repeated. Peter wondered what on earth was going on. 'We can't find the virus any more. It isn't there,' reported the medical staff. Peter was so shocked. Truly he felt that the old life had gone. 'Then you will know the truth, and the truth will set your free' reads the Bible.

Peter Dungey now attends Heaton Chapel Community Church, Stockport.

Jodi Whitehouse

THE CHARITY WORKER

Every time I go to the airport or the bank I carry with me something that will prove my identity. I will need to prove who I am. A photo or a signature that is uniquely mine is required. But what is it that defines you or me as a person? I wonder what we would say? Would it be our job, our appearance, our religion, our family, or our position in society?

The first time I saw Jodi was at a public meeting in one of Britain's big cities. She walked out onto the stage undaunted, it appeared, by the large, expectant audience facing her. Taking the microphone with confidence, this beautiful young woman – with long blonde hair, a bubbly personality and totally dressed in black – told her life story. It was one that was full of hope as well as challenges to her identity.

> *'My life has been full of ups and downs. When I was born, I had a very rare skin condition*

– and still have it. A very large, dark-brown, hairy birthmark covers 80 per cent of my body. It starts at the top of my back, comes down way past my bottom and then goes round past my stomach. I have a few other marks too, covering my arms and legs. At birth I had a mark on my cheek that looked like a tomato that had been cut in half, plus many others on my head and elsewhere. When my mum and dad were handed me all wrapped up in a blanket, the doctor's initial response was, 'She has a birthmark, but its nothing to worry about.' '

When her mum saw Jodi's back, she thought she looked like a little monkey. No explanation was given to her parents as to what was the matter with her skin. Other doctors said that they had never seen anything like it before and that she might not live for very long, and advised them to make the most of her life.

So when her parents took Jodi home, they left with a bag of bandages to help cover some of her wounds that were still open. For the first 15 years of her life Jodi had over 30 operations to try and remove the birthmark. Since the doctors didn't know what the condition was, the only thing that they could do was to try and remove it because they feared it could become cancerous. The operations were, in fact, simply attempts at 'shaving' the birthmark off but, because it was so deep, it would just grow back – 'rather like cutting grass' is the way Jodi explains it. They did manage to remove the birthmark on her face, though, and if you were to look carefully you would see a scar that looks like a lightning bolt. So when curious children ask her about it, she replies, 'I am Harry Potter's sister!'

In fact she still has lots of scars all over her body. When she was 17 years old, she was admitted to a London hospital for major surgery to carry our skin grafting. One of the nurses said at the time that she had never seen such a big graft done in one operation, and there is still a mark there today.

When curious children ask her about it, she replies, 'I am Harry Potter's sister!'

For Jodi growing up was really difficult. In her primary school years, whenever there was swimming or PE, children would ask what the mark was. 'Dunno, just a birthmark' was her reply.

One day when she was sitting in the bath aged eight, she put her little hands together and prayed, 'Dear Lord, please will you get rid of my birthmark?'

Her parents had always taken Jodi to church so she had heard about Jesus and the Bible. She knew something about praying; she knew God could hear and answer prayer; and she knew that God loved her. Therefore she felt sure that He was going to get rid of the mark. Having prayed, she decided that she would just open one eye and have a look round, expecting it to have gone. But it was still there!

We are coy about admitting it but, as we look back on our lives, many of us have prayed similar types of prayers for others or ourselves that were not answered in the way we had hoped. As a child Jodi couldn't understand why God was saying 'no', but then she began to learn early lessons about faith in God. Someone taught her an acrostic on the word 'faith' that helped her then and has been a mainstay throughout her life: FAITH means:

***F**orsaking*
***A**ll*
I
***T**rust*
***H**im*

Jodi remembers going on holiday to Perranporth in Cornwall and her younger sister, who at that time was probably about seven, asking if she could wear a bikini on the beach. So her mum bought her a tankini-type thing. Jodi, being older, thought, 'well if her sister could, she ought to be able to as well'. When she asked her dad, he replied, 'Well, Jodi, you know if you did, people on the beach would stare at you. Would you be able to cope with that?'

Confidently she boasted that she would be fine and she was going to wear it whatever, but her heart was pounding. She put on the tankini and for the first time revealed to all who she was. It was as if Jodi was acting out a truth she knew to be true. It is very easy in life to hide our real characters. We say 'Good morning' to everyone and give the impression that life is brilliant, maybe we even turn up to church on Sundays and do the same when inside we know life is not good. We think bad thoughts; we do wrong deeds; we are not as great as everyone thinks we are. Jodi remembers walking on that beach and revealing her skin in public for the first time – her lumpy, very dark, hairy skin. People stared. Children asked their parents about her. Then the child would be pulled away but continued just staring at her. She walked along the beach pretending that everything was all right but actually, inside, she found it very tough.

It is very easy in life to hide our real characters.

On account of all her operations at Alder Hey Children's Hospital, Jodi lost three years of her education. Throughout school she kept quiet. She hated speaking out loud – it was really uncomfortable for her. But now she speaks, as she puts it, 'not in my own confidence but in the confidence and strength that God Himself gives me'.

As a child she had attended junior church and learned that when she died she could go to heaven or hell. She preferred to go to heaven! She asked what she would have to do to go there. The answer was that there are no lists of what you have to do. It is not a question of having to go to church each week, good as that may be. So again she asked how she could get to heaven. It was explained to her that she needed to trust in Jesus. He came to earth with the purpose of taking on Himself, as He was crucified, all that would condemn us and keep us out of heaven. He died as the substitute sin-bearer. Heaven is not a reward for good works, it is a gift purchased by Jesus and is offered to all who will receive Him. She may only have been a child, but it seemed quite straightforward to her just what she should do.

When she arrived home, Jodi sat on the stairs and prayed, 'Dear God, I am sorry that I am a sinner and not good like I am pretending to be. Please forgive me when I do selfish things. Please will you come into my life and live in me?' She explains, 'And that was it. Amen. No big flash of lightning or anything like that. But from then on I trusted Him that He would know what is best for my life.' Later, as Jodi continues:

'At the age of sixteen a 'miracle' happened. My mum's friend knocked on the door to tell us that a Scottish newspaper had been put through their door. A local Glasgow newspaper had been delivered to a house in Liverpool! Inside was an article about a little boy who had just been born with exactly the same condition as me. I had never met anyone else like me in my life. My doctors still didn't have a name for it. This story gave me hope. There was a doctor in Great Ormond Street Hospital in London who had started to do some research into the condition. I went with my family down to his clinic where for the first time in my life I learned what it was called: Congenital Melanocytic Naevi or CMN.

'This particular doctor was just starting to meet patients who had CMN, which was an extremely rare disease. Because I was

older than others who had it, he requested permission to take my telephone number to pass it on to others so that they would not be left on their own. That very night I received a call from a mother in a desperate way and in tears. By the time I was 20 we had about 100 families all across the UK that we were supporting. Since then the support has developed into a big charity, partly due to the need to fund the Great Ormond Street clinic which was due to close unless more money could be found. I volunteered to help.

'During the months following we raised more than £80,000. The doctor who took over the research wrote a paper, which has been distributed worldwide, revealing the discovery of a gene that causes CMN. As a result they have been able to look at how to treat CMN properly. It is now known that the disease also grows internally, which has caused some children to die. So it is more than a birthmark; it is a syndrome. As a consequence we now seek to support bereaved families through the charity. We also share our struggles and help people along the way.

So it is more than a birthmark; it is a syndrome.

'People ask me how I have coped having this condition, knowing that even I don't know if it is going to grow internally in me. I won't lie or pretend. Honestly I can say I have no fear of death because as a child I learned, and then experienced, the simple truth of the song, 'Jesus loves me, this I know for the Bible tells me so'. I hate reading so looking at the Bible has not been easy for me, but the Bible is amazing. Get your head into the Bible and, trust me, you can't put it down. In it are wonderful promises that God makes to us through Jesus. I know its true.

'When I left school, my teachers were a bit worried about me as to what my future might hold. I actually went to university, after which I was appointed as the Disability Liaison Officer at Liverpool Football Club. One time I had the wonderful opportunity to go to Liberia with the charity Samaritan's Purse. I was used to being around footballers who had everything and yet were not content, yet there was I in the middle of jungle with kids who had been child soldiers and who had seen terrible things but were now going to a church there. As we walked up to it, we heard loud singing, praising God. These were people who had very little material things

or worth in this life and yet I have never seen such joy. Then, thinking back to Liverpool to those with so much and yet who were not content, it made me think, 'Who would I rather be?'

'Life can be rubbish, and full of pain, difficulty, suffering and problems. We are not immune to life's struggles, even though we are Christians. Yet when we come to know God, underneath it all there is a foundation found in the Bible that helps us stay secure throughout. In heaven God promises that there will be no more pain and suffering. However, the only way to get there is through Jesus, who is 'the way and the truth and the life', as it says in John chapter 14, verse 6 of the Bible. No one comes to the Father except through Him. God sent Jesus to die so that He could take the punishment we deserve for our sins. He rose again from the dead to make the way for us to go to heaven. We enter Heaven not by what we know, our intellect, but rather by who we know, Jesus our Saviour.

It is only with hindsight, when I look back to when as an eight year old I prayed to be healed and I wasn't, that now I can see why. God had *a purpose for me. Not only did He enable me not to be bitter about my situation, but also He was to use me to help others, for which I am so thankful.'*

Jodi still continues with her charity work, including an appearance on daytime television. Earlier this year she managed to squeeze a very special occasion into her busy schedule – her wedding!

If you would like to know more about the CMN charity, go to:

www.caringmattersnow.co.uk

Alternatively you can contact them as follows:

email: info@caringmattersnow.co.uk

Caring Matters Now, PO Box 732,
Cambridge, CB1 0Q

For a free course entitled IDENTITY (which looks at what the Bible has to say about who we are and who God is) or to meet up with a group near you contact www.10ofthose.com.

‘Mina’

THE DENTIST

Within the cauldron of a Middle Eastern country a conflicting mixture of politics, religion and culture was swirling. Even the climate was showing no mercy as the sun beat down day after day, parching the earth.

A little girl bowed to pray to Allah. But this day was different in that she actually said, ‘Where are you? I can’t sense you.’ All she knew was that this god was watching every move she made and was going to come down hard on her. In the religion she was being taught, there was a god of judgement, with no love being mentioned at all. Allah was very powerful, but distant.

Mina (as we shall call her) belonged to a very close-knit family of two boys and three girls. Being the youngest, Mina had a lot of support from her siblings. With much hard work her father worked his way up from a post as a caretaker to a high position in an oil company. Mina’s mother was barely 16 when she married her cousin, who was only two years older than her, having been brought up in his household since the death of her own mother. While not being an arranged marriage, they grew up realising that it was the expected thing to do.

Life became comfortable for the family due to the many privileges they received from the oil company. A house was given to them, their bills including utilities were paid for them, and if anyone wanted to travel to visit family members in other cities or towns, they simply phoned the oil company and tickets were booked without charge.

Within her culture Mina was able to experience other freedoms besides unrestricted travel. She loved school, especially competing academically with boys in her class because they were felt to be the clever ones. Her family were strict in the areas of prayers and fasting, and Mina remembers praying five times a day when she was quite young, but they were not a mosque-going family. However, while they may not have been devout, Islam actually impacted every decision and action they made in life.

She was almost 12 when her country was convulsed by an uprising. Mina recalls this event:

'I remember it vividly. I remember actually

being in the street while rioting was happening all around me. It seemed that the whole country was turning against the government. There were soldiers in the street after us. One really kind shopkeeper pulled up the shutters of the shop and called in 20 or 30 of us. Pulling down the shutters, he kept us all safe until everything went quiet. I vividly remember it: the anger, the shouting and the hatred in the faces of those who wanted to turn over the regime.'

Her older sister had taken up a strongly political stance in her thinking. Mina had just been following her sister that day, although her parents had told her not to go. But they nearly got killed. Mina's sister didn't expect her country to become as rigidly Islamic as it did. All the people who went out to protest simply wanted something better. They did not want to see it become as oppressive as it eventually became. There was, and still is, bitter disappointment from many who were fighting for change.

Normal life, as the family had known it for many years, was about to suffer from the devastating effects the uprising had on the ordinary people of their country. One brother emigrated, with no problems at all in getting out, and settled in the UK. But another brother had to escape from the country having reached the age when he would be conscripted into National Service.

Friends could not believe that the family was actually going to get on a plane legally.

He was called to go out to the front, but because he did not believe in war, he felt it was the wrong thing to do. The family did not hear from or see him for two months. As far as they knew, he could have been killed. Other family members elsewhere had left their areas and ended up coming to live with them.

By now the government was looking quite closely at people like them who were on the move. It really was dangerous for them as a family to live where they were, especially as it became known that they were not all supporting the new Islamic regime. So as a family they decided it might be safer to move north to live with an uncle for a year until they managed to get visas for the UK. These visas were a miracle because, at the time, things were so difficult for even one person to get a visa, let alone a whole family, especially when the authorities knew that two members of the family had already left the country. Friends could not believe that the family was actually going to get on a plane legally and be met at Heathrow in London. A two-month visiting visa was given for them to stay with their relatives in the UK. As Mina says, 'We just wanted to get out of the place.' They left home with suitcases of photographs and some clothes, leaving everything else behind. They hoped they would return someday but deep down didn't think it would ever be possible. It was a case of 'let's see what happens'.

Inevitably they faced a couple of hours of questioning by officials at Heathrow Passport Control. Every one of them feared they would be sent back. Mina's brother, who had come to meet them, had an anxious wait as they were not permitted to see him. Finally, though, they were allowed through. A new life was about to begin, even if no one was quite sure what to expect.

Mina found it quite surreal to be out of the Middle East and to not be forced to cover her head if she didn't want to. She was allowed, quite simply, to be herself. She was 15 years old and had left behind a new regime that told her that she couldn't go to school because there were boys there, stated that head coverings were mandatory, and dictated what she could or couldn't wear. 'Even white shoes were banned! We didn't have freedom for anything. We weren't allowed to have joy, happiness, music, laughter or anything.' So it took quite a while for Mina to settle into a new culture.

For the first year they all lived with her brother. She had to learn the language, and found that she was still reacting automatically in the way she would have done in her country of origin. For example, if a visitor came to their home she would instinctively cover her head and turn off the radio. Their time in the UK was to be long-term, though, as Mina explains:

> *'Obviously we had just come as tourists but we soon realised that our lives were in danger. By now 'they' were looking for my younger brother who had not completed his National Service. We had disappeared; my dad left behind 30 years of living and working for the oil company. He left everything, all he had worked for and owned, in order to flee. We lost a lot, but it was to save us and give us an opportunity to actually do something here and have a life of freedom.'*

A possibility came up for them to enquire about gaining refugee status, which started the process for them to become British citizens. This involved endless queues, interviews and much waiting around over a period of five years. During that time they received permission to study, but only part-time. Eventually they were accepted on humanitarian grounds.

For the time being, though, gone were the days of luxury and the space she had enjoyed in her home country. When they first moved to the UK, circumstances meant that the whole family had to share living quarters with Mina's brother, his wife and child in their two-bedroom house. Despite the obvious difficulties, Mina managed to study part-time for A-levels in biology, chemistry and maths as she had an ambition to eventually to eventually study medicine. All her study books and personal possessions were in a box under her bed because that was the only place she could find to put them. Without a desk she had to study lying on the floor behind her door, often being interrupted by people coming in and out and banging into her. She was a very determined student.

Eventually they were accepted on humanitarian grounds.

Since she was a child Mina's dream had always been to train to be a cardiologist; but, although she had worked her hardest, her grades were not quite sufficient. When faced with such cruel disappointment, her reaction was, like many others, to ask the questions, 'Why?' and 'Why has god let this happen to me? I don't deserve this.' Although she would have been allowed to repeat the A-levels, she decided to accept an unconditional offer to study dentistry at the nearby university.

Her brother, R, would argue with anyone to prove a point. He would invite anyone who was willing to chat about religion over a coffee. It didn't matter which religion it was because he was interested in them all and reading books about them. Finally he met someone who was just a straightforward Bible-believing Christian. On occasions he had discussed matters with Mormons and Jehovah's Witnesses, so thought he knew all the answers, but this person was different. He believed the Bible without directives from Salt Lake City or Brooklyn in the USA. This man was a follower of Jesus Christ, the Son of God, and was trusting Him rather than following an organisation or a system. He knew God in an intimate way.

This man introduced R to someone from a similar background to himself who had become a Christian. They met and had lots of discussions, and R started bringing home Bibles and other books on the subject. In time Mina's brother, trusting in God's love for him, asked the Jesus who had died on the cross for his sin and risen from the dead to forgive him and become his Lord and Saviour.

The wider family thought he had gone crazy. They didn't oppose him, but they were concerned and wondered both what was going on and why was there such a change in him. They had been repeatedly been taught, in Islam, that people don't change like that because when someone is born a Muslim they are always Muslims – it is just in their nature.

Nevertheless, within a month not only had R become a Christian but also his brother. He was staying with them on a visit from the USA, having also been converted to Christ. The two of them decided to be baptised – to publicly declare their faith in Jesus – and invited the whole family to the church service. None of the rest of the family had ever been in a church before. The conversations in the car on the way to the church were very revealing.

One of her sisters, in anger, asked R, 'What are you doing this for?'

R replied, 'I can just tell you one thing. Jesus has said, "I am the way and the truth and the life. No-one comes to the Father except through me (John chapter 14, verse 6).” If you’ve got a problem with that, ask Jesus.’

That was the challenge he gave them, and that was only on the way to church! So there they were, sitting in a building, not knowing anyone or understanding what was going on. The sister was sitting at the back adamantly muttering, ‘I’m not getting involved in any of this.’ Mina was not taking much notice of what was going on because she was video-taping the whole thing for her brothers. But by the time the service had finished, Mina’s sister was actually having an argument with God saying, ‘R is telling me that you are *the God*. Why don’t you show me? I’m not leaving here until you show me.’ By the end of the baptismal service there were tears rolling down her face. Running down to the front of the church, her 30-year-old-sister was shouting to her brothers, ‘I’m a Christian girl! I’m a Christian girl!’

‘If you’ve got a problem with that, ask Jesus.’

Try to imagine being in that very full, little house. They were still all living together. At one end of the settee was R reading his Bible, while the father was sitting at the other end reading his Quran. He was only doing so because he felt obliged to. Yet it wasn’t long after that both her parents also put their trust in Jesus and became Christians too, as Mina recounts:

> *'It was a big decision for my parents but they could not ignore the changes that they were noticing in their children. There was joy in their faces. They had no restrictions as such. They had liberation almost. The salvation Jesus gave them was something we Muslims never had, even though we did the five times a day prayer and one month of fasting routine. We gave to the poor – we always did so as a family. My parents were very generous. I often remember loads of people being fed by my mum. We gave clothes away. We didn't want to be happy just because we were comfortable. My parents were really kind people and still are. They remained loving people but now they had come to know the true God, the God of love, in whose image they were made.'*

Being an avid reader, Mina was picking up and pouring over R's books. But for her lots of questions came into her mind. As a logical, scientifically-minded person, she required proof. It wasn't enough just to read the books putting forward Christianity; she wanted to read the arguments against as well. She went to the library to look for answers.

R had gone as far as he could take her in trying to answer her questions so recommended that she met up with a retired medical doctor who also taught the Bible at a college. Having listened very carefully to her story, he gently said to her, 'It seems to me that you are struggling to understand something. It seems to me that the Shepherd is looking very hard for you.' At the time that didn't make sense to her, but it did strike a chord.

A couple of days later Mina tagged along with others to a meeting where the Christian message was being proclaimed and explained by a third-world preacher. It wasn't because of what he said or even what she heard that day, but she had a sudden realisation that she was a sinner in God's sight, and that He is a loving, holy God. He is the Shepherd looking out for her, and was offering the gift of eternal life through Jesus Christ the Lord. Mina explains more:

> *'In Islam I can be as good as I want to be, try as hard as I can; I could be a very good person, trying not to lie or steal, living my life as best as I can. But I would still not have a guarantee that I would go to heaven when I die. It depends what Allah wants to do on the day I am judged. I didn't like the belief in Islam that lots of people try to do good to cancel out the*

bad things they have done. How can that be right? Christianity says something completely different. A person goes to heaven not because he or she is good, but because they have received the gift of salvation that Jesus has bought for them because He loves them.'

That day something 'jumped in her heart'. She wanted to be converted. Mina had investigated the evidence and was convinced, but at that particular event she wanted 'her heart to be converted' too. She wanted to belong to Jesus so she trusted her life to Him and follows Him day by day.

Mina has since qualified as a dentist specialising in treating children with special needs, is married and now has children of her own. Following Jesus kept her from abusing the freedom that she so relished when she first came to the UK. It was as a Christian that she went to university, where all sorts of wild excesses were expected and encouraged by the student fraternity. While there she met someone with the same name but from a different country. They had conversations about faith. On one such occasion they examined the question, 'If you died tonight, would you go to

That day something 'jumped in her heart'.

heaven?' Her friend replied, 'I hope so. I don't know.' Mina replied, 'Only a year ago I would have said the same as you, but now that I am a Christian I know for sure that I will go to heaven, not because I am better than you but because I know that I have got salvation through Jesus. That's the difference.' As far as Mina knows, this girl stayed a Muslim.

Mina muses on the huge turnaround in her life:

> *'I remember as a Muslim little girl praying to God and actually saying, 'Where are you? I can't sense you.' because it seems in the East that Allah is very distant and very powerful but there is no love. Whereas obviously now I know the God of the Bible, and know for myself that He is the God of love. In Islam god is one of judgement. He's watching every move you make and he's going to come down hard on you. There is no love mentioned in Islam at all.*
>
> *'The true and living God heard my prayer and brought me to know Him as my Lord, my Saviour. My Heavenly Father knows all about me, and yet still loves me. He gave the Lord Jesus to die for my sins, and then went on to conquer death by rising from the dead. He*

showed me Himself, and made me His child forever.'

David

THE DAD

Slowly yet deliberately, David swirled the amber, alcoholic liquid in the glass as he inhaled the nicotine from his cigarette. Alone, sitting at the kitchen table, he gazed upwards to the ceiling. Unheard by anyone, David's thoughts wandered over all the areas and experiences of his life. Was there a God? If so, was anyone listening?

Although David had been born in Belfast, his family moved up to Annalong, which is a tiny little fishing village along the County Down coast. Behind it stretches a beautiful, lush-green landscape. His dad was a fisherman by trade, with his own trawler. He would go up and down all over the Irish Sea and into the North Channel to catch prawns, herring and mackerel as well as hake, cod and haddock. Sometimes David would go with him but the fishing industry had no attraction for him as a career. As he puts it, 'As much as I loved it out on the waves, the social life of a fisherman was terrible. You never knew when you would be back from a trip so it was no good making plans. Out at sea it was a great place for escapism, for thinking your own thoughts – away from everything.'

As well as relishing the sea, David loved getting up into the mountains of Mourne, from where there are spectacular views across the fields and beyond. This caused David to conclude, 'I just thought that all this beauty could not have come about by accident. But that was as far as it went about believing in God.'

Fortunately a boat answered the mayday call before his boat sank.

Three times he was in life-threatening situations. The first was when he suffered appendicitis as a child. The second was when a car in which he was a passenger turned over. Amazingily he emerged from this unscathed. However, a couple of hundred metres further down the road was a long drop over a cliff. If the accident had happened there, he would have died. The third incident happened when he was out fishing. The boat took on water and started to sink. It looked like he was going to have to swim a mile to the shore on a cold, windy night. He probably wouldn't have survived this ordeal but fortunately a boat answered the mayday call before his boat sank.

In Northern Ireland everyone seemed to have an opinion about religion. Culture dictated that, right from their early years, young people would be exposed to teaching about religion of all varieties. Knowing about God is very different to believing in God, though, as the latter requires an engagement with the heart in a relationship. David went to church because his parents did, but he always preferred the informal youth stuff to the actual church services. Then by the time he reached 15 or 16 years of age, he decided that he had had enough. He didn't like church – it was a trial.

After David left school, Queen's University Belfast offered him a place to study electrical and electronic engineering. The following years found him becoming a heavy drinker and a self-confessed party animal. His degree result reflected that since he got the bottom end of an honours.

The political troubles were evident across the city. Big bombing campaigns, disruption and threats often brought the place to a standstill. Sometimes it was not worth taking the car as it was quicker to walk. After graduation David managed to gain a position with BT. (British Telecom had had its fair share of bomb scares.)

Life for David moved on inexorably to getting married, settling down and starting a family of his own. Sandra, his wife, liked to go to church, so David got into the routine of taking on the job of cooking Sunday lunch while she was out. Nevertheless, David was thinking about God, as he explains:

> *'I suppose the thing that really started to speak to me about God was when my first son was born. I just remember that day seeing this new life being born, and realising how perfect this little boy was with his small fingers and toes. He was an absolute human being; he was absolutely perfect. I thought that his life could not just be an accident. It was not chemistry, not physics, not any of the sciences. There was genuine life in the child.'*

Life was not the only thing that was sparking David's interest in God; death too came along to jolt his thoughts in the right direction. His uncle died, and David recalls the impact this had on him:

> *'He was a very generous man who cared practically for my family and others. In Belfast he owned a shoe shop. After they had had a sale, there would obviously be shoes that didn't sell, some of them very good shoes. Instead of*

donating them to the Salvation Army, which in itself would have been good, he went around looking for down-and-outs to personally fit them up with shoes. This Christian man showed his Christianity in a very practical way. He was gentle, kind, loving – a real reflection of Jesus.

'I thought, 'If I were to die today, where would I go?' So I would end up in the evenings sitting in the kitchen pondering all these things in my head, asking God questions but not knowing if they were going beyond the ceiling. I remembered things from Sunday school, such as how Jesus loved us so much that He came to take the punishment for all the wrong things we had done in our lives. I found it harder to believe in evolution than creation. I couldn't take seriously the idea of two big balls of gas coming together, blowing up and out of this coming something as sophisticated as a human.'

So David began to reason with God. He said, 'Right, I have been brought up in Northern Ireland with all this background but how do I know that Christianity is the way? I see on TV about Hindus, Muslims and other world religions. How do I know that I will be right? God, show me. If You are truly God and Your Son is real, show me right now.'

David looked around the room. Something caught his eye. Something was stuck behind a cookery book. He continues the story:

'I pulled out an A4 sheet of paper that was beautifully decorated with flowers round the edges. It was actually a verse from the Bible. About a year before it had been put through our letterbox. The only reason it had not been put in the bin was because it was so attractive looking. I hadn't the heart to throw it away.

It was a life where I came first and I was the centre.

'It read, 'For God so loved the world that he gave his one and only Son, that whoever believes in him shall not perish but have everlasting life.' In a nutshell it said, 'I am God. I love you so much that I sent my son to die on a cross for you so that you can be saved.' '

David dropped to his knees on the kitchen floor and prayed. 'I just asked God to forgive me, although not too bad, I had lived for myself. It was a life where I came first and I was the centre. I knew in my head that was wrong.'

Both David's head and heart engaged in belief in the God of the Bible. Instead of religion, he now had a real, personal relationship with the God who made him. He was 35 years old. From then on David grew inwardly in his spirit as he learned and read more of the Bible. Compassion for others accompanied his new-found faith, resulting in him becoming a youth worker with a local church. David now wanted to share with his own kids and those in his neighbourhood how young people could know God for themselves, understand His plan for them and live life to the full as God intended. Hope and certainty could come even on the streets of his own country that had suffered such a troubled past.

David has become a full-time youth worker in the country area of Annalong.

Rob

THE RAPPER

Reggae, rap, hip-hop, break dancing and body popping were all part of the family and cultural life of a boy born in ... Bedford, England. Rob is a first-generation Jamaican. Both his parents were born in the Caribbean but, like many others in the 1950s, they moved to England for economic reasons. Blessed with two boys, his parents should have been happy, but sadly the marriage was not a happy one.

'When I was about eight years old, my mum and dad had really difficult marital issues,' Rob explains, and he vividly remembers there being domestic violence. At one point the family returned to Jamaica, hoping for a fresh start. This was Rob's first experience of the island. No doubt he appreciated the contrast in weather conditions to those in Britain. The intention was to live there for a few years but things didn't work out, so within a year and a half they were back in the UK with their mother, leaving their dad behind.

Rob remembers coming back to live in London, which is pretty much where he spent most of his time until he was 18 years old. His mother and father did not resolve their differences. Actually Rob feels glad that his mum split up with his dad because the marriage 'peaked' as he would say, meaning that it got very dangerous for his mother, though his dad never laid a hand on Rob as far as he can remember. Rob had seen his dad knock his mum down flights of stairs, and the possibility that this deeply scarred him explains the hatred he had for his dad. He despised him and even intended to hurt him if he had opportunity. The hatred was really very deep and dangerous. But he remembers his mum saying to him back then when the abuse was going on, 'One day you are going to reap what you sow.' Later on, when Rob's life had changed quite dramatically, he was able to go and find his dad, who by then had Parkinson's disease and couldn't even hold a cup of tea.

Rob's mum was a God-fearing woman but didn't attend church. She worked as a nurse on nights and, as a single mother bringing up two children, didn't have time to go. She did, however, talk much about the Bible. For a very short time Rob went along to church, but only because his mum sent him, then in his mid-teens he stopped going.

Music has always been a big part of his life, as he describes: 'My biological dad had what you call a sound system back in those days. It consisted of big speaker boxes, which he would hire out to venues to play music. It was kind of like the beginning of the experience of going out to a nightclub in the early days. I grew up around seven-inch singles and vinyl discs.'

Reggae was his first introduction to music, but by the time he was 12, hip-hop had arrived on the scene. It had come over from the States to the UK in the late seventies. Naturally Rob was curious as to what this was. But it just captured his heart. Then he got into break dancing and body popping. When he hit 16 he could afford to buy some music of his own.

A career as a DJ was a big step for Rob. It started to take off, first with a London-based set now called Rampage. Back then there was only him and one other person involved in it but now Rampage Sound is a successful organisation. Rob would like to say that this was how he earned his money as it sounds glamorous, but in reality he was a postman who DJ-ed in his spare time!

Hip-hop is a collection of things. A guy called Kool Herc, in the 1970s, started scratching and using break beats, which led to the beginning of hip-hop in New York. Rob did the up-rock stuff like body popping and rap, which stands for Rhythm And Poetry. However, he was heavily influenced by the Caribbean and their reggae music as well as hip-hop.

Rob always had a respect for God. Perhaps that influence came from his mother. There were always things he wouldn't say. For instance, he would not use God's name as a swear word. However, other parts of his life he would describe as definitely being ungodly. While there was still an underlying respect for God and belief in Him, that was as far as it went. He had no interest in finding out more or asking more specific questions. Rob adds, 'I always had a Bible at my bedside, always opened at Psalm 23. I never read it but it would always be there.'

He had no interest in finding out more or asking more specific questions.

If Rob met someone on the street who wanted to give him an invitation to a church event, or even just a Christian leaflet, he would always give him or her time. Jehovah's Witnesses used to come to his house regularly for about six months. Four o'clock every Sunday afternoon they would arrive and have a cup of tea. His girlfriend at that time was worried that he was going to become a Jehovah's Witness. 'Thankfully I didn't,' sums up his thoughts now.

Meanwhile Rob was busy with his day job at the post office. At his particular office at 9 Elms Lane in Vauxhall they worked in what is called 'mechanised letter offices' rather than delivering letters. While working in the sorting office, he met Helen, who became his girlfriend. After what happened to his mother's marriage, Rob had no intention of making such a commitment himself, so they just lived together, spending three nights or so at her place and four nights at his house.

She was not the only person he met at work. A guy called Harry Hanks came to his office. He was a chaplain from the London City Mission. Six foot and four inches tall, Harry was an ex-builder with massive hands but very much a 'gentle giant'. Helen and Harry got chatting together about what Harry believed. This was remarkable considering that Helen's lifestyle was one of one of drugs, drinking and casual sex! So she initially said to the chaplain, 'Harry, I'm not interested in God and I'm sure God wouldn't be interested in me.' Harry was not so easily put off and for the next two or three years continued to chat to Helen about Jesus Christ. Still she wasn't interested, though, saying, 'Harry, you're a nice man but I am not interested in God, thank you.'

Then one day, out of the blue, she decided that she was determined to go to church. Rob, probably surprised, encouraged her and said, 'Hey, good for you, Helen.' He continues, 'She was brought up as a Roman Catholic but she knew nothing about God. I at least had a Bible, unlike Helen. I told her to go to church. I was cool.' So she did.

Rob was still DJ-ing but also playing football with the lads. He would come in late on a Saturday night with boxes of records from DJ-ing. Then on Sunday morning he would pick up his football boots while Helen would be getting ready for church. He just pretended that church was of no interest for him. Then one day she startled Rob by saying, 'Rob you're going to football and it is Sunday, why don't you come to church?' Rob comments, 'She got me that morning. I'm like, I'm cool. No problem, I'll go to church.'

Near the Oval cricket ground in London there is a massive Church of England Church called St Mark's,

Kennington; it is directly opposite the Oval tube station. That is where Helen took Rob.

Rob had already seen a change in his girlfriend's life. The change was so stark that he was a bit nervous, as he explains: 'I thought that she was in a cult. She had changed overnight; she stopped drinking and smoking and had even got to the point where she said, "Rob, no more sex!" I was like "What?"' Rob had never been into drinking because in DJ-ing a clear head is needed. But when she told him 'no sex', he thought there was something definitely wrong.

The change was so stark that he was a bit nervous.

So when Rob eventually turned up at St Mark's, he was very suspicious, thinking that the church people were brainwashing his Helen. He even took along a friend from the post office and warned him to be wary of what was happening at the church.

The three of them walked in and sat down. But Rob found it was quite overwhelming. He felt ... humbled. There must have been about two hundred people inside. It was strange to him that 98 per cent of them were white. Feeling a little unnerved in that environment, he just sat down and behaved himself.

There was a lovely carpet and very comfortable seats – Rob had thought the church would have hard benches and be freezing. The people were very pleasant, welcoming and warm. The guy up front, who was doing all the speaking, made complete sense. Rob had imagined that there would be some chanting or singing in Latin but there was nothing like that. Instead, Rob continues:

> *'It seemed like the guy was just talking to me personally. As I sat there, it was as if he was saying things I had been thinking about in the weeks before, having seen such a change in Helen. She had not become a Christian, but since going to church and being given a Bible, she had begun to change even if I don't think she even fully understood Christian beliefs yet. But that day when the three of us were there, first we heard some bad news and then some good news.*
>
> *'The guy at the front was telling us that, because we are all sinners, we can't get into heaven. Now, I believed that God existed, that there was a basic right and wrong, and that there was a devil, heaven and hell. But when he said that unless we have trusted in Jesus as our Saviour we can't get into heaven, I wanted*

to put my hand up to challenge him ... but I didn't. I wanted to say that I am not that bad. Anyway, the guy went on to explain from a book in the Bible called Romans that though the bad news is that I am cut off from God by my sin, God has a gift for me by making provision for me, and he began to talk about Jesus being a substitute on the cross for me.

'That made sense to me because I remembered that as a child I had seen on television the film Jesus of Nazareth starring Robert Powell. When I saw in the film Jesus being nailed to the cross, I asked my mum, 'Why are they doing that? He hasn't done anything wrong.' At the time I remember crying my eyes out.

'When the preacher began to talk about Jesus dying on the cross for my sin, everything just came into focus. The good news is that I don't have to go to hell because Jesus took the punishment I deserve. At the end of the talk, we all bowed our heads while the man at the front prayed. I put my head down and I was like, Wow!' By the time I lifted my head, my girlfriend and my friend were at the front of the church. I wondered what was going on! The preacher had invited anyone who wanted to become a real Christian, to know Jesus as his *or her own personal Saviour, to come to the front to pray with him. That is why they had gone.*

'I thought to myself, 'I am not trying to go to hell on my own,' so I raced to the front to stand with my friends. The guy said this simple prayer and I prayed honestly for the first time from my heart: 'God, I know that I am a sinner. I realise that I deserve punishment but that Jesus died for me, in my place. Would you please forgive me?' '

Rob walked out of that church a different man. He looked the same on the outside but inside, in his soul, something had happened. The transaction was done, the penalty for all his sin had been paid, not by being religious or trying to live a good life but by trusting in Jesus Christ alone.

Everything seemed different from then on. Brought up in the West Indian culture, Rob had been disillusioned with marriage so he had had no intention of getting married. But after he became a Christian, he not only married his girlfriend but also faithfully stayed married to her. They have two children.

The DJ-ing ended as he decided to get rid of his

music collection. That was part of his old life that he had replaced with something better. But music did reappear later in his Christian life. One day at a home Bible study group he asked if he could share a poem that he had written. Everyone was amazed, saying that it sounded like a rap.

That really started his journey into writing. At church he met a producer, who wrote music for him. Then he hooked up with another Christian brother called Efrem, who was originally a singer but began rapping along with Rob in a group called M.O.D. – Ministri of Defence. They began getting very involved in ministry, using Christian rap in evangelism, youth and children's work. Later Rob and Efrem became Christian ministers at Calvary Chapel South London. Next Rob went back to 'school' at the PT Cornhill Training Course for preachers and then later at Oak Hill Theological College in order to equip himself for pastoral ministry. In reality he did the 'life-stuff thing' back to front!

Rob's mother was really thrilled to see her son so transformed.

Rob's mother was really thrilled to see her son so transformed. She had been a little nervous at first about what was happening to her son. Being more of the 'old-school type of Pentecostal lady', she expected Rob to dress in a three-piece suit. 'Robert, you haven't changed your appearance one bit!' exclaimed his mother when he became a Christian. 'Well,' he told her, 'you know that the Bible says that there are wolves in sheep's clothing (bad guys that look like good guys), so just see me as a sheep in wolves' clothing!'

Rachel Waddilove

THE NANNY TO CELEBRITIES

....

Everyone wants a good night's sleep – especially those with, or in earshot of, a child under five years of age! In order to help with sleep deprivation and other issues, parents who can afford to choose to employ a nanny. Those of us of lesser means can buy books on the subject.

Sleep Solutions: Quiet Nights for You and Your Child by Rachel Waddilove sounds an ideal read. Her website www.rachelsbabies.com is definitely the place to search if you are looking to employ a nanny. But just who is Rachel? What are her credentials? Does Rachel bear any resemblance to Mary Poppins or Nanny McPhee?

Well, yes and no! Rachel does love children, but has no magic solutions and cannot fly. What she does have, though, is common sense and a gifting that she believes God gave her, which has enabled her to help many families from all sorts of backgrounds.

It comes as no surprise to learn that Rachel was raised in a large family. No doubt this experience would have provided an excellent hands-on, practical background before she embarked on a career in childcare.

Her own mother had been notable in bringing up six children, Rachel being the eldest child and with only ten years between her and the youngest. The home was a very happy one, full of comings and goings, especially as they lived on a busy working farm. Rachel also recalls,

> *'When I was growing up, Father would come in off the farm from milking in the mornings and sit down at the table with us. Before we went to school, all six of us children knelt at the chairs by the table while father prayed. Afterwards I can remember impatiently running up the road, thinking I was going to miss the bus. Why had we got to pray before we went to school? It was only much later that I realised that these things are invaluable.'*

It was such a happy home. Although Rachel was actually born in Wiltshire, the family lived in

Oxfordshire on a farm and then later moved on to another one in Kent, which is still in use as a dairy cattle business today.

Rachel freely admits that she was not much of an academic. Up until the age of 11 she attended a private school, her grandparents having funded the fees. After that, as she hadn't passed the exams to get into a grammar school, she went to a senior school. Rachel loved all the practical subjects there, such as needlework, cookery, art and music, plus all the running about outside, but she wasn't too good when it came to history, geography and maths.

Leaving school at sixteen, she was to go off to Tunbridge Wells in Kent to a nursery training college that was run by Barnardo's, the children's charity. Before the Abortion Act had come in and before the contraceptive pill was used widely, there were very many illegitimate (as they were then called) babies born. Young, unmarried women who were having babies were not encouraged to keep them as it was considered to be socially unacceptable to have a child where there was no husband. Homes like Barnardo's took in the babies and looked after them until they were adopted, while at the same time giving training to nurses.

So Rachel commenced a two-year course leading to an NNEB Certificate (National Nursery Examination Board). As it was a private college and her parents could not afford to support her, she worked for a year as a cleaner, scrubbing floors and cleaning students' rooms, to pay for her tuition. She received no wages but was then able to go on to complete her training. 'It didn't hurt me,' she says. 'It was very good for me. Coming from a farming background, it was fine.'

During her course, Rachel went to St Thomas' Hospital in London to work on the maternity unit. As part of her training she had to see babies delivered, be there at the birth, and teach mothers how to feed and bath their babies. Very differently from today, mums often used to be in hospital for one to two weeks back then.

She worked for a year as a cleaner, scrubbing floors.

While she lived and worked in Tunbridge Wells, she came to know a wonderful family who befriended her as well as other nurses. Invitations would regularly be given to join them for amazing refreshments, with their time together being rounded off by listening to someone share how he or she had become a Christian. This was not at all unusual for Rachel as her own family were

God-loving and read the Bible and prayed together. She explains more:

> *'When I was about 13 years of age, I heard someone preach and then we all sang a lovely hymn about Jesus, about how He had died in our place to take away our sins. I decided to put my trust in Him at that early age. It was a personal decision. I wasn't just living off my parents' faith.*
>
> *'But later, when I began my work at St Thomas' Hospital in London, I got involved in all that was going on and it was great fun. There was a lot of partying among the medics, but perhaps I was overdoing it a bit. I was a country girl and there I was in London! My faith suffered but God somehow wooed me back.'*

Of course, fun is great and to be encouraged, but we know that certain things don't build character and can be dangerous or become a distraction from what is important. Rachel admits, 'I think I gradually realised that I wasn't in the right place. I wasn't happy. After college and getting a job, I sorted things out between God and me. I truly believed that He loved me and gave Himself for me, and I thoroughly trusted in Him to deal with my sins and take me though life then death to be with Him forever. I trusted Him for whatever he wanted me to do.'

Rachel never guessed then that her future career would involve being employed by royalty, top government officials and world-famous celebrities. At first she did private work in Kensington. She absolutely adored newborn babies so when a doctor and his wife requested her services to look after their first-born, a premature little girl, she was delighted. She worked for them for about six months, but became bored so left them and moved to work for a theatre producer. He and his wife had three children less than three years of age. They went off to America and left her in charge of their offspring for six weeks. She hadn't been trained very long but coped fine and just got on with it. When she thinks about it now, though, she feels they must have been mad to do such a thing. Life was rather surreal as people such as John Cleese and his wife would pop in, as did Jane Asher, Yoko Ono and other celebrities. At first being in their company was strange to Rachel, but then after a while she just became used to it, finding that they are really like everyone else. They were guests and she was the nanny who was there to look after the children.

Rachel's own life took a romantic turn a little later, although events were not straightforward and caused some pain within her family. She was still very young and quite headstrong, but she had met a man, John, who was ten years older than her. He was very charming and she fell for him and really loved him. The problem was that he was already married, although it turned out that his wife was having an affair with someone in the village. It was all a very painful time, so she took a backwards step. Then his divorce went through, so they married. Yet her parents were unhappy that she should marry a divorcee and there was a lot of family sadness.

John was a farmer so life had a familiar ring to it and was comfortable. They lived in Kent, near Sevenoaks. Her parents slowly accepted their marriage and were fine about it in the end, loving John as their son-in-law. They 'moved on' and didn't let their own strict upbringing spoil the relationship. Instead they supported John, being mindful of his own situation of having gone through a broken marriage. On reflection Rachel wonders if perhaps it would not have been better for her to keep away for a bit while John 'got the skeletons out of the cupboard'.

It was all a very painful time, so she took a backwards step.

There had been no children from his first marriage

but for John and Rachel a boy, Ben, and then a girl, Sarah, arrived on the scene, followed later on by another girl, Jayne. John's parents lived down the road from them. However, sometimes things were somewhat tense, as both his parents were quite a dominant influence on their lives. Mr Waddilove Snr had been a private secretary for the Duke of Windsor for 13 years, before going to work in the city of London.

For various reasons, not least the building of a motorway close by, John and Rachel sold their land and relocated to Devon. This involved a massive move of 19 lorries, cattle, machinery, children and belongings. Then their new property needed a lot of work doing to it, but gradually they managed to get things done.

Rachel learned to lamb ewes, among other things, before starting up a bed and breakfast business. But farming is hard work. Besides coping with the changeable climate, there are milk quotas to deal with, long hours to work, changing markets and fluctuating prices to contend with, disease and pressures from all quarters. So life was a battle and even the marriage was feeling the strain. Eventually they decided to sell up. Strangely the man who made the purchase had actually been born in the very same house, and then only lived in it for one year after the sale before he died.

They came right out of farming but carried on with the bed and breakfast business and Rachel went back to looking after babies again. Sadly in 1996 John and she split up. They weren't communicating and things were bad between them. John was in a difficult place and was far away from God, struggling with lots of issues. As a result the marriage broke down and they were divorced in 1999.

Suddenly Rachel was a single mother and with a daughter who was facing her own serious issues. Having worked together closely with her husband in the farming environment, to then be on her own was a challenge. There was a whole load of things to deal with. That's not an experience she would wish anyone to have to go through, and she has enormous empathy with those who are going through this right now.

With regard to John, despite her hurt, she felt that God had some 'unfinished business' with him. About a year or so after their divorce, they met up again on a few occasions. God had been changing them both and slowly they realised that He had relit the flame of the relationship, so much so that they decided to remarry! They still have ups and downs but, when things happen nowadays, they are reminded of God and all His dealings with them over the years. They are certainly not perfect 'but we are forgiven by a loving Heavenly Father and seek to walk with Him together day by day,' Rachel says. 'We have been married now for twelve years.'

When she returned to her work as a maternity nurse, Rachel began with just local jobs and did not do them for money. One of the first people she started working with was Noel Edmonds, who had bought an estate nearby. Rachel and John themselves had a big house so entertained and threw large parties. Outwardly it must have all looked as though she had it all. She was like the lady of the manor and probably, she honestly admits, had become a little proud. Yet in the beginning she worked for Noel and Helen as a mother's help, and that meant cleaning floors on her hands and knees. She felt that God was using this to keep her humble and servant-hearted.

One of the first people she started working with was Noel Edmonds.

Most of her work then came in as a result of personal recommendations. Having trained as a nanny, her main job grew into becoming a maternity nurse, which is totally different in the sphere of responsibility. A nanny looks after all the children but a maternity nurse moves into the family home when a baby is born. Usually Rachel will live in a family home from immediately the baby is born and then stay for up to four to six weeks. She is also present at the delivery, though she does not actually do it. Some of her clients have home deliveries but most of them go into hospital.

Rachel will be on duty 24 hours per day. The new baby will be with her throughout the night. She is there with the mum at all times to help her and teach her how to feed and care for the baby – and helps to teach dad as well! As well as helping with a variety of things, her role is also just to be there giving support and encouragement, getting the baby off to sleep and settling them into daily and nightly routines.

Rachel will be on duty 24 hours per day.

As her role is specifically with mum and baby and making sure that they are all right, she is not there to look after any other children. Obviously if a mum is breast-feeding the newborn and there are two or three other children around with no nanny, Rachel would not ignore them but would read to them or do whatever was necessary to give the mother a bit of peace. However, very often in many of the houses there is a nanny as well.

Nowadays Rachel is called a childcare expert. She is not away from home as much as she used to be but is still working with all sorts of people – television celebrities, lords and ladies of the realm, the royal family, MPs or anyone really who feels she could help them. Sometimes the granny and grandpa will pay for her to go into assist families who just need some extra help for a short time.

Job descriptions change or evolve so now she has a website: www.rachelsbabies.com. She also does consultancy work via the telephone as well as home visits, day visits of two or three hours or even perhaps overnight stays.

According to Rachel there seems to be a national epidemic of sleeplessness in babies and young children. She feels that there is a lot of bad advice about and probably too much unhelpful information on the web. For example, she has to counteract misleading advice that leaving a baby to have a 'shout' and self settle will lead to a baby becoming psychologically damaged. Older mothers particularly seek and are grateful for her help. Musing on this,

Rachel says,

'I think that we have a lot of parents who are having their babies later in life and mothers and families tend to get too 'precious'. The baby becomes the kingpin and everything falls around this little person, instead of he or she being part of the family and fitting in with the family. There are lots of reasons for this but socially I think we have lost our way of parenting. I am always talking to parents about boundaries. The first boundary they put down with their babies is sleep. I say to parents that that is nothing compared with the temper tantrums that come later on! You and your husband, or partner, are the ones who are going to put those boundaries in. Nobody else is going to do it. When you start talking to parents, they realise that the responsibility is with them.'

In her books the publisher has allowed her to add a chapter at the end of each of them about the emotional and spiritual needs of the baby or child; this is an important but often neglected or untaught area of their little lives. As Rachel explains,

'Jesus is the centre of my life really. I give God

my diary and ask Him, 'Lord, where do you want me to go?' Sometimes faced with a tricky situation I ask, 'Lord, what do I do now? Help, what do I say?' I know that the Lord is with me and will never leave me or forsake me. Even though I let Him down, He always keeps His promises; He is always faithful. Really God is with me through my working day and beyond – 24/7 in modern parlance!'

If you would like to read some books by Rachel, she has written:

Sleep Solutions: Quiet Nights for You and Your Child: From Birth to Five Years

The Baby Book: How to Enjoy Year One

The Toddler Book: How to Enjoy Your Growing Child

Rob Dean

THE SUBMARINER

....

Every night, while you and I fall asleep peacefully under duvets, sheets or blankets, there are people working night shifts to ensure our personal and national safety. For the most part we do not know their names. They may or may not wear uniforms but include policemen, nurses, firemen, doctors plus a variety of personnel who serve in the armed forces on land and sea. Have you ever thought that right now there is a top secret mission being played out beneath the waves, as well as above, involving men and women who are dedicated to keeping our land and its people free and safe from all kinds of attack and disaster?

Rob Dean cannot tell us everything about the part he has played in securing national security for his country. If he did, we would be shot! His 'underworld' activities were those experienced during his long career as a submariner.

Every time submarines rise, whale-like, from the

depths of the ocean to the surface of a merciless sea, there seems to be a sinister, mysterious air about the whole process. Where has it been? Who were these anonymous sailors secretly monitoring during their stealth operations?

Rob was not unfamiliar with military life, as his father had served in the Royal Marines faithfully for about 38 years. This had practical repercussions for his family, who moved 25 times, causing them to be extremely experienced in house removals. Rob's place of birth was Weymouth, Dorset. Portland Harbour was nearby, sheltering a large number of the country's fleet of submarines. Any young boy standing on the rocks by the lighthouse on Portland Bill surely could not fail to be impressed or inspired by the sight of some of Her Majesty's Fleet when they visited this important maritime harbour.

However, although the sea was in his blood, first Rob had to get an education. This was not easy for a lad whose parents moved around so much. Despite changing schools 14 times (including attending five grammar schools, three of which were while in the sixth form), Rob went up to Aberystwyth University to study Physics and Geology. It took him a year to work out that really he wanted to join the Royal Navy, his first love. After this he took up the offer of sponsorship by the navy as a university cadet.

While still in Aberystwyth, Rob undertook an intellectual exercise concerning Christianity. His personal history of the subject until then had been limited to occasional Sunday School visits or the odd baptismal service or Christmas communion. 'The only thing that stuck in my memory', Robs says, 'was part of the creed that states "I believe in God ... I believe in Jesus Christ ... I believe in the Holy Spirit."'

When his father was at home, they never had any contact with church. When he was away at sea or in Aden (one of our country's former military bases in the Middle East), people would call to take the children to Sunday School. 'At such times,' Rob adds, 'I would hear the more familiar Bible stories and the gospel message.' In teenage years he met a very genuine man called Robin Hall, who would take his sister and him to Aggie Weston's.

'I guess that not many people have heard of this lady,' Rob explains. 'Dame Agnes Weston was a wonderful Victorian lady who established the Royal Sailors' Rest. This was commissioned to help sailors to preach the gospel, the good news of Jesus Christ, and to keep their fellow sailors out of the pubs!

As an organisation Aggie Weston's still exists in Plymouth, and there is another in Portsmouth.'

But it was at university that he started thinking the big thoughts about life. He wondered whether he really did believe in God: Father, Son and Holy Spirit. He also questioned whether this was of any relevance to him and pondered if it is important that God exists. Those issues were the start of him talking about faith.

Rob's intellectual exercise into faith during his university years most memorably involved reading Mere Christianity by C.S. Lewis. Renowned for writing the Chronicles of Narnia books, Lewis wrote up what had been his radio broadcasts in the 1940s into what we now know as Mere Christianity. It has become one of the most influential books worldwide over the last 75 years. In it C.S. Lewis argues that Jesus Christ is either a lunatic, a liar or the Lord, the Son of God. Carefully considering the arguments of Lewis, Rob concluded that Jesus must be the Son of God.

Rob concluded that Jesus must be the Son of God.

1973 was an important year in Rob's life. He married, graduated and passed out of the Royal Naval College in Dartmouth. Another important step was when he was confirmed at an Anglican church. One condition of his course as a navy cadet was that he had to commit himself to five years to the service. This was no problem for him and seemed quite a natural career for him taking into account his upbringing. At this stage of his life he would still not consider himself to be a Christian, despite his confirmation, but felt that he was very much on the way and moving in that direction.

As part of his general naval training he served on board HMS Blake, a cruiser. It had a very beautiful chapel with oak panelling. Every Sunday there was a church service that included Communion. This was quite old-school in content. The Armed Forces Prayer Book follows The Book of Common Prayer but also repeats comfortable words of Jesus from Scripture, such as 'Come unto Me all you who travail and are heavy laden, and I will refresh you' and 'So God loved the world, that He gave His only-begotten Son, to the end that all that believe in Him should not perish, but have everlasting life.' Through the liturgy, words of Scripture became embedded in Rob's memory, for which he was grateful.

It was a foundation in the Word of God that would help later, not only in his own personal faith in the resurrected Jesus Christ, but also in those long periods of separation from his loved ones while at sea. It was, by Gods Spirit, a defining constant through his life, even when, as Robs says, 'I did dumb and stupid things in my life and sinned.'

One incident, early on in his career, made such an impact on his life that it was to take him in a different direction – underneath instead of on top of the water. He was on board HMS Blake, crossing the Atlantic, when a submarine came alongside. It was one of the roughest seas he had ever seen – a force ten gale was blowing. The Blake was a big cruiser but boats on the upper deck, as well as radars and the masts, were being smashed by the high seas.

The whole crew of the submarine had just crossed the Atlantic in these terrible conditions and they were really tired as it had been tough going. Leaving the duty officer on board the submarine, the captain and crew came on board the Blake. They were a professional, tight, efficient unit; altogether they were very impressive. There was a difference in the navy between the submarine and the big ship, the latter of which Rob regards as very much 'spit and polish and brass'.

Having encountered this group of men, Rob decided

to try a few days on a submarine – and that was it. For the next 25 years he was a submariner. Starting off in diesel boats, he progressed to become the navigator of HMS Repulse, which was the third Polaris Missile submarine of the Resolution class and went on to be the longest-serving craft of its kind. On average Rob used to be away from home 210 days each year.

He was three times down in the Falkland Islands. During the conflict with Argentina he was a student on the Submarine Commanding Officers' Qualifying Course between April and August 1982. As soon as he qualified on 1 September, he was on a plane down to the South Atlantic where he flew out to be the Submarine Element Coordinator and Controller in the South Atlantic onboard the aircraft carrier HMS Illustrious. He did that for a couple of months and then took charge of HMS Osiris. The first thing this crew did, with about four days' notice in January 1983, was to go back down to the Falklands again.

He was three times down in the Falkland Islands.

His later service involved a lot of interesting and exciting things that demanded utmost secrecy. He cannot talk about those times. Suffice it to say that he was one of those who were commonly referred to as Cold War Warriors working anywhere between the Mediterranean and the North Pole!

Throughout these years of danger, stress and separation from family, Rob feels that on reflection God, by His Spirit, had been working in his life in different ways. Home life was, of course, precious, as it is to all those in our armed forces. Rob and his wife have three children. His eldest, Tim, is a Surgeon Commander Dentist in the Royal Navy; Katie is married to a Christian minister who has recently left St Ebbe's Church in Oxford to become the chaplain at Canford School; Joanna, the younger daughter, also joined the navy and is a Naval Lieutenant.

When Joanna was in her early teens, she was diagnosed as having scoliosis, which is a major curvature of the spine that requires surgery. Katie, meanwhile, had gone up to Oxford. Rob went along to church with her, being a regular church attender himself.

Actually when Rob had been in command at sea, one of the responsibilities under the Articles of War is to 'encourage pursuant of religious observance in one's command'. So he was obliged by law to hold church services. On board they would meet in the fore ends of the submarines. Standing next to torpedo compartments and singing (or trying to!), Rob used to get frustrated that people wouldn't want to come and join in but was encouraged that a lot did indeed attend. There was a slow progression in his own coming to true faith in Jesus Christ.

Anyway, Rob discovered that his church was one where the Bible was preached and taught faithfully and engagingly. When he had been to the USA he went to a church that used the old King James Version of the Bible but e didn't always understand its old-fashioned English. The New International Version – a more modern translation of the Bible, which St Ebbe's used – was much easier to understand. He was given his first copy of the Bible in 1998. He listened to people preaching what the Bible was saying. They looked first at what it meant verse by verse; second at what it meant at the time it was written; and third at what its relevance is now and how it should be applied to one's life. The preacher's messages were them simply working their way through the Bible in a systematic way, and Rob thought, 'There is something here I've not been getting.'

At about the same time Rob was living at Sandhurst so attended a church in Camberley. It was there that he attended a course which explores the Christian message over a number of weeks. People get together for food, watch a video looking at one aspect of Christian belief and then chat about it. It is very informal, and the participants can chat about any issues that may arise. Rob found this particularly helpful, looking forward week by week to the next part of the course.

Towards the end of the course Jo went into hospital for her serious operation. This meant Rob spending a lot of time by her bedside, so he took with him his copy of the Bible and read the New Testament. That was when he became a Christian. He read the gospel for himself in a Bible that he could understand ... and he got it! He understood! It was as though there were curtains that were taken away from his mind and everything became clear. He understood that he was a sinner but that Jesus had died for him so that he might to be reconciled to God. As Rob puts it, 'I made the decision that I would serve Him and follow Him in all I did. To use a military expression, Jesus Christ to me is front and centre.'

'Jesus Christ to me is front and centre.'

Rob left the navy with some regret in 1999 but transferred his leadership and managerial skills to work, with much enjoyment, in schools and later with churches. 'Although a scary prospect, it is a privilege to lead and to teach others, helping them to understand how much God loves them. It is as exciting as that former submarine life – well almost,' he adds with mischievous intrigue.

Deborah Kelly

THE SURVEYOR

Have you ever tried to do a jigsaw without seeing the picture? It's confusing and frustrating, maybe, but satisfying on completion.

Deborah likens her journey to the Christian faith to pieces of a jigsaw – they didn't mean that much to her as a random selection of pieces, but when put together made a precious picture. Later on, when life dealt her the 'curve ball' of multiple sclerosis, that picture was to be her interpreting framework.

From the start of life our homes influence us greatly. For Deborah this was a good and stable one. Her family encouraged her to get the most out of life and enjoy learning and socialising with family and friends. For Deborah's family this included reading the Bible at home and going to church. Together with a large and lively group of contemporaries at the local church, she happily joined in with church services, kids' groups and activities. Along the way she learned and believed in God as the Bible teaches about Him. She understood, even as a child, that being a Christian isn't something that happens to us just because of the family we are born in, or because of the church-going habit, but it is the response of our hearts to a generous God. Deborah recalls how her young mind felt:

'I didn't need telling that I wasn't perfect. Even as a child, lots of times I was really disappointed with myself. But although I had learned about Jesus and heaven and that God made the world, it was all a bit disjointed. It all came together when I went on a children's camp. There I heard, and for the first time understood, that when I did wrong I wasn't just letting myself down, I was letting God down. I was letting down my loving Creator. But I also then understood that God sent His Son Jesus to deal with this. He lived in this world but never did any wrong, so He could take my punishment in my place. That's how come He could forgive my sins.

'The gospel was explained in simple terms to us children on that camp. I had a choice to go on living my own sweet way and be an enemy of God or I could say 'sorry' to God for all the wrong things that got in the way between

me and God; then I could say 'thank you' for sending Jesus to take my punishment; and last I could ask Him 'please' help me to live a life that pleases Him rather than make Him sad. 'Sorry', 'thank you', 'please' – they explained it that simply. I could know God there and then as my heavenly Father and I could look forward to one day being with Him in His wonderful heaven. This simple explanation meant that all the bits of the jigsaw, all those different bits about God and Jesus that I had heard over the years, now came together into a picture that made sense.'

So as a young child, with all her life ahead of her, she left one particular camp in the sure knowledge that God had forgiven her sins through the death of His son. She knew that He would never leave her and that she was trusting in the Lord Jesus as her personal Saviour. She was confident in her faith as life unfolded for her.

The usual milestones cropped up – exams, growth spurts, change of schools, more exams, career advice and leaving home for the first time. All too soon it was time for Deborah to leave college, having nearly completed her training as a chartered surveyor.

I suppose with a good qualification 'in the bag' she could have picked a number of places in which to settle and ply her trade, not only in the UK but also abroad. But she landed up, to the envy of a lot of people her own age, with a job right in the City of London, the Square Mile, the prestigious business sector of London. Deborah specialised in the point where law and property interact. She loved her job and even gained a few promotions. For her it was important to have an easy commute so she could have a life outside of work as well. Involvement in her church was important to her and was included in the list of things she enjoyed. Squash, cycling and getting out of London to climb mountains were special hobbies too for a very active, busy young woman with exciting business prospects.

She loved her job and even gained a few promotions.

Aged 25, a series of unexplained injuries and a patch of illness led her to a few visits to the doctor, followed by the inevitable round of medical tests. When the diagnosis of multiple sclerosis was confirmed, it came as an immense shock. The possibility hadn't crossed her mind and her thoughts immediately went to a lady with MS whom Deborah had known while she'd been growing up. She had been in a wheelchair, had become gradually more and more disabled and had died while only in her 40s. Deborah was now facing the knowledge that the road ahead could lead to disability and death.

On the other hand, though, she couldn't get out of her head what she knew and believed from the Bible: that God is the loving ruler of the world and that nothing happens outside of His control. So in her heart Deborah knew she could trust Him for whatever might lie ahead while she was still living, and moreover she could trust Him for what happens beyond death. She felt the assurance of knowing that the Bible makes it plain that for all who belong to God, life beyond death will be in His wonderful new creation. This will include, among other things, having new bodies that aren't corrupted by disease and disability. She says, 'I am not sure how I would have coped with MS without the knowledge that this life is not all that there is. The importance of this world fades in the light of the hope of what is to come.'

Over 20 years on from that initial diagnosis, Deborah is conscious of the challenges she faces because of MS but is also well aware that her suffering is nothing compared to what many of her friends have faced.

Many of them have encountered bereavement, illness, emotional pain and family breakdown. She says,

> *'My mobility, balance, vision and general strength are all impaired but so far MS hasn't been as tough on my body as I feared. Eventually I had to give up my job in the City, I am not playing any sport, I am no longer allowed to drive a car, and my walking is much slower, and over shorter, flatter terrain! But I am sure that in His wisdom God has brought me to precisely this point. I have tried to make the best use of the time and strength given me and to focus on the things I can do. Trusting God's plan means I don't see these things as second best, but as God's best plan for me in this life.*
>
> *'That's not to make it sound easy – there is a lurking fear that comes from an uncertain disease. And there is grief that comes from the awareness of things lost – my career, my independence, and the thrill of climbing a mountain or beating someone at squash. I'm aware that the sense of loss can generate bad things in my heart and I do sometimes struggle with jealousy and bitterness. But as*

well as giving me the hope of life to come, remembering what Jesus suffered on the cross for me reminds me that no experience of mine is greater than what He endured for me. God is good.

'I have always had food on my table and a roof over my head. I don't take them for granted. There have even been blessings as a result of having MS – actually there are good things about having to slow life down!

'More than that, as a result of my path changing, I have been able to be involved with people and places that I never would have been had my life carried on its previous trajectory. The Bible teaches that God's ways are above our ways, and that He works out His good purposes for the whole of His world.

The Bible teaches that God's ways are above our ways.

Sometimes things don't make any sense at the time we are going through them. At one stage I was made redundant. It seemed like a disaster at the time (it was three days after I had bought my first property), but in hindsight I could see God's hand in this as it led me into working for a different firm, one much better placed to look after me in the later years when

I was unwell but still working.

'So sometimes we can look back and see God's purpose; but at other times we simply have to trust that He is good and faithful and that is the way He is working. But both in the good and really tough times of life, God is always good.'

There are those who react to Deborah's confident faith by suggesting that for her Christianity is a crutch. This is true to the extent that Deborah senses her own weakness while also relying on the fact that God is very strong. She remarks, 'It is so wonderful to lean on Him and trust Him to get me through.' But she also feels that describing her faith as a crutch is a poor picture because that implies a sort of temporary thing, a passing help, not a full remedy. For her Christianity is so much more than a crutch. Faith in Jesus solves once and for all the biggest problem we all face, namely our sin and the issue of what happens when we die.

Faith like this does not minimise the problem of suffering. There is an interesting verse in the Bible that states, 'The secret things belong to the LORD our God, but the things revealed belong to us and to our children ...' In other words, there are many things in the twists and turns of life, as well as the goings-on in our world, that we cannot understand or explain, but what we do know about God enables us to trust Him in all we do not understand about life.

If you would like to read more about the issue of suffering from a Christian perspective, try Where Is God in a Messed-up World? by Roger Carswell (published by IVP) or Enough by Helen Roseveare (published by Christian Focus).

Bill Peartree

THE TATTOO ARTIST

David Beckham has many, my dad had one put on his arm during his army days and today they have become indispensible accessories. Fashion statement, fad or foolish, whatever you think of tattoos they are not new. They are even mentioned in the Bible. Previously found in dark, dingy, downtown premises, nowadays tattoo artists ply their trade often next to a respectable hairdresser or optician.

Able Seaman Bill Peartree stood to attention. A matter concerning him had come to the attention of the Naval Command in Gibraltar, where Bill was based. 'It is against regulations to conduct a business while serving as a member of the armed services,' Bill was informed in no uncertain terms. 'You must close down your tattooing operation immediately!'

Bill, who had been operating very successfully from a flat in town, had no intention of closing down as it was making more money than he was as a serviceman. Instead he applied to his captain for discharge by purpose – he wanted to try to buy himself out of the navy.

A few months later the Divisional Officer sent for Bill again to tell him that his request had been granted. He would shortly be returned to England to complete a discharge routine. Also, on payment of £200, a sum well beyond the resources of most servicemen in the early 1960s, he would be discharged. Sailor Bill, as everyone had come by then to know him, was both surprised and delighted. Discharge by purchase was very rare in those days.

Bill looked a strong man, very strong. He was someone you would not want to cross. A typical sailor, Bill went to sea as a lad and soon indulged in the excesses the world so readily offered, without considering the consequences.

Having made a successful exit from the navy, Bill returned to his native Colchester, where naturally he opened a tattooing studio in that garrison town. He worked long hours among both servicemen and civilians. In 1970 the Royal Anglian Regiment was about to commence a tour of duty in Belfast, stationed at Sunnyside barracks on the Ormeau Road. Some of their members invited him to join them over there. He had established himself as a very popular tattoo artist, but in January 1971 he arrived in the Province, intending to stay for only three weeks. He soon discovered that there was plenty of work for him to do in Northern Ireland, where he stayed touring around and working from a caravan.

Four years later a request came in for him to travel to Germany to work among the Irish Rangers. Following a tour of European countries, Bill managed to find work on the island of Malta. Heavy drinking and chain-smoking were taking their toll on his body, leading to his collapse one night in a casino. Some hours later, in hospital, he regained consciousness. Following an exploratory operation a rather sombre surgeon explained what they had discovered: 'You have alcohol poisoning, Bill. If you ever take another mouthful of alcohol, it will kill you.' They were shocking words. From then on Bill decided never to touch the stuff again.

'If you ever take another mouthful of alcohol, it will kill you.'

Worse news of a different kind was yet to come. One of Bill's customers tipped him off that the police were planning to raid his caravan and impound his equipment. Bill had apparently been operating on the island without a work permit. He would have to leave straightaway or face prosecution.

Bill chose to return to the Province, as it had been one of the most lucrative places he had been to. Eventually he opened up a tattooing shop in Coleraine. It was there, also, that he met Irene Leighton, whom he later married. For a number of years they enjoyed a life of socialising together.

One night in February 1982 Irene and her friend Joy decided to go to a special event being held in Drumadragh, some miles away. Bill wasn't too bothered about going as he was working late that night anyway, so the girls went by themselves.

When Irene returned, she had a big surprise for Bill. It turned out that the women had been to hear a man called Billy Parke, who was speaking at a Christian mission hall. Irene told her husband that she had been 'saved' that night – and so had Joy. There was no doubt that something had happened to her, but what exactly? Irene explained to Bill what the preacher had said in the meeting. The message was simple yet profound: 'We've all done wrong, every one of us. That cuts us off from having a relationship with God. But, because He loves us, Jesus took the punishment we deserve for that wrong so that we can go free ... to save us from our sins.'

Bill didn't understand what had happened to his wife but she had come back a different person. From then on he noticed that instead of heading off to the pub she had started going to church. Through her influence it wasn't too long before Bill started going with her. And the more dealings he had with Christians, the more he liked and respected them. He felt that they genuinely cared for him, which, of course, they did!

Alongside the tattooing business, Bill opened a garden nursery, as he loved gardening and had a vast knowledge of plants. But one day back in his shop, while tidying up, a magazine was knocked to the floor from the shelf above. As Bill went to pick it up he noticed that it had fallen open at a page on which were highlighted words that were straight from the Bible: 'Do not cut your bodies for the dead or put tattoo marks on yourselves. I am the LORD.' This command was given because of pagan connections or tendencies.

One of his own needles could not have pierced his heart and conscience any more than those words from the Old Testament. Bill felt so challenged by what he had read that he wanted to finish his personal involvement with the tattoo business. But what would happen then? Bill struggled with this for nearly a year until one day he made the decision to hand over the keys of his shop Sailor Bill's to Bruce, his son from a previous marriage and his business partner.

The next day was Sunday, so he went along to church with his wife for the morning service, which included a communion service.

Bill explains, 'I had never taken communion because I knew that a person must be a Christian to take part. So after the first part of the service and before the communion service began, I left, whispering to Irene, "Please pray for me!"' Afterwards Bill went home alone, as Irene was involved in an afternoon activity at the church.

Bill could get no inward peace ... so he went to his greenhouse and sat down among the beautiful fuchsias.

In turmoil Bill could get no inward peace ... so he went to his greenhouse and sat down among the beautiful fuchsias. There, of all places, he dropped to his knees and prayed a simple prayer: 'Lord, save me!' He asked God to come into his life. Straightaway he jumped into his car and drove to the church to tell them what had happened! 'I will never forget that day as long as I live,' Bill says. 'I knew that it would not be an easy road to walk, but that with Jesus at my side all things would be possible.' Bill and Irene were now united, not only by marriage but also in their relationship with Jesus Christ.

Bill struggled with his health, particularly with his heart, but in spite of this he managed to find work as a part-time gardener for the National Trust, which he really enjoyed. Sadly he had other health issues related to his lifestyle in previous years that, combined with cardiac illness, eventually caught up with him.

So Bill, the former tattoo artist, is now in heaven, in the presence of the One who has marks in His hands and side – not marks of fashion, but wounds suffered out of sacrificial love for the world.

(This chapter is adapted from an article that first appeared in Lifetimes *magazine, with permission from Noel Davidson.)*

Passion for Life

THE 'NUTS AND BOLTS' OF FAITH

....

As 'no man is an island', so too are we not men of stone who are not moved by the noble passions of love, friendship and human compassion?

(Nelson Mandela)

It is great to be passionate. Our emotions are part of what makes us human beings.

Passion lets us know that we are alive. Without passion life would seem very overcast and drab. Passion demonstrates what really matters to us. Be it sport, food, relationships, politics, hobbies, chocolate or you name it, somewhere somebody will be passionate about it.

Passion, though, is not enough in itself. Passion can be both good and bad. We know that for we see both love and hate exemplified in society. Nor does passion guarantee success. No matter how strong our feelings are about sport, victory one year can be snatched away the next. Passion for the family is no guarantee that the family will stay together. Too often we see and experience broken hearts. Politics, for some, raises emotions to great heights; but high ideals to change people's standard of living, sadly, can soon be corrupted by power or extremism.

Passion in religion, however, is not really encouraged or particularly admired in today's society. Rather it is often feared, especially when leaders behave in ways no different from leaders of other areas of society. Yet there is a passion that can satisfy our greatest longing.

Mel Gibson's film *The Passion of the Christ* shockingly depicted the physical horror that Jesus endured at the hands of Roman soldiers. In the film's opening moments, a verse from the Bible is shown on the screen. These words were written 700 years before Jesus' crucifixion. They prophesied what Jesus would accomplish by his death: 'But he was pierced for our transgressions, he was crushed for our iniquities; the punishment that brought us peace was upon him, and by his wounds we are healed.'

Whether we are aware of it or not, each one of us carries around a huge burden of guilt, shame and regret, feeling that we are not the people we could or should be. But Jesus has provided the means for us not only to be forgiven, but also to start again with the living God at the centre of our lives.

Yes, Jesus was spat upon and mocked before being nailed to the cross. But hanging on the cross, He was carrying our sin, shame and guilt. Because of His great love for us, He died paying the penalty for all that would condemn us.

One balmy summer's evening while on holiday in France, I, and hundreds of other people, were seated in the open air in a town square overlooking the Mediterranean Sea. The spotlights were turned onto a young man dressed immaculately. Silence descended as Sergey Khachatryan, the celebrated Armenian violinist, took up his instrument and treated us to the most amazing display of pure genius for over an hour. Everyone was stunned by his performance. To me, it appeared faultless.

Everyone was stunned by his performance. To me, it appeared faultless.

In the multitude of my thoughts I contrasted that wonderful scene with those terrible hours of Jesus on the cross. He was without sin, alone, with the spotlight of eternity on Him. He bore in His own body all the sin of the world – the sins that hit the headlines and the sin that simply hardens the heart were all laid on Him. The scene was so horrendous, it was as if God had switched off the lights – a great darkness covered the face of the world for three hours, even though it was midday. God the Father turned away from His darling Son.

Yet Jesus was forsaken so that we could be forgiven and never forsaken by Him. As it says in the Bible, 'For God so loved the world that He gave His one and only Son, that whoever believes in Him shall not perish but have eternal life.'

Jesus died for us, and then three days later He rose again from the dead, leaving His grave empty. Jesus' resurrection, which is so greatly attested by the historical data of His day, was God's seal of approval on the way back to God that Jesus had made through His death.

'I have come that they may have life, and have it to the full.'

The most passionate love the world ever saw was Jesus dying on a cross. The greatest news the world has ever heard was announced by an angel in a graveyard: 'He is not here ... He has risen from the dead!'

Jesus said, 'I have come that they may have life,

and have it to the full.' He invites all of us to trust and know Him: 'Come to me, all you who are weary and burdened, and I will give you rest.'

There is a passion for life when you know:

- that God made you and has given you life
- that despite everything, God loves you
- that you have been made right with God
- that your sins have been forgiven through Jesus' death and resurrection
- that God, by His Holy Spirit, lives within you
- that God is in control of everything in your life
- that when you die, instead of the hell you deserve, you are going to be with God forever

In the preceding chapters we have seen how people from very different backgrounds have come to a living relationship with God, and how real, precious and dynamic it is. Despite their circumstances – and some are battling huge issues in their lives – they have a confidence about God, who is equipping them to face each new day as well as death one day. They know that they are in the loving care of God their Heavenly Father. They have a passion for life.

It may be that you too are at the stage where you

are ready to trust Jesus as your Lord and Saviour; you want to start to follow Jesus. It is not going to be easy in today's society to live for Him, but it is vitally important to make sure that you are at peace with God. There is no magic formula of words that can make you a Christian, but many have found praying words similar to those below has helped them put their trust in and make their commitment to Christ. Would you be willing to pray like this now?

> *'Dear God, Thank you for the life that you have given me. I am sorry for all my sin and, with your help, I want to turn from it. Thank you that Jesus died for me, and rose again from the dead. Please forgive me. By your Holy Spirit, please come to live within me. Please give me your new life and become my Lord and Saviour; help me to follow you. Thank you for hearing this prayer, which I pray in the Name of Jesus. Amen.*

If you have prayed like this, please get in touch with me via the publisher so that I can send you helpful information about starting to mature in your newfound faith.

'Passion for Life' is an initiative arranged by many churches of different denominations throughout the UK who, this year, are having a variety of events designed to explain the Christian message to today's generation.

Books in the same series by DJ Carswell include:

a passion for life
Real life stories about faith
D.J.Carswell

ASTRONOMY

igloo

This edition published in 2009
by Igloo Books Ltd
Cottage Farm,
Sywell,
NN6 0BJ

www.igloo-books.com

Cataloguing in Publication Data information
10 9 8 7 6 5 4 3 2 1

ISBN: 978-1-84817-742-0

Printed and manufactured in China

Produced by Metro Media Ltd
Author: Paul Sutherland
Images provided by: NASA, ESO, ESA, SOHO, Paul Sutherland, Shutterstock.com, istock.com, Clipart.com
Star maps created in conjunction with Stellarium software (www.stellarium.org)/American Association of Variable Star Observers
American Association of Amateur Astronomers, Anthony Ayiomamitis, Neil Bone, Fred Bruenjes, Celestron, Sebastian Deiries, Colin Ebdon, Yoji Hirose,David Graham, Peter Grego, Yoko Kikuta
R. Ligustri and Herman Mikuz, Meade Instruments, Optical Vision
Dave Pearson, Philipp Salzgeber, Juergen Schmoll
Nik Szymanek, Dave Tyler, David Strange, Leo Stachowicz

ONTENTS

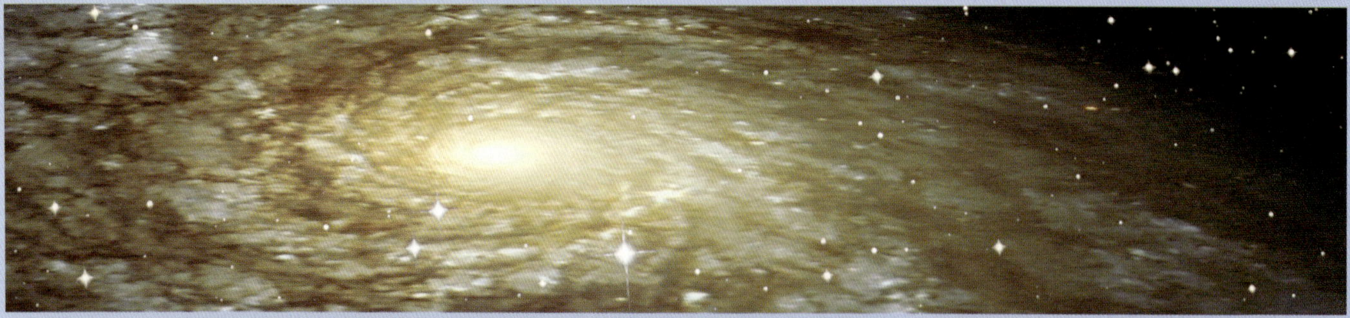

INTRODUCTION

We on planet Earth are infinitesimally tiny specks on the cosmic stage. But, by looking out, we can marvel at the nature of the universe and appreciate the wonders of the heavens for ourselves.

The study of everything beyond the Earth is called astronomy. This is clearly an enormous subject, but it is also makes for a fascinating hobby. There is so much out there, so much to see. To lose yourself in space is a great antidote to the stresses of everyday life.

Astronomers have long shed the image of old men with long white beards. And you don't need a brain the size of a planet and a bottomless wallet to take up stargazing.

There is so much to discover by watching our sky. There are constellations to identify and planets to spot. To do this all that is required is enthusiasm to learn about the vast universe that surrounds us.

This book will help you in your exploration of the universe by explaining the basics of what it is all about, in plain English. It will also show how you can become an astronomer, with beginners' guides on taking up different areas of stargazing.

Above all, we hope to show that astronomy is much more than complex research. As a hobby, it's tremendous fun!

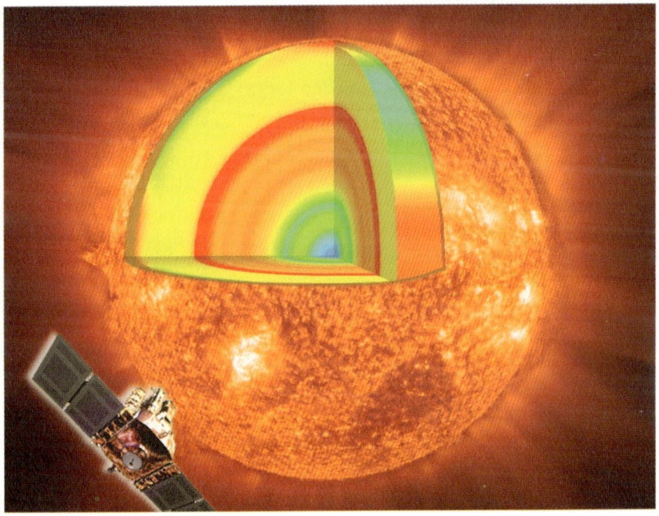

NATURE OF THE HEAVENS

Our view of the sky is like looking out from the inside of a goldfish bowl.

Our view of the sky is not fixed. It changes as time passes, from hour to hour and day to day. Stars and planets are visible at some times but absent at others. To understand why, we need to appreciate a few basic concepts. First, the Earth is a ball in space, surrounded by all the objects in the universe. From any one point on its surface, we can look up and see around half of the sky at a time. But the Earth is also rotating. As the Earth turns, the sky seems to wheel in the opposite direction. The most obvious indicator of this to us is the Sun, which we see rising, crossing the sky and setting each day. We may not have noticed it, but all the other objects such as stars, rotate across the sky in a similar way.

It's as if they are all fixed to a spinning goldfish bowl that we are observing from the inside. Of course, it is we who are spinning and not the bowl, but we get the impression that it is turning rather than us.

Astronomers term this virtual goldfish bowl the Celestial Sphere. It appears to rotate around two Celestial Poles directly above the Earth's own North and South Poles.

An imaginary grid can be drawn on this sphere, matching the longitude and latitude grid that was created for the Earth.

An observer at a mid-northern latitude sees stars rise, cross the sky and set. But stars close to the North Celestial Pole always stay above the horizon. Others around the South Celestial Pole never rise at all.

Yoko Kikuta

Leaving a camera's shutter open for many minutes shows clearly how circumpolar stars revolve around the celestial pole as the Earth rotates.

Lines joining the two Celestial Poles – the equivalent of longitude – are termed Right Ascension and are measured in hours and minutes. Lines parallel to the Equator, similar to our lines of latitude, are termed Declination and are measured in degrees. The line at 0 degrees running directly above the Equator is called the Celestial Equator. Positions north of it take positive values up to +90 degrees at the North Celestial Pole. Points south of the Equator count down to -90 degrees at the South Celestial Pole.

Although the whole sky appears to rotate around an axis, not all stars rise and set (unless you live on the Equator). Our location determines which stars set and which do not.

Before the invention of mechanical clocks and watches, man invented sundials which used the moving shadow cast by the Sun's daily motion across the sky to tell the time.

From the North or South Pole, all the stars appear to move parallel to the horizon. From the Equator, they all appear to rise vertically from the horizon, pass over the sky and sink below the opposite horizon.

If you are at a spot somewhere between the North Pole and the Equator, the North Celestial Pole will appear to lie in the sky at an altitude equal to your own latitude. Stars close to the North Celestial Pole will never set. Conversely, the South Celestial Pole will always lie below your horizon and stars close to that will never rise at all. The diagram on page 6 shows this. The situation is reversed in the southern hemisphere.

The entire Celestial Sphere appears to rotate in a little under 24 hours, with everything moving from West to East. Each star will make a complete journey around it and return to its original point in exactly 23 hours 56 minutes, which is the time it takes the Earth to rotate on its axis. This is called the Sidereal Period. But we all know that the day is actually 24 hours long, so where do the extra four minutes fit in?

The answer is found in the Earth's journey around the Sun in its orbit. This year-long trip makes the Sun appear to move from day to day against the starry background. It is highest in the sky at local noon but takes

The other planets can be seen to move from night to night against the starry background in their orbits around the Sun. But the planets outside the Earth's orbit appear to backtrack, creating little loops in the sky, for a period of time every year.

Of course, they don't really change direction. The effect is similar to when you are in a car that overtakes a slower vehicle on the motorway. The other car appears to move backwards against the background. When we overtake the more distant planets, the same thing happens. This is called retrograde motion.

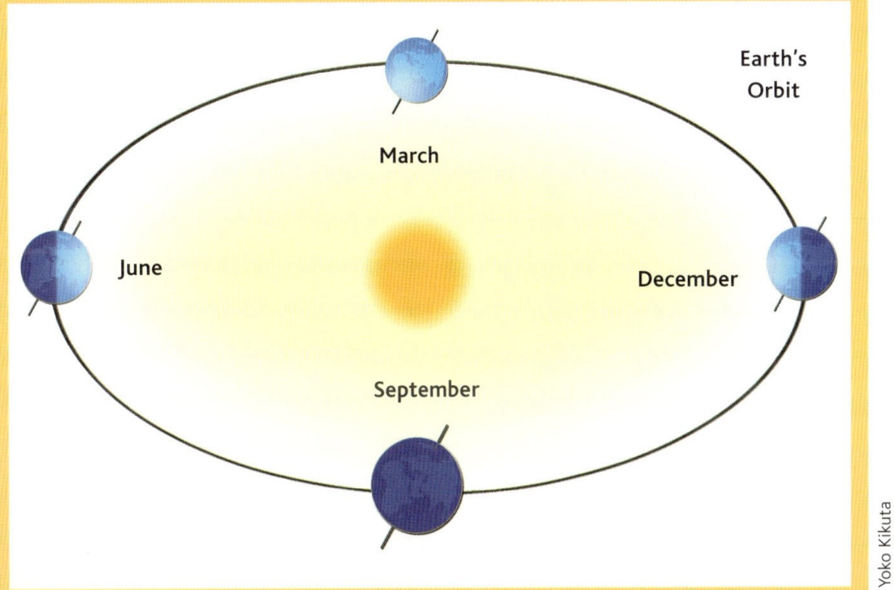

The Earth's axis is tilted to the plane of its orbit around the Sun, giving rise to the seasons. The northern hemisphere is tilted towards the Sun in June, the time of its summer, but the position is reversed six months later when the southern hemisphere enjoys more sunshine.

24 hours to reach its highest point the following day.

The path that the Sun seems to follow against the sky is skewed against the lines of Declination that we encountered earlier. This happens because the Earth's polar axis is tilted by 23.5 degrees to the plane of its orbit around the Sun.

This means that the northern hemisphere is tilted towards the Sun in June (northern summer) and the Sun climbs high in the sky at noon.

The South Pole is tilted towards the Sun in December, when the southern hemisphere enjoys summer and the Sun is high at noon there. The path along which the Sun appears to move against the Celestial Sphere is termed the Ecliptic. It runs through the constellations of the Zodiac and crosses the Celestial Equator at the Equinoxes in March and September.

Because the planets have orbits that are more or less level with the Earth's, they too appear to move through the Ecliptic. So too does the Moon.

THE SOLAR SYSTEM

The Solar System is made up of the Sun and its family of planets, plus the other natural objects that circle it, condensed from a spinning cloud of dust and gas created more than four and a half billion years ago.

The Solar System includes the natural satellites or moons that orbit many of those planets, as well as countless smaller objects ranging from asteroids and comets down to tiny particles of dust.

In recent years we have discovered that our solar system is by no means unique. Telescopes on Earth and in space have detected planets in orbit around close to 200 stars, plus disks of dust where planets might be forming around others.

Astronomers today consider there to be eight main planets in our own solar system after Pluto was demoted in 2006 by a controversial gathering of the scientific powers that be, the International Astronomical Union.

The planets are named after Roman gods, continuing the tradition set by ancient man who were aware of the existence of all planets out as far as Saturn.

Earth is the third planet in order from the Sun. The two that lie between our parent star and us are Mercury and Venus. They are known as Inferior Planets because of their position relative to us. They are solid, rocky worlds like our own. The five major worlds that lie beyond Earth – Mars, Jupiter, Saturn, Uranus and Neptune – are known as Superior Planets. Again, that is due to their position rather than any decree as to their

importance. All except Mars are giant balls of gas with no solid surface.

When viewed through a telescope, the inferior planets can be seen to change their appearance, like the Moon. They will resemble a not-quite-full moon when their orbit takes them further from Earth than the Sun, but as crescents as they close in between us and the Sun.

The point when Mercury or Venus lies between us and the Sun is called Inferior Conjunction and that where either lies at its furthest position beyond the Sun is described as Superior Conjunction.

Planets beyond the Earth are said to be in Conjunction when they lie on the far side of the Sun but at Opposition when the Earth lies between them and the Sun.

None except Mars – which resembles a nearly full moon at certain positions in its orbit – can show phases when viewed from Earth.

A Full Moon shows the dark lunar seas, or maria, as well as bright material ejected from more recent impacts, though the lack of shadows renders most craters invisible.

THE MOON

Apart from the Sun, there is one other object that clearly dominates the skies – our celestial partner the Moon.

The Moon may be pretty insignificant on the grand scale of the cosmos, with a diameter of just 2,160 mi/3,475 km, but there is no astronomical body that shows itself to us in such detail.

The Moon is the Earth's only natural satellite and lies so close, at an average distance of just 240,000 mi/385,000 km, that we can enjoy wonderful views of its mountains, valleys and other formations. It is the only world other than our own that humans have visited and explored.

The naked eye is enough to detect some of the features on its surface, but any small telescope and even binoculars will bring into view the spectacular craters that have permanently scarred its surface.

Generally speaking, we only get to see the features on one side of the Moon because it keeps the same face toward us throughout its orbit. A gentle rocking, called Libration, does allow us to peek around at some of the far side, but more than 40 percent of the lunar surface remains permanently out of view from Earth.

The side of the Moon that we can see offers a wealth of features to keep backyard observers happy for a lifetime, though there is not an awful lot going on there because the Moon is basically a sterile rock devoid of any of the weather or other events that make many of the planets so interesting.

This means that the lunar landscape has barely changed over millions of years. For an observer, however, the features may put on a different appearance from night to night, and even hour to hour, as the angle of sun-light on them varies.

The Moon has no light of its own and shines purely because of reflected sunlight. As the Moon travels in its orbit around the Earth, it shows different phases. To be strictly accurate, the two worlds rotate around one point marking their center of gravity, but it lies beneath the Earth's surface. Parts of the Moon move from darkness into daylight as the Sun rises over the local lunar horizon. This "daytime" period lasts for two weeks for any one spot on the Moon before the Sun sinks below the horizon again and the area is plunged into two weeks of gloom.

This darkness comes suddenly. There can be no twilight without any atmosphere. Temperatures plummet from more than 212°F/100°C to less than -275°F/-170°C. Inside some craters near the lunar poles are shadows that the Sun never reaches. Space scientists speculate that there may be ice buried in these permanently dark areas from cometary impacts long ago.

We see the phases change from a fine crescent in the evening sky through a half phase, then gibbous (as the waxing and waning are known), until Full Moon when the whole face presented to us is lit up. The process then reverses as the Moon continues its orbit and wanes back to a crescent in the morning sky. For a few days, the Moon becomes invisible as it lies in the same general direction as the Sun. This is the time of New Moon, when the Sun's light falls entirely on its far side.

The Moon, which always keeps the same face towards the Earth, produces no light of its own. As it makes its month-long orbit, half of its surface is always illuminated by the Sun. The diagram shows how the changing phase of the Moon appears at different stages in this orbit.

Yoko Kikuta

As the diagram above shows, half of the Moon is always in sunlight throughout this orbit. It's the changing position of the Moon relative to the Earth and the Sun that produces the phases. It can be a surprise to people to learn that the the Moon's orbit means it spends as much time in the day-time sky each month as it does the night.

When the Moon is showing as a fine crescent, it is often possible to make out the rest of it too. This phenomenon, dubbed "the new Moon in the old Moon's arms", is produced by sunlight reflecting off the Earth and illuminating the area of the Moon in shade.

The Moon is a lot less dense than the Earth, which rules out the idea that they might have formed as twin worlds. Instead, astronomers' favorite theory is that the Moon formed when another giant body collided with the Earth billions of years ago, throwing a vast quantity of our planet's outer layers into space. The material came together and slowly solidified into our satellite.

Until around a billion years ago, the Moon still had a hot interior. Major asteroid impacts would cause its outer crust to crack open, allowing molten lava to flood out. It formed the huge flat plains that we call the maria, or lunar seas. The seas are, of course, dry; there is no water.

Although there may still be a molten core, the Moon is today largely a solid, inactive world. It is covered with a lunar soil, called regolith and around 30ft/10m deep, made of pulverized rocks and dust from billions of years of impacts. Occasional activity has been reported in some craters. Called Transient Lunar Phenomena, or TLPs, these may be signs of gas venting from the interior.

Recently, other genuine flashes have been detected in the part of the moon in shadow. These are thought to be due to tiny meteors exploding as they strike the Moon. They would burn up as shooting stars if they entered the Earth's atmosphere.

When observing the Moon, note that the best time is when the dividing line between its illuminated side and its dark side, called the terminator, is passing across the visible disk. At this time, lunar features nearby will cast strong shadows, showing them in dramatic relief. When the Moon is full, all the detail is lost because no shadows can be seen from Earth. The only features that stand out at this time are the maria and brilliant white rays crossing the surface that mark the ejected material from a few, relatively young impact craters. The Moon looks brilliant when full despite the fact that its rocks are actually very dark. The Moon has weak gravity, a sixth as strong as on Earth, which explains why the Apollo astronauts appeared to bounce along as they walked on its surface. But the pull is enough to cause the tides that raise and lower our seas every day. The Earth's own gravitational pull on the Moon is what locked its rotation over the years, so that the same side is always presented to us.

The Moon has an eccentric orbit, meaning that its distance from the Earth varies in distance by around 25,000mi/40,000 km. It appears larger in the sky when closest (called at perigee) than furthest (apogee), although the casual observer would find it difficult to notice the difference.

Robotic space probes have continued to study the Moon since the last Apollo astronauts walked on its surface in 1972. But NASA is working to send humans there again by 2020 and set up permanently manned colonies, as a first step to going to Mars.

The Moon is the only other world to have been visited by humans. Here the second man on the Moon, Buzz Aldrin, steps down the ladder from his lunar module to set foot on the lunar surface. Twelve astronauts walked on the Moon between 1969 and 1972 during the Apollo missions and NASA is making plans to go there again.

NASA

ESA

When astronauts return to the Moon, they may well stay in or near Shackleton crater. Scientists believe that ice may exist in craters like Shackleton which have areas permanently in shadow. If ice is there, it would make it easier to supply nearby moonbases with water.

THE SUN

The Sun is the great powerhouse at the center of the solar system around which its extensive family revolves.

It dominates our lives, its diameter of 864,950 mi/1,392,000 km is around 50 times greater than that of Jupiter, the largest planet in the Solar System. It is big enough to swallow up a million Earths.

On a cosmic scale, however, the Sun is not particularly special. It's an average star like the thousands of millions of others in our own Milky Way galaxy and the untold billions within the countless other galaxies in the universe.

Yet the Sun is special, indeed vital, to us because it provides the light and heat on which we all depend for survival. It does this not by burning like a fire, but by acting as a giant nuclear furnace, where atomic reactions occur on a vast scale. These processes turn 7,000 million tons of hydrogen into helium every second, releasing the enormous amount of energy that makes the Sun shine.

NASA/ESA

Scientists have been putting the Sun under close scrutiny, using satellites such as SOHO to monitor flares and solar storms which could threaten Earth.

What is incredible is that the Sun has already been converting hydrogen in this way for more than 4.5 billion years, and is expected to carry on doing so for a similar length of time.

Unlike other stars in the sky, the Sun is dazzlingly – indeed dangerously – bright. It also shows a sizeable face that astronomers can study in detail. Despite this, we know a lot less about our parent star than we would like, although a number of satellites are currently returning data that should improve our knowledge considerably.

The common perception that the Sun is yellow, is based on an illusion: it is really a white star. It is a ball of gas with no solid edge, so when we view its surface, called the photosphere, through filters, we are actually looking into a fog 300mi/500km deep. The temperature here is a staggering 9,900°F/5,500°C and photographs reveal the surface to be granulated like a pile of sugar: each cell is around 600 mi/ 1000 km across.

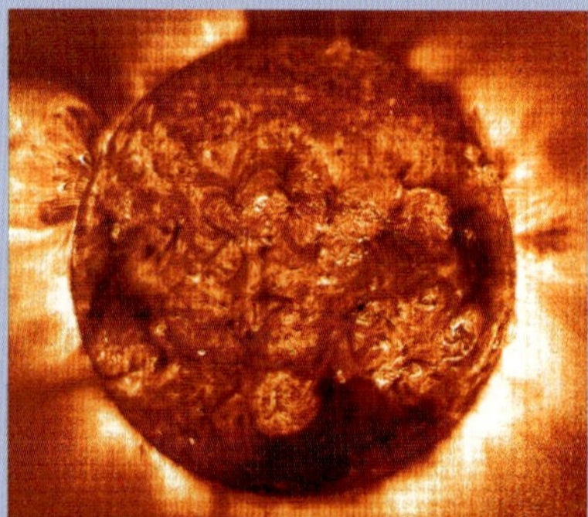

EIT Consortium (ESA/NASA)

This dramatic image is a map of the Sun's corona indicating the different temperatures in its atmosphere. Brighter areas show the hotter regions of gas. It was made by the SOHO satellite on June 21, 2001, while a total solar eclipse was visible from southern Africa, allowing astronomers to compare observations from space with those made from the ground.

This photosphere can be seen to be brighter towards the center than near the edges because we are looking at the hotter central regions of the Sun – it is thought that the temperature at the Sun's core may be as much as 60,000,000°F/ 15,000,000°C.

Notable features on the photosphere are the dark blotches that seem to appear suddenly and at random. These are called sunspots, a kind of solar acne formed from convection currents – regions 1,800°F/1,000°C or more cooler than the rest of the surface. They are surrounded by a lighter and warmer fringe that is termed the penumbra. Sunspots only look dark because they contrast with the solar disk's general brilliance. If one could be viewed in isolation, it would glow brightly.

Studies of these sunspots show that their appearance is not quite as random and unpredictable as one might think. They are caused by disturbances in the Sun's magnetic field and are far more frequent at certain times than at others. Indeed, there is an 11-year cycle during which such solar activity grows and wanes.

Over that period, as well as changing their frequency, sunspots also tend to appear more at particular latitudes on the Sun's disk. This phenomenon is known as the Butterfly Effect due to the pattern created when spot occurrences are plotted on a graph.

Some sunspots are so big that they are several times the size of the Earth. Occasionally they are big enough to be seen with the naked eye – providing an appropriate solar filter is used. Ancient man was aware of sunspots and they were studied by the astronomer Galileo and others after the invention of the telescope.

These observations showed that the Sun spins on its axis and helped determine how long it takes to do so. Matters are complicated because the rotational period differs across the disk, but we now know that the Sun turns once every 26 days at

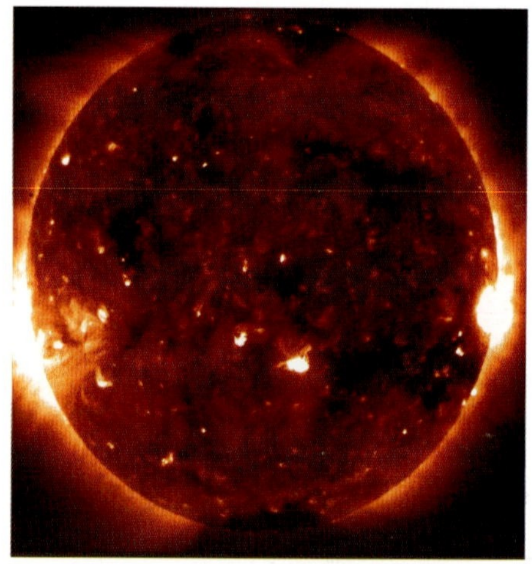

Hinode JAXA/NASA/PPARC

An X-ray view of the Sun from the Hinode satellite shows intensely bright regions where huge explosions of gas, powered by the Sun's magnetic field, are taking place. These coronal mass ejections hurl highly charged particles into space and can wreck satellite electronics.

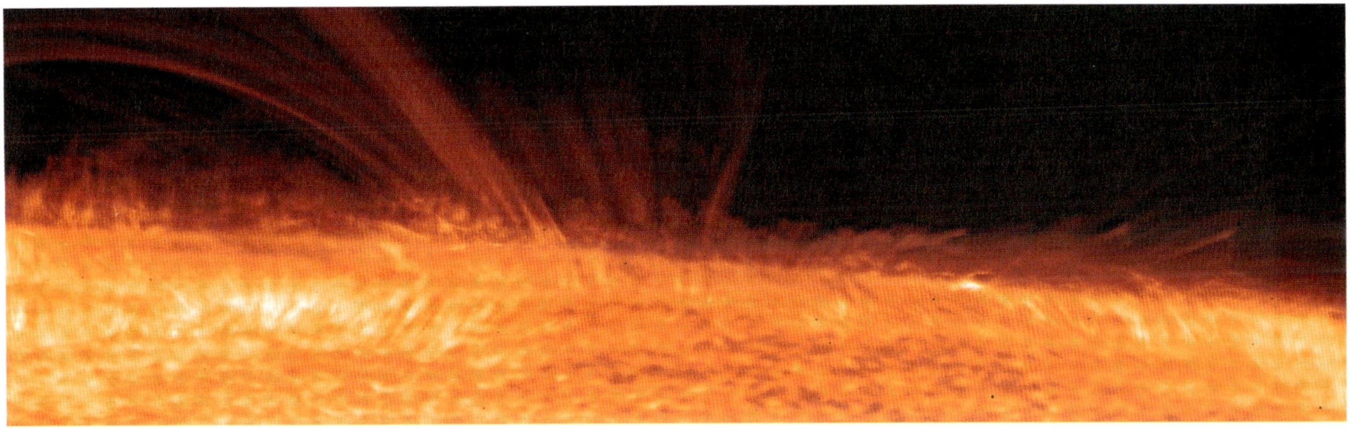

Hinode JAXA/NASA/PPARC

Long strands and wisps of gas stream from the thin layer of the Sun's atmosphere called the chromosphere.

the equator and between 30 and 36 days as you get nearer the poles.

Spots are not the only feature to be seen on the Sun. Faculae show like bright rivers of light and plages are other bright regions. Explosive events occasionally occur in the form of intense flares.

Flame-like prominences that specialist equipment reveals around the Sun's edge are invisible in normal daylight. These eruptions, which can form strands or loops reaching thousands of miles/kilometers into space, also reveal themselves during a total eclipse of the Sun, when the solar atmosphere, called the chromosphere, also comes into view. Beyond the chromosphere is the corona, an extensive outer atmosphere, and beyond that streams the solar wind, a continual flow of high-speed gas.

Observatory satellites have detected another form of event called coronal mass ejections. These hurl electrically charged particles out into space and are the main cause of the aurora, the celestial light show that we call the northern and southern lights, when they hit the Earth's magnetic field.

Scientists have sent twin satellites called Stereo to watch for these ejections, from either side of the Earth, because they pose a real threat to satellite electronics, power grids and even the lives of astronauts.

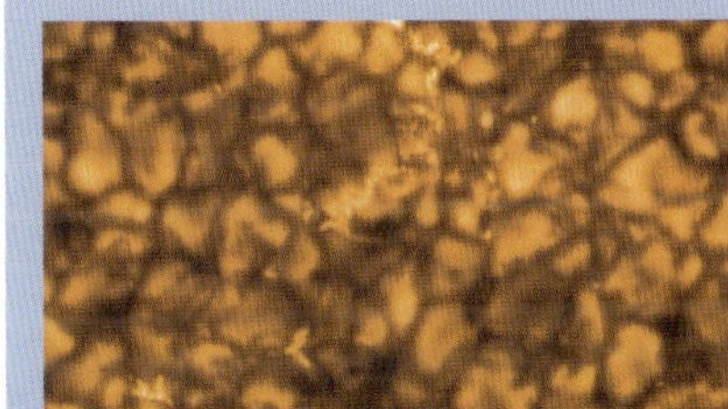

Hinode JAXA/NASA/PPARC

The granulated surface of the Sun is clearly revealed in an image from a Japanese solar satellite called Hinode. This mottled pattern is caused by convection currents which carry hot gas from below the surface and then send it sinking again as it cools.

OBSERVING THE SUN

The size and proximity of the Sun make it attractive for amateur astronomers. However, observing the Sun is highly dangerous unless you follow safety rules to the letter.

Traditionally, the safe way to observe the Sun has been to use a technique called projection. This entails aligning the telescope with the Sun so that its light shines down the tube, like any other object, but is then projected out of the eyepiece and onto a piece of card held a short distance away. The Sun is so bright that this will produce a clear image. Focusing the telescope in the normal way allows this image to be made sharp.

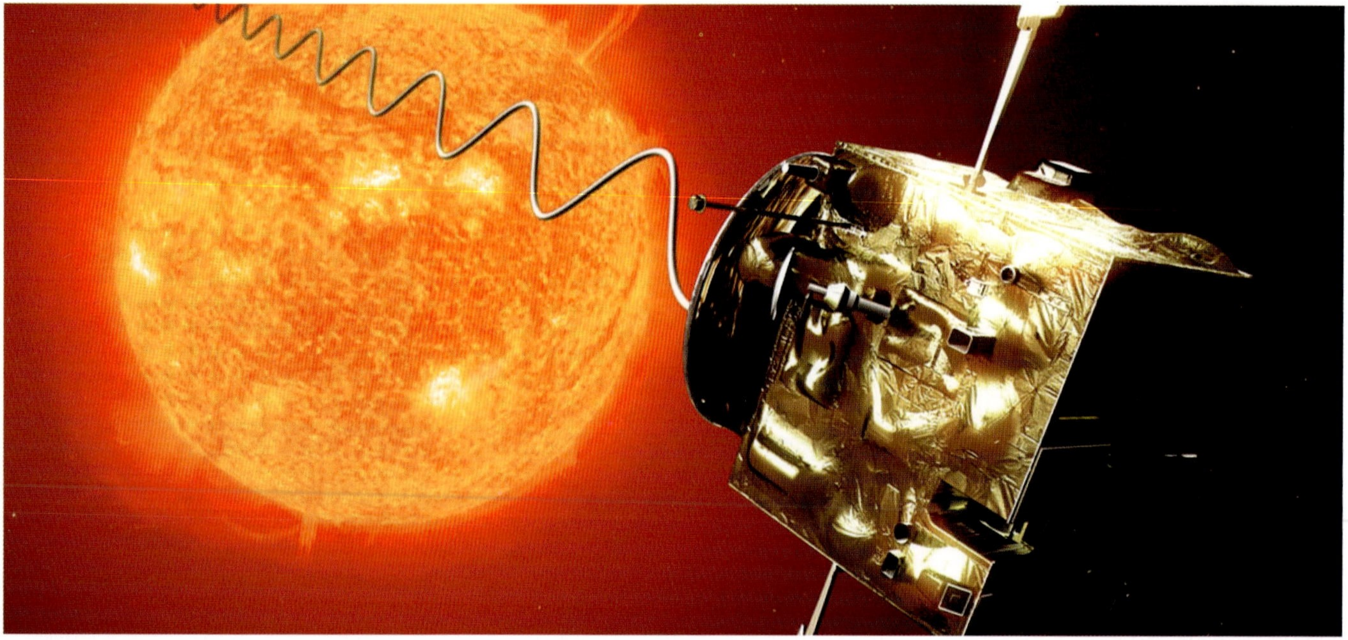

ESA - AOES Medialab

Many sophisticated probes have been launched to investigate the Sun's mysteries – including the Venus Express shown here. But a properly prepared telescope can still provide fascinating insights.

Putting the card in shadow will help the projected image to stand out more clearly. Some observers use black card instead of white, claiming this gives a much clearer image. Regular solar observers buy or build special projection screens to make life easier. This may be lined with a special graded disk to help to log the precise positions and sizes of any sunspots and so build a record of solar activity.

Some words of warning. Don't align the telescope by looking through it or along it. Use the instrument's shadow to tell when it is directed the right way. Also, put caps over the lenses of your telescope's finder, if you have one, so that sunlight does not pass through; it could burn you or set fire to clothing while you are observing. You should also check carefully that your telescope is suitable for projecting the Sun. Many contain plastic rather than metal in the telescope tube and eyepieces, and this can melt under the magnified heat. Larger telescopes, particularly reflectors or SCTs, may need to have their apertures reduced, or "stopped down", to cut the amount of sunlight entering the tube. You may find that the cap that came with your scope has a smaller cap covering a hole in part of it for just this purpose.

In recent years, special filters have been produced, made in glass or of specialist coated film, that are placed over the main opening of the telescope to cut its light to a safe level for normal viewing. You can even buy miniature binoculars with filters built in purely for keeping an eye on the Sun. Only buy such filters from a reputable source and always check them for damage, such as holes or scratches.

Some telescopes used to come with a so-called solar filter for the eyepiece end of the telescope. If you have one, throw it away. They are not safe and can crack in the intense heat. Never try to make home-made filters, either. Colored film, dark photographic slides or CDs are not suitable. Even if they appear to filter the sunlight, they will let through invisible solar radiation which can permanently damage your eyes.

An observer snaps the Sun through a compact telescope fitted with a dense protective filter to cut its powerful rays.

Special telescopes filter out most of the light spectrum, so the Sun's prominences may be viewed in hydrogen alpha light. These used to be prohibitively expensive because of the engineering involved, but today some mass-produced models are available at relatively affordable prices.

ECLIPSES OF THE SUN AND MOON

Eclipses are among the rarer events in the sky, and they are also among the most dramatic. There are two major types both of which involve alignments of the Sun, Moon and Earth.

SOLAR ECLIPSES

An eclipse of the Sun occurs when the Moon passes directly between us and the Sun. Technically, this is an occultation rather than an eclipse, which normally involves a body moving into shadow. A solar eclipse can only occur at New Moon.

By an amazing coincidence of nature, the Moon appears almost exactly the same size in the sky as the Sun, although this is solely because it lies so much closer to us.

It means that from parts of the Earth, the Moon can completely obliterate the Sun in broad daylight, temporarily turning day into night and revealing our home star's atmosphere, or corona, shining as a ghostly band around it, with perhaps a few prominences also in view.

An eclipse is the only time we get to view the corona from Earth. Its shape changes depending on the point the Sun has reached in its 11-year cycle of activity.

Around solar minimum, the glow stretches mainly from the equatorial regions and much less so towards its poles. Around solar maximum, the corona is more evenly spread all around the Sun's disk.

Because the Moon just covers the Sun, the area from which a total eclipse is visible is very small, perhaps 100mi/160km wide, on the Earth. This stretches into a lengthy eclipse track that can run for thousands of miles across continents as the Moon travels in its orbit and the Earth rotates below. But it means that from any one point on Earth, total eclipses are extremely rare. Partial eclipses which may be seen for hundreds of kilometers around, are more common. From these regions, the Moon only partly covers the Sun.

Key moments during an eclipse are called contacts. First contact, as the name suggests, is when the Moon limb first encroaches on the Sun.

Second contact is the moment when it completely covers the Sun and totality begins.

At third contact, the sun's light breaks through a lunar valley, producing the famous Diamond Ring Effect and marking the end of totality.

Fourth contact is when the Moon glides completely off the solar disk.

Only during the period of totality is it safe to look directly at the eclipse. Be sure to do so because it's an amazing spectacle. Look away, or use your eclipse specs again, the moment the Sun reappears.

A total eclipse of the Sun is one of the most dramatic spectacles in nature and the only time when the solar atmosphere, or corona, can be viewed from the ground. Red flame-like prominences may also be spotted leaping from the edge of the Sun. Totality is the only time when it is safe to look at the Sun wth the naked eye.

There is a further type of solar eclipse, called an annular eclipse. This occurs when the Moon is around its furthest distance from Earth and does not appear quite big enough in the sky to cover the Sun completely. When the two bodies align directly over a point on Earth, a ring of sunlight is left around the Moon's edge. This is the so-called Ring of Fire. Although they lack the subtleties of a total eclipse, annular eclipses are incredible to witness. You will need to protect your eyes throughout.

Solar eclipses do not happen every New Moon because the plane of the Moon's orbit is tilted by about five degrees to that of the Earth around the Sun, so that it normally passes above or below it. They occur at the points where the two orbits cross, called the nodes. Solar eclipses may be observed using the techniques described on pages 20 and 21. Alternatively, you can project a tiny image of the eclipse without a telescope by making a pinhole in a piece of card and allowing the Sun's light to shine through it on to a second piece of card.

A total lunar eclipse is a dramatic sight with the Moon turning red from sunlight scattered onto its surface through the Earth's atmosphere. It can take on a 3-D effect.

LUNAR ECLIPSES

Eclipses of the Moon are true eclipses because they are caused when our natural satellite passes into the shadow of the Earth in space. They can only occur at Full Moon, but they do not occur at every Full Moon for the reasons of tilted orbits explained above. As it's the Moon's own appearance that changes during a lunar eclipse, the event is visible from any part of the world from which the Moon can be seen. You will therefore get the chance to see a lot more lunar eclipses than solar during your lifetime.

The Moon usually shines from reflected sunlight. The Sun also causes the Earth to cast a shadow, which is normally invisible in the sky. When the Moon drifts into the shadow, its light begins to fade.

At first the effect is only slight because the eclipse is penumbral – from the Moon, the Earth would appear only partly to be obscuring the Sun. During some eclipses, the Moon only enters this twilight zone of the shadow. But when it passes through the central shadow, the Sun's light is completely blocked from falling on the Moon.

Or almost. During most total eclipses, the Moon remains visible, displaying a glow that ranges in color from orange to a deep red. This is because the Earth's atmosphere scatters sunlight, directing the longer reddish wavelengths on to the lunar disk and allowing it to remain in sight.

Astronomers watch in fascination to see how dark or bright a total lunar eclipse will be. It often gives a clue to the state of our atmosphere, because dark eclipses tend to occur in months following a major volcanic eruption that has ejected dust to high altitudes. Sometimes variations in the light can give the Moon a three-dimensional glow.

The total phase can last up nearly two hours, depending on how far into the center of the Earth's shadow the Moon has traveled. Passage through the entire shadow, including the penumbra, can take several hours.

How the Full Moon's appearance changes as it gracefully enters the shadow of the Earth in space. Longer exposures at totality reveal the colors on the lunar surface in shadow.

MERCURY

Mercury – the closest planet to the Sun – is a rocky terrestrial world like Earth. In size and appearance, however, it more closely resembles the Moon. It has a heavily cratered, mountainous surface that has been untouched by weathering, because the planet has only a very tenuous atmosphere.

At a distance averaging around 36 million mi/58 million km from the Sun, Mercury experiences enormous contrasts in temperature. The side facing the Sun gets a severe roasting, reaching 800°F/430°C. The dark side of Mercury becomes a deep freeze, with temperatures plunging to -290°F/-180°C.

Highly reflective areas within the craters lead scientists to believe that there might well be ice within the crater walls, permanently frozen in areas that never receive sunlight.

Mercury spins slowly on its axis, with a day that is around 59 Earth days long. That's not much less than the length of its year, because it zips around the Sun in just 88 days. This orbit, incidentally, is the most eccentric of the planets, with the Mercury-Sun distance ranging from 28.6 million to 43.5 million mi/ 46 million to 70 million km. Mercury is unique in the solar system in that its axis is is at a 90 degree angle to the plane of its orbit, so that there can never be any seasons on the planet. Mercury, named after the winged messenger of the gods, is believed to have had a particularly violent birth. The planet is known to contain unexpectedly high levels of iron. The theory is that this is because it was formed from an impact between a giant asteroid and a much larger world that was orbiting the Sun more than four billion years ago.

Only one space probe has so far visited Mercury – more than 30 years ago – although things are about to change. America's unmanned Mariner 10 probe made three flybys of the planet in 1974 and 1975, and those brief approaches transformed our knowledge of Mercury.

The probe was able to photograph less than half of Mercury's surface, but the pictures revealed its lunar-like craters plus a system of ridges hundreds of km long which are thought to have formed when the planet originally cooled and shrank. Most prominent among the features is the Caloris basin, a ring of mountains 807 mi/1,300 km high.

Two more robotic missions will unlock more of the secrets of Mercury. A NASA mission called Messenger has been en route there since 2004, but will not go into orbit around the planet until 2011.

Another mission to Mercury, BepiColombo, will carry two orbiters, one European and one Japanese. The craft is not due for launch until 2013 and the probes will not arrive until six years later.

NASA Jet Propulsion Laboratolry

OBSERVING MERCURY

Mercury is one of the brightest objects in the heavens, yet many people go through life without ever seeing it. This is because it clings to the so Sun that it is never visible in a truly dark sky. It never manages to get more than 28 degrees from the Sun at one of its elongations and so, from most of the world, it never stands very high above the horizon in the twilight sky. Even when these favorable apparitions occur, the planet is often hidden in low cloud, haze or murk.

The times to look for Mercury are when it reaches its eastern elongation after sunset or western elongation before sunrise.

However, celestial geometry means that the angle of the ecliptic – the imaginary line through the sky along which the Sun and planets appear to travel – is steeper to the horizon at certain times of year than others. The steeper the angle, the better your viewing chances.

For observers in the northern hemisphere, the best evening (eastern) elongations occur in the spring and the best morning (western) elongations are in the autumn.

The reverse is the case in the southern hemisphere. If you are viewing in the evening, start looking for Mercury while the sky is still bright. Binoculars will help, but no attempt should be made to use them to sweep for the planet until after the Sun has set.

When you do spot Mercury, it resembles a bright star. A telescope with a high-power eyepiece will allow you to distinguish the moon-like phases, but don't expect to see any detail such as mountains and craters –

Europe and Japan are planning a joint mission to explore Mercury. Two probes will be launched in 2013 and will take six years before they go into orbit around the heavily cratered planet.

ESA - C.Carreau

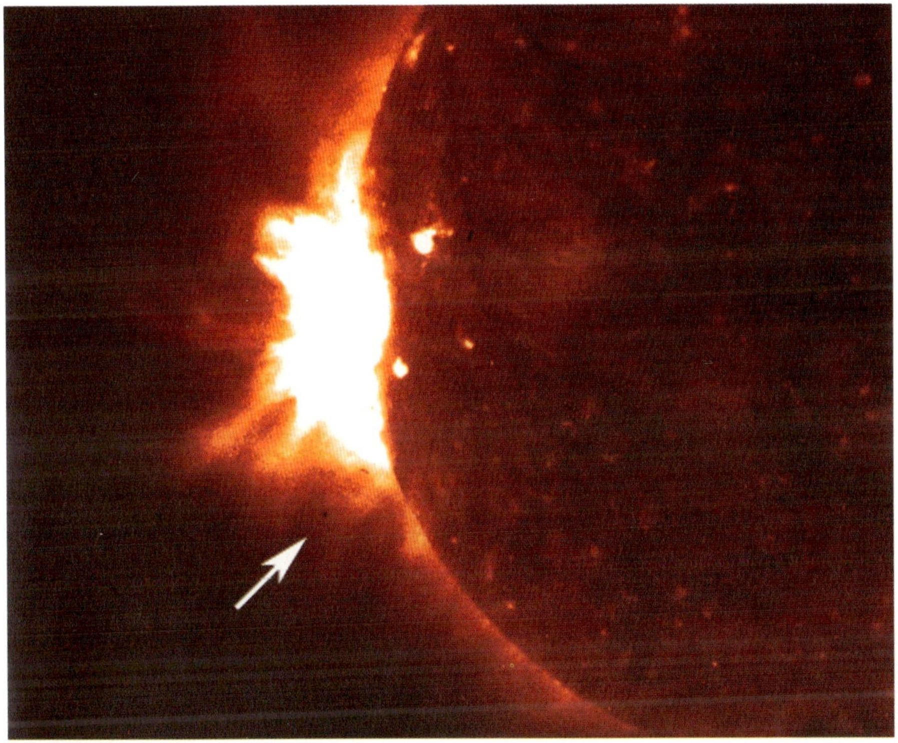

NASA/ESA

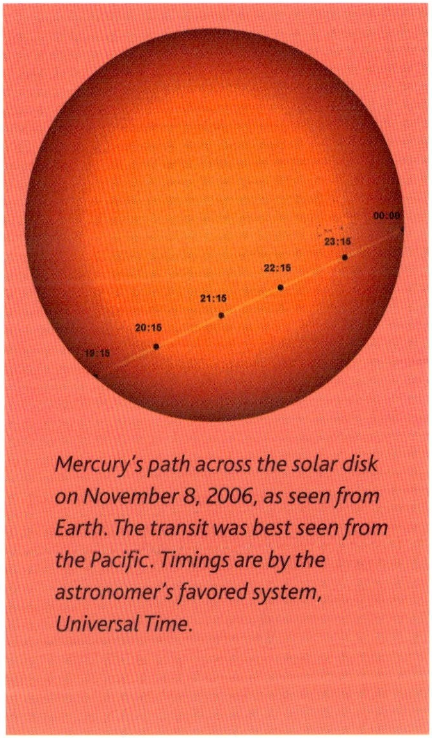

JAXA

Mercury's path across the solar disk on November 8, 2006, as seen from Earth. The transit was best seen from the Pacific. Timings are by the astronomer's favored system, Universal Time.

the planet is too far away. Experienced observers sketch Mercury, however, recording subtle shadings on its tiny surface.

There is another rare occasion when it is possible to view Mercury – during a transit, when the planet passes directly in front of the Sun and appears as a silhouette. These are rarer than one might imagine because Mercury's orbit is tilted slightly with respect to ours and so usually passes above or below the Sun.

Transits only occur in May or November, with May events happening at intervals of 13 and 33 years and November events at intervals of seven, 13 and 33 years. The next transit will not occur until May 9, 2016, and the next one after that will be on November 11, 2019.

Observing transits requires the same critical care as observing eclipses of the Sun. Use similar techniques to those described earlier in this book . Mercury will appear as a tiny dark dot crossing the solar disk.

VENUS

There can be few more beautiful sights in nature than that of Venus shining brilliantly in a twilight sky. The second planet from the Sun has a serene splendor explaining why it is named after the Roman goddess of love.

Appearances can be deceptive, however. Venus is, in reality, a planet in poisonous climatic turmoil.

Scientists are fascinated to know why that should be, because it was once believed that Venus could be like Earth. The two worlds are approximately the same size, are both made of rock, have atmospheres and inhabit a similar zone of the solar system. But our closest planetary neighbor is a world whose climate has gone out of control.

The air is heavy with sulfuric acid, the surface glows at 750°F/400°C, twice the maximum temperature inside a domestic oven. Anything surviving that heat would be crushed by the pressure of the atmosphere.

It was only comparatively recently that we learned this, because Venus is enveloped by a dense cover of clouds. The surface of the planet is completely hidden from us and, before the advent of space probes, astronomers could only speculate as to what lay at the surface. Some imagined vast oceans as the source of the clouds. Others suggested it was covered by Saharan-type deserts.

The clouds must reflect around 60 percent of the Sun's light and heat, so its fiery conditions are thought to be due to a runaway greenhouse effect.

Early clues that all was not well on Venus came when the former Soviet Union sent a sequence of probes named Venera to the planet. It was not long before they sent back data revealing Venus's searing temperatures, extreme atmospheric pressure at the surface (90 times greater than on Earth) and raging thunderstorms. Two probes even transmitted images of the planet's rocky terrain in the minutes before they were crushed to destruction.

Later probes managed to lift the veil from Venus even more. Two American Mariner missions learned more about the make-up of the atmosphere – mainly carbon dioxide with some nitrogen – and photographed the patterns in the cloud tops. But the greatest flood of information came when the US spacecraft Magellan sailed into orbit around Venus in 1990 and began to chart its surface in detail, using cloud-penetrating radar.

Europe's Venus Express probe is orbiting the planet and sending back valuable data about its atmosphere, including observations of a powerful double vortex above Venus's south pole.

Venus's landscape has volcanoes spewing sulfur dioxide into the atmosphere.

Magellan was a stunning success, allowing planetary scientists to draw up high-resolution maps of Venus, before the probe was deliberately plunged into the atmosphere in 1994. The maps showed that the totally dry surface was made up mainly of smooth plains with two continent-sized highland areas: one in the northern hemisphere, now named Ishtar Terra, and one in the southern, called Aphrodite Terra.

Most of the mountains and other surface features were named after historical and mythological women, in keeping with the planet's own female persona. The features detected include 167 giant volcanoes and nearly 1,000 impact craters.

In 2006 a European space probe, Venus Express, went into orbit around the planet and began returning fascinating new data, including close-up images of a swirling double vortex over the south pole.

For the amateur astronomer, Venus is an easy if inscrutable target. It can become as bright as magnitude -4.7 – enough to cast a shadow – and is then even visible in daylight in crystal clear skies.

Its moon-like pattern of phases can be seen through a telescope, as Galileo first showed in the 17th century. When Venus lies beyond the Sun, it shows a gibbous (i.e: waxing or waning) face but, when it's at its brightest, it displays a crescent shape that may be seen in binoculars.

Paul Sutherland

Brilliant Venus, the third brightest object in the sky, makes a beautiful pairing with the crescent Moon in one of its appearances as the so-called Evening Star.

Some amateurs have sketched subtle shadings in the atmosphere, but there are not the striking details seen on other planets.

One phenomenon seen by various experienced observers is the so-called Ashen Light, a mysterious glowing of the dark part of the planet that is in shadow and should therefore be invisible. Discounting the possibility of an illusion, it has been suggested this could be due to lightning in the continually raging thunderstorms. Others wonder if it is caused by volcanic eruptions or is perhaps a glow from the baking landscape.

Venus lies an average of 68 million mi/ 109 million km from the Sun and, from Earth, appears to venture as far as 47 degrees from it in the sky when at either its eastern elongation, in the evening, or western elongation, in the morning. This means that, unlike Mercury, it may at times be seen shining in a dark sky.

Because Venus's orbit is inclined slightly to our own, it usually passes above or below the solar disk when at inferior or superior conjunction. However, at rare intervals, it may be seen gliding across the Sun's disk as a large black dot. This last happened on June 8, 2004, and will happen again on June 6, 2012.

Venus takes 224.7 days to complete one orbit of the Sun. But a final oddity is that its own day (the time it takes to spin on its axis) is 243 days – longer than its year. It also rotates in the opposite direction to other planets in the solar system. Venus is a strange world indeed.

MARS

Mars, often known as the Red Planet, fascinates people because it most resembles Earth. Although a lot smaller – just 4,222mi/6,795km wide – it is made of rock, has an atmosphere, albeit thinner than ours, and experiences weather. Why is it red? Because the surface is covered with rust – or iron oxide.

Mars has a day just 40 minutes longer than Earth's, and on its nearly two-year long journey around the Sun it enjoys seasons similar to ours because its axis is tilted 25 degrees, in a similar way to our own.

There are also, we are beginning to discover, significant reserves of water on Mars. Scientists are intrigued to know, therefore, whether the planet might ever have been home to life – and whether life might still exist there today.

It's no surprise, then, that Mars has been put under greater scrutiny by space probes than any other planet. Several are already in orbit around it and others have landed and sent robots trundling across its surface. The planet is also a target for a manned mission within the next few decades.

Thanks to the probes' cameras and other instruments, we are being deluged with detailed information about our planetary neighbor. Martian features include the biggest volcano in the solar system, the 16mi/26km high Olympus Mons, plus Valles Marineris, a vast chasm 2,500mi/4,000km long that dwarfs the Earth's Grand Canyon.

ESA/DLR/FU Berlin (G. Neukum)

A large patch of water ice is photographed by Europe's Mars Express probe on the floor of a crater in the Vastitas Borealis region in the high northern latitudes of Mars.

The planet is also dotted with craters from asteroid impacts, first spotted when NASA's Mariner 4 flew past Mars in 1965. Recent monitoring of the surface shows that smaller impacts are still occurring today.

Unlike the Moon, Mars' surface is constantly weathered by winds. Deserts reveal the familiar patterns of sand dunes, and little whirlwinds called dust devils whip across the surface. Every couple of years or so, and thanks to seasonal temperature changes, much bigger dust storms blow up, sometimes enveloping the entire planet.

ESA

The Exomars rover is just one of the ways space agencies are planning to explore the surface of Mars further.

The notion that aliens might exist on Mars received a major boost in the late19th century when Italian astronomer Giovanni Schiaparelli announced that he had seen channels on Mars. His Italian was wrongly translated into English as "canals". USA astronomer Sir Percival Lowell "confirmed" their existence and claimed there was vegetation growing alongside waterways.

We now know these Martian waterways were simply an optical illusion. But the truth, we are learning, is no less exciting. There is plenty of evidence for water on Mars, and planetary scientists believe it was once a blue planet under vast oceans, just like Earth.

Many Martian features, including channels and gullies, appear to have been sculpted by running water. Other features show sediment deposits. An area near the equator resembles a frozen sea, with the shapes of ice floes clearly visible through the sand. And most remarkably, the American space agency NASA revealed picture evidence in 2006 of fresh deposits that indicated water was still bursting from below the surface and running down crater slopes before evaporating into space.

Certainly, there is still much water at the poles. Studies by a ground-piercing radar instrument on Europe's Mars Express orbiter showed that the southern polar cap holds enough ice to cover the planet with a sea 36ft/11m deep.

Two robot rovers, Spirit and Opportunity, which landed on Mars in January 2004, both found conclusive evidence of features formed by the presence of water. Future international missions are being planned to land on Mars and bring rock samples back for detailed analysis. Strict quarantine measures will have to be observed to protect the samples from terrestrial contamination.

However, it appears there are samples of Mars already on Earth. We know of a number of meteorites with a chemistry that shows they must have been blasted out of the Martian surface, perhaps by an asteroid impact, and then floated around space for aeons before falling to Earth.

One such meteorite lay preserved in Antarctica, and caused a sensation in 1996 when NASA scientists claimed it contained microscopic, worm-like bacteria.

Closer inspection has led most scientists to conclude that these aliens are the result of contamination on Earth.

Even if that is the case, more and more scientists now believe we will find evidence of microbial life forms on Mars, especially as organisms have been found to survive in the most extreme conditions, including volcanic vents, radioactive sites and even the vacuum of space. Future exploration of Mars will be fascinating.

NASA

NASA's Mars Reconnaissance Orbiter pictured dunes inside the half-mile wide Victoria Crater. A close-up revealed one of the US rovers, Opportunity, and even its tracks in the Martian sand.

DEIMOS AND PHOBOS

Mars has two moons, named Phobos (top) and Deimos (bottom). Their small sizes and irregular shapes mean they appear more like asteroids captured by the planet's gravitational pull, and indeed most astronomers believe that is what they are. Phobos, which is just 16.8mi/27km long, has distinctive groove markings thought to have been gouged out by material ejected from Mars in an impact. Deimos is even smaller, at 9.3mi/15km long. Both moons are covered with craters.

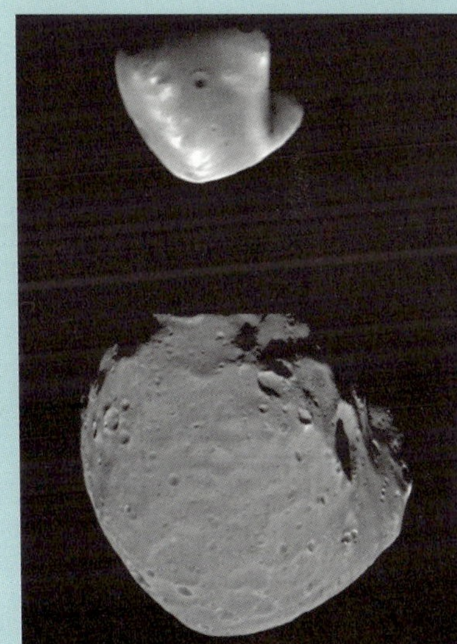

NASA

David Strange

Mars hangs brilliantly in the night sky close to the Pleiades and Hyades star clusters in Taurus around the time of one of its favorable Oppositions. At other times Mars is seen much fainter.

OBSERVING MARS

Mars can be explored with even a small telescope, particularly for a period of a few weeks every couple of years or so, when Earth and Mars come closest together. In the intervening year, Mars lies on the far side of the Sun during its 687-day long journey around it. The circumstances of our neighboring orbits means that the distance between the Earth and Mars varies hugely.

But when Mars is at Opposition and therefore at its closest, it becomes one of the brightest objects in the sky, sometimes reaching a magnitude of -2.8. It is then easy to see why it was dubbed the Red Planet and given the name of the Roman god of war, because it hangs like a drop of blood in the heavens.

Around opposition, Mars becomes a sizeable object that is rewarding to observe even through a modest amateur telescope. Its apparent diameter can reach as much as 25 arcseconds across, compared to a tiny 3.5 arcseconds when it is on the other side of the Sun. Some oppositions are better than others, because Mars' elliptical orbit means its closest distance from Earth can vary between 34 million and 62 million mi/ 55 million and 100 million km. At the most unfavorable oppositions, it can reach a diameter of only 14 arcseconds.

During these close encounters, amateur astronomers can spot the white patches marking the polar ice caps and the dark shadings of major features such as Syrtis Major, a V-shaped region resembling the Indian sub-continent.

These dark markings were first noticed by Italian astronomers in the early 17th century, following the invention of the telescope. Galileo viewed Mars through his in 1610, noting its sometimes gibbous shape. In 1636, his countryman Francesco Fontana made the first recorded sketch of the planet's features.

Traditional observers still make sketches of Mars, filling in printed templates provided by national astronomical societies. There is undoubtedly a great sense of achievement to be had from making one's own visual log in this way. But the development of webcam-style devices and more sophisticated CCD cameras, as well as software with which to process images, are leading more and more amateurs to keep a photographic record of the Red Planet.

NASA Jet Propulsion Laboratory (NASA-JP

Olympus Mons, pictured here by NASA's Viking 1 orbiter, is the largest volcano known in the solar system. It has a diameter of around 360mi/600km and the caldera at the summit stands 15mi/24km above the surrounding plains at three times the height of Everest.

ASTEROIDS

Hundreds of asteroids of varying size travel on orbits which pass just a few tens of millions of miles from that of the Earth.

Automatic telescopes constantly monitor the sky to detect and track threatening objects, and space missions are being planned to fly out and deal with them.

Many hundreds of asteroids of varying sizes travel on orbits that cross or pass close to that of the Earth. But the vast majority – probably 95 percent – steer well clear of us as they orbit the Sun in a zone called the Asteroid Belt.

This cosmic highway lies between the orbits of Mars and Jupiter and is littered with hundreds of thousands of rocks half a mile or more in size, and usually irregularly shaped. They fill a gap in the solar system where one might expect another planet to lie. The first were discovered after a group of 24 astronomers with the wonderful name of the Celestial Police searched for such a missing planet in the late 18th century. The first spotted – by Giuseppe Piazzi, in Sicily in 1801 – was Ceres. It is the largest asteroid, with a diameter of about 590mi/950km, and it orbits the Sun once every 4.6 years.

Subsequently other large asteroids were discovered, including the 380mi/610km wide Pallas and the 340mi/540km wide Vesta. The latter is the only asteroid that usually which bright enough to be seen by the naked eye. Hundreds of thousands of asteroids have since been discovered, usually in photographs; the current rate of detection is around 5,000 a month.

NASA

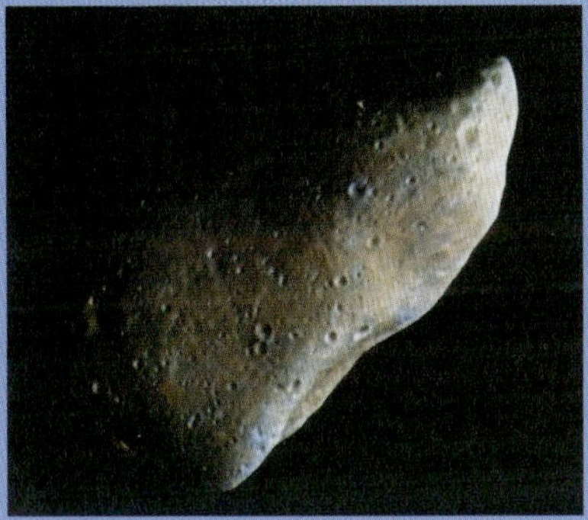

Gaspra was the first asteroid to be seen close-up, pictured by the Galileo probe to Jupiter.

Still, it's estimated that even if they were all combined in one, they would form a body less than half the size of the Moon.

It was thought that asteroids were produced when a planet was pulled to pieces by collisions or gravitational forces but modern thinking is that the rocks are remains of the early disk of material that collected to form the solar system. The rocks in the asteroids' space lanes never managed to combine because of the disruptive gravitational effects of mighty neighbor Jupiter. Jupiter has also managed to shepherd clusters of asteroid into special regions ahead and behind itself in its own orbit. These clusters, at regions known as the Lagrangian points in the orbit, are known as Trojans.

Asteroids are often referred to as Minor Planets, but in 2006, our contemporary celestial police force, the International Astronomical Union, decreed that they be officially known as small Solar System bodies. At the same time, Ceres was promoted to a new category: Dwarf Planet.

Though the largest and earliest-found asteroids, like the planets, have classical names, they are also identified by catalog numbers. It has become traditional also for the myriad of smaller rocks to be awarded names of living people, in recognition of their achievements.

Space probes have given us our first close-up views of asteroids with a number of fly-bys. The first came in 1991, when Galileo, on the way to Jupiter, sped past a space rock called Gaspra. It showed it to be a tumbling, elongated body, solid and about 11mi/17km long, its surface dotted with impact craters. Other probes have checked out Ida, which was found to have its own tiny moon called Dactyl, and Eros, among others. In 2005, Japan's Hayabusa probe

ESO

Asteroids drift through the space lanes between Mars and Jupiter, far from the Sun.

touched down briefly on Itokawa, collecting samples from its surface.

Many asteroids, including Ceres, Pallas and Vesta, can be spotted easily with binoculars. You can check where to find them in astronomical magazines or via national societies. The number on view increases vastly when you use a telescope. None will appear as any more than a point of light, but it can be fascinating to watch how they move against the starry background from one night to the next.

JUPITER

Jupiter is the undisputed king of the planets and the first of the so-called gas giants. It has a diameter at the equator of almost 88,860mi/43,000km although, rather oddly, the distance measured between the poles is a lot less at 83,260mi/134,000km, making the planet resemble a pumpkin. This is due to Jupiter's rapid rotation – the planet spins so fast that a day is under 10 Earth hours long.

Jupiter lies an average 485 million mi/780 million km from the Sun and its light takes more than 40 minutes to reach us. Such is its size that it is one of the brightest objects in the heavens, earning it the name of the chief Roman god.

The gas clouds at Jupiter's surface are impenetrable by any telescopes, but it's thought that, deep inside the planet, there could be a solid rocky core up to 12,500mi/20,000km across. Those veils of cloud – mainly hydrogen and helium with traces of methane, ammonia and ethane – offer a fascinating canvas of color.

A look through even a modest amateur telescope will reveal that Jupiter shows a pattern of horizontal stripes. Close-up photos show these to be a multi-hued extravaganza of weather systems, with bands of high-speed winds blowing in opposite directions. Following the changing shapes and intensities of the swirling features makes Jupiter fascinating to study.

None of those features is more dramatic than Jupiter's famous Great Red Spot, a raging storm so vast that it has been observed for centuries and shows no sign of diminishing. This spot, which varies in redness over time, is up to 24,850mi/40,000km long and 8,700mi/14,000km wide. It is big enough to swallow the Earth three times over.

In the early 21st century, another, smaller red spot was seen to form, but most storms on Jupiter tend to be white or brown in color and last days, months or years.

Johns Hopkins University Applied Physics Lab

Although the main mission of NASA's New Horizons is to explore the Pluto system and the Kuiper Belt of icy, rocky objects, the spacecraft first flew by the solar system's largest planet.

NASA/JPL/University of Arizona

Io, one of the four major Galilean satellites of Jupiter, casts its shadow on the planet's colorful cloudtops close to the famous Great Red Spot.

Jupiter shines by reflecting sunlight. However, it emits more than twice as much energy as it receives from the Sun and radio telescopes find it one of the noisiest objects in the sky. Astronomers believe Jupiter's energy is produced from the forces of it shrinking from a much larger world many millions of years ago. The planet also has a powerful magnetic field.

Space probes, either in orbit or passing by, have helped us learn a lot more about Jupiter. They have discovered that it has faint rings, which are made up of tiny dust particles fed into them from meteor impacts on satellites in its own extended family.

This family consists of 63 natural satellites, although many discovered in recent years are tiny fragments of rock captured by the planet's powerful gravitational pull.

There are, however, four sizeable moons. They are so big that they would have ranked as planets if they had orbited the Sun alone. These Big Four – Io, Europa, Ganymede and Callisto – are called the Galilean satellites because it was Galileo who discovered them in 1610. They are clearly visible through binoculars, stretched in a line around Jupiter like a string of pearls. It can be fascinating to watch their changing pattern as they orbit their home world.

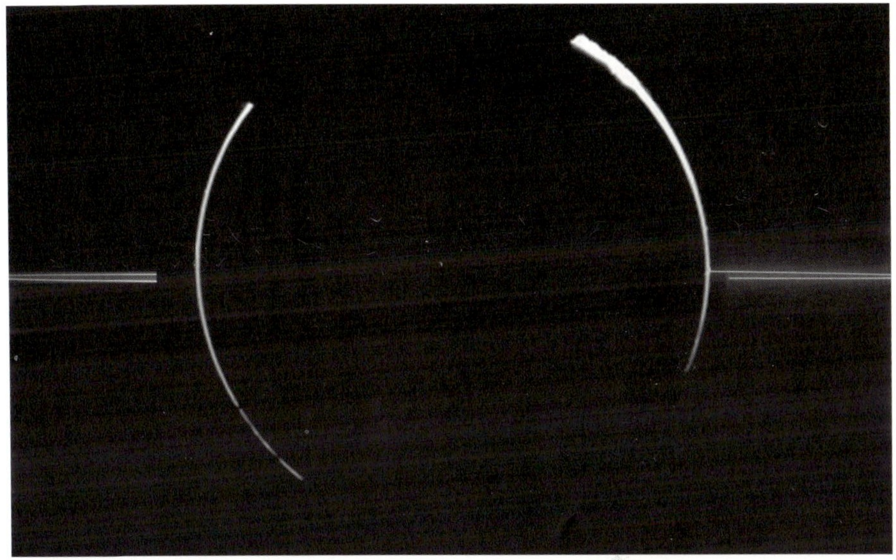

A dramatic view of the rings of Jupiter taken by the Galileo probe as it flew around the back of the planet, viewed from the side in shadow from the Sun. Its limb is lit up by scattered sunlight.

Ganymede is the biggest moon in the solar system, with a diameter of 3,270mi/5,262km. Its surface is covered with craters, grooves and ridges.

Callisto is 2,996mi/4,821km wide. Jupiter's second largest moon has a heavily cratered surface covering a thick layer of ice.

Spacecraft views of Io show it resembling a pizza, due to the eruptions that make it the most volcanically active world in the solar system. It has a diameter of 2,264mi/3,643km.

Europa – 1,940mi/3,122km across – fascinates planetary scientists because it is a smooth satellite spewing geysers of water ice. Some believe a vast underground lake could contain simple aquatic life.

SATURN

The sixth planet from the Sun, Saturn is a fast-spinner like Jupiter, with a day less than 11 hours long. It is the second larg planet, with an equatorial diameter of 74,898mi/120,536km and resembles its larger neighbor, being squashed at the pole and completely circled by bands of cloud.

Saturn's most striking feature, however, is a spectacular ring system marking it out as the most beautiful object in the heavens. The smallest telescope displays the rings. Galileo was first to spot them in 1610, although he thought he was observing three separate round objects. He must have had a better telescope in 1616, because his sketch made then clearly shows the ring system.

Larger instruments confirmed that there is more than one ring, including the 2,485mi/4,000km wide Cassini Division. But photos from space probes have shown that there are countless rings made up of tiny particles of pulverized rock ranging in size from specks to boulders. These are held in check by the pull of Saturn's many satellites.

Saturn itself is a gas giant like Jupiter. The cloud bands are less colorful than Jupiter's, and the features more subtle, but they include oval storms which break out occasionally and a Great White Spot which was first noticed in 1876 and appears to recur at roughly 30-year intervals.

NASA Marshall Space Flight Center

The rings around Saturn are thought to have formed from material that was unable to form into a moon because of tidal forces from Saturn, or from a Moon that was brokenup.

Our knowledge of Saturn, its rings and its moons has been given a huge boost by the arrival of the space probe Cassini in 2004. This American-European mission has been viewing the Saturn family from every angle since then. Among its discoveries are odd storm systems at the planet's north and south poles. The southern hurricane is two-thirds the size of the Earth, with a well-developed eye. The one at the north pole is shaped like a hexagon with six straight sides. Nothing like it has been observed on any of the other planets.

Saturn has a vast retinue of natural satellites – at least 56 discovered so far. Of these, there are six major moons: Mimas, Enceladus, Tethys, Dione, Rhea and Titan.

With a massive crater Mimas resembles the Death Star from Star Wars. The crater, blasted out by an asteroid impact, is named Herschel after William Herschel, who first spotted Mimas in 1789. The moon is only 246mi/396km across. Herschel also spotted Enceladus, a 311mi/500km wide world which fascinates scientists investigating the possibility of life elsewhere in the solar system. The Cassini space probe showed plumes of water ice erupting from its smooth, reflective surface, indicating that it is

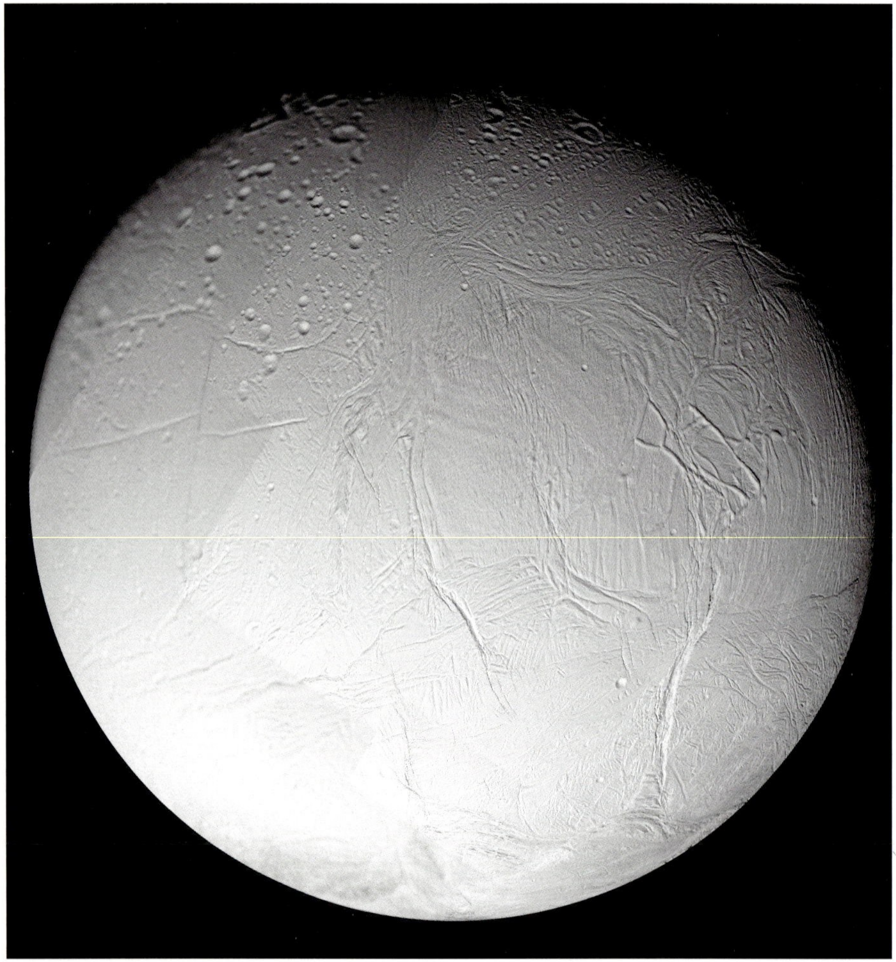

NASA/JPL/Space Science Institute

This 16-image mosaic of Enceladus was taken during Cassini's first close flyby of this moon of Saturn on February 17 2005.

An artist's interpretation of the area surrounding the Huygens landing site on Titan based on images and data returned on January 14 2005.

ESA

geologically active. There could be an underground sea where primitive life might exist or be evolving.

Tethys, discovered by the astronomer Cassini in 1684, is another icy world, 665mi/1,070km in diameter and covered with craters and cracks, the largest of which is the 250mi/400km diameter Odysseus. Another striking feature is the 60mi/100km wide valley Ithaca Chasma, which is 1,240mi/2,000km long and runs about three quarters of the way around the moon.

Dione – width 700mi/1,120km and also discovered by Cassini – is another world with vast amounts of water ice. As well as extensive cratering, there are also long streaks which indicate cliffs of ice.

Rhea is the third of Cassini's moons and Saturn's second largest with a diameter of 950mi/1,530km. Like Dione, it is covered with craters and ice cliffs. Saturn's biggest moon, Titan, is also the second largest in the solar system. With a diameter of 3,200mi/5,150km, it is half as big again as our own Moon and larger than the planet Mercury.

Titan has recently come under greater scrutiny than any other moon because it appears in many ways to resemble a young Earth. The research has culminated with the landing of a European space probe, Huygens, in January 2005, after it had flown piggyback to Saturn on NASA's Cassini orbiter.

Titan is the only planetary satellite with a dense atmosphere, which shows as an orange haze in photographs. After floating to the slushy surface by parachute, during which it recorded the winds and photographed coastlines, rivers and deltas, Huygens took images of a landscape covered in icy rocks and pebbles. One rock appeared broken and may have been fractured when the probe bounced off it.

Radar images from the Cassini mother-ship showed seas and lakes in Titan's northern hemisphere. These are not lakes as we know them, but filled with liquid methane or ethane. Scientists believe there may be an underground sea on Titan where the organic ingredients for life are present. It could be a balmy place to live in another four billion years, by which time the Sun is expected to swell into a red giant.

URANUS, NEPTUNE & PLUTO

Until little more than two centuries ago, we only knew of the planets visible to the naked eye; those that stretch as far as Saturn.

Uranus was spotted in 1781 by William Herschel, a scientist, telescope builder and musician, as he was observing the night skies from his garden in England's historic city of Bath. Others had previously noted it in their observation logs but thought it just another star.

Herschel wanted to name his planet Georgium Sidus, in a tribute to King George III. But protocol dictated that the new world was given a classical name just like the rest.

Uranus is 32,000mi/51,200km wide and 1,800 million mi/2,900 million km from the Sun, and just bright enough to be glimpsed with the naked eye on a clear, dark night. It is, however, so close to the limit of visibility that it's not difficult to see how it remained undetected for so long.

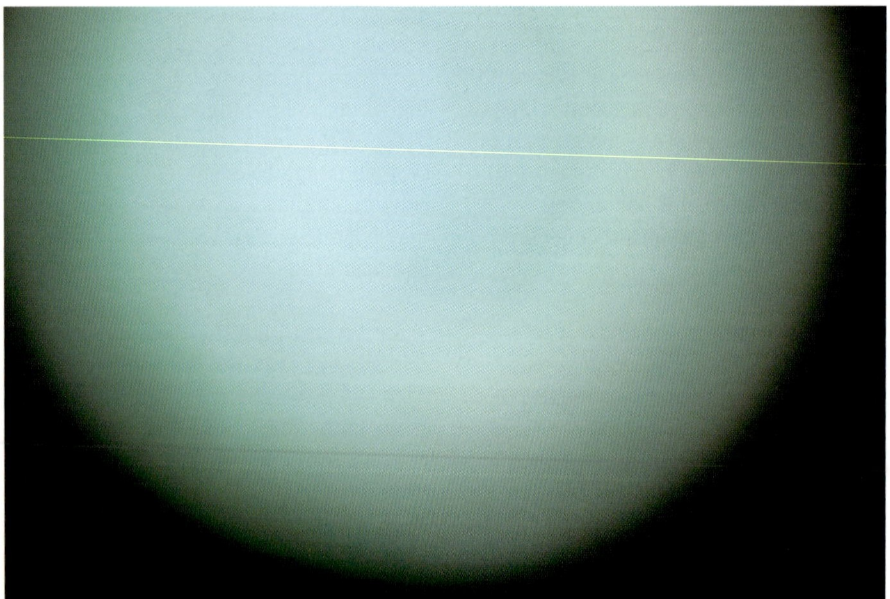

Uranus is bright enough to be glimpsed by the naked eye.

NASA Jet Propulsion Laboratory (NASA-JPL)

Uranus's atmosphere viewed by Voyager 2.

NASA Headquarters - Greatest Images of NASA

NASA's Voyager 2 probe has given us our only close-up view of Uranus's moon Miranda.

Binoculars show it easily and a telescope will delineate a tiny blue-green disk. They won't show any details, but a few nights of noting Uranus's position against the stars will reveal the slow movement on its 84-year journey around the Sun.

Uranus is another of the gas giants of the solar system, being made mainly of hydrogen and helium plus a hint of methane, though its cloud tops are pretty bland visually, compared to the multi-colored Jupiter.

It has five main moons: Ariel, Umbriel, Oberon, Titania and the baby of the group, Miranda. Larger amateur telescopes will show them as faint dots. There are at least another 22, much tinier satellites in orbit.

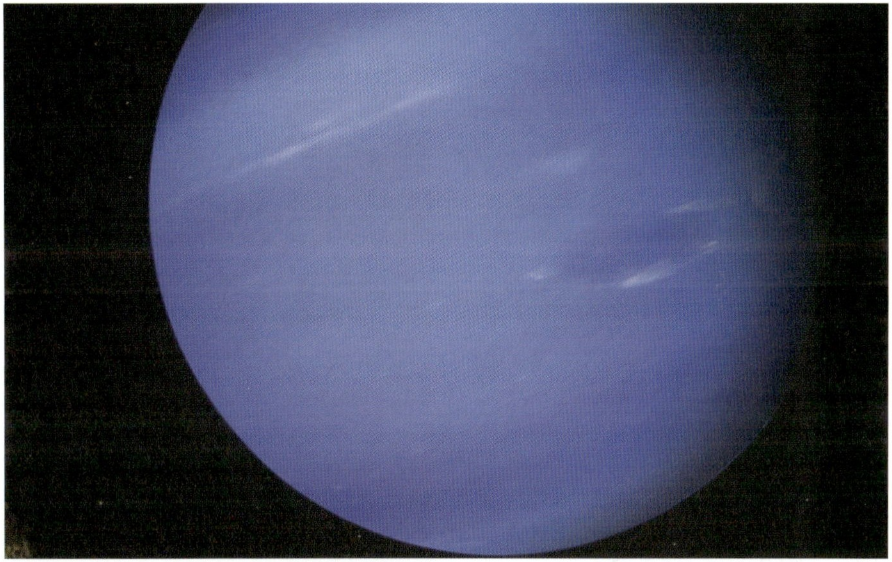

Neptune was found by maths before it was seen.

Another development occured in 1977 when astronomers were watching Uranus pass in front of a star in what is termed an occultation. The star blinked on and off repeatedly, revealing the presence of rings around it. The space probe Voyager 2 confirmed their existence in 1986. As with Jupiter's rings, they are totally inconspicuous, unlike the splendid rings around Saturn.

Uranus has another curious feature. Its polar axis, around which it spins in a day lasting 17 and a quarter hours, is tilted right over at nearly 98 degrees. It is likely that it collided with another giant body long ago.

A matter of 60 or so years after Herschel's discovery the solar system grew once again with the confirmation of the eighth planet, Neptune, in 1846. This find was remarkable because it came as a result of mathematical calculation rather than a sweep of the heavens.

Observations of Uranus had shown that it was not maintaining its expected orbit. The pull of another, as yet unknown body, was blamed. Astronomers in the UK and France independently predicted where the culprit lay, and Frenchman Urbain Le Verrier just beat Englishman John Couch Adams to the declaration. Final confirmation came when astronomers at Berlin Observatory spotted Neptune close to the spot where it was predicted to lie.

Yet another world of gas, Neptune could easily pass as a twin of Uranus. It is slightly smaller at 31,000mi/49,500km wide and so far away at a distance of 2.8 billion miles/4.5 billion km that it takes 165 years to orbit the Sun.

Neptune reaches magnitude 7.8 at its best, but it may be picked out with binoculars. Like Uranus, Neptune has a faint ring system, which was first detected during an occultation of a star in 1983. Its day is a fraction over 16 hours long.

Neptune has two main moons – Triton and Nereid – and at least 11 much smaller ones. Triton is the biggest, with a diameter of 1,680mi/2,700km, and orbits the "wrong way" around Neptune. It is also slowly spiraling in toward the planet, and will eventually shatter to form another ring of debris.

Triton is the largest of Neptune's moons and was photographed by NASA's Voyager 2 spaceprobe when it flew past in 1989, revealing that the moon is a rocky world covered by an icy mantle. This montage shows Triton in the foreground with gas giant Neptune itself in the distance.

Nereid is only 211mi/340km across and has an extremely stretched orbit that takes it nearly seven times further from Neptune at certain times.

Neptune is the last of the Sun's main family of planets. Until August 2006, there was a ninth planet, Pluto, which was demoted by the astronomical authorities to the new status of Dwarf Planet.

This controversial decision sparked a wave of protest, particularly in the United States, where Pluto was discovered by Clyde Tombaugh in 1930. Legislators in New Mexico passed a motion declaring Pluto to be a planet again in 2007, although they had no authority to do so.

The decision to reduce Pluto's status was, in fact, logical. Astronomers had begun to discover a number of similar new icy bodies in the same outer fringes of the solar system, suggesting Pluto had received special treatment for historical reasons. More than 800 have been found so far, and some may turn out to be larger than Pluto.

An artist's impression of Pluto ,which will be visited for the first time by a spaceprobe in 2015.

This region of space it termed the Kuiper Belt, and it is thought the giant planets hold a vast number of small icy bodies in position there. They are unlike the asteroids but are probably one source of the comets which frequently fly in toward the Sun.

With a diameter of 1,500mi/2,400km, Pluto is smaller than many of the solar system's moons, including our own. Its eccentric orbit means its distance from the Sun varies between 2.7 billion and 4.5 billion miles/4.3 billion and 7.3 billion km, and it takes 248 years to complete one revolution.

Pluto has three natural satellites. Charon is just over half Pluto's diameter. Two much smaller moons, Nix and Hydra, were spotted by the Hubble space telescope in 2005.

A NASA mission, called New Horizons, is currently on its way to explore Pluto and the Kuiper Belt but will not arrive until 2015.

COMETS

On August 7, 2006, Rob McNaught, a Scottish astronomer living in Australia, spotted a faint smudge on a photo of the sky taken with a large telescope. Later photos showed the smudge had moved slightly – it was a comet heading towards the Sun from the depths of space.

Comet McNaught: spectacular in January 2007.

Sebastian Deiries (ESO)

The comet became lost from view as it moved into the daylight from Earth, but when it was next seen against a dark sky, in late December, it became clear that it was going to be a bright object in the New Year's skies.

For observers in the northern hemisphere, Comet McNaught became a lovely sight low in the evening twilight. Then, as it rounded the Sun, its head became so brilliant that it could be seen in broad daylight. In the next few days, the comet put on a spectacular show for lucky viewers in the southern hemisphere.

As Comet McNaught moved away from the Sun again, it was a stunning sight in the dusk, sporting a long, sweeping tail that stretched far across the sky. So far, in fact, that though the comet's head was out of sight from northern latitudes, parts of the tail could be viewed in dark skies north of the equator.

Over the next few weeks, Comet McNaught gradually faded and the tail became less glorious as it began to head into the depths of space to become once more a faint, distant smudge.

McNaught had not been seen before, and it may never again return to the heart of the solar system. The last Great Comet, Hale-Bopp in 1997, came as a similar surprise. But a study of its orbit revealed that it had passed through our skies before – 4,200 years ago. During the last flyby,

A close-up of Comet Hale-Bopp shows its tails of gas and dust.

Hale-Bopp's orbit was disrupted by the gravitational pull of giant planet Jupiter, so that its next return will be somewhat sooner, but still not until around 4380.

Many comets are known to appear at intervals of a few to several years because they, too, have fallen under the spell of Jupiter. In 1993, one of these periodic comets, called Shoemaker-Levy, was seen to break into a number of fragments which the following year crashed one by one into Jupiter's atmosphere, leaving it with long-lasting "black eyes".

The periodic comet with the shortest orbital period is Encke, which takes just 3.3 years to travel around the Sun.

RIDING A TRAIL OF DEBRIS

NASA Jet Propulsion Laboratory

This infrared picture taken by NASA's heat-seeking Spitzer Space Telescope shows Comet Encke riding along the diagonal dusty trail of debris that it leaves as it orbits the Sun between Mars and Jupiter. Two bright jets of freshly ejected material can be seen streaming from the comet's head.

By tradition, comets take the names of their discoverers. Automated cameras are beginning to pick up more and more of these celestial wanderers, meaning that there is an ever-growing list of comets called Linear or Neat. Each is given a catalog description too, such as C/2006 P1 in the case of Comet McNaught.

Perhaps the most famous visitor is Halley's Comet, which has been witnessed since early historical times and returns to the Sun's neighborhood every 76 years. The closest it came in recent times was 1986 and will be back in 2061. In this case the comet is named not for its discoverer but for Edmond Halley, the man who first recognized that comets seen in the past were one and the same, and so predicted its reappearance in 1757.

Comet Hale-Bopp was a fine subject for photographers. Here is it seen above a tree on the Istrian coast of Croatia. The Andromeda Galaxy can be seen faintly beneath it.

McNaught and Hale-Bopp were truly Great Comets of the kind that come along a handful of times in a lifetime. Less magnificent comets appear fairly often, and one or two a year may become bright enough to be seen with binoculars, or even occasionally with the naked eye. The vast majority appear simply as fuzzy blobs; this is the halo around the head that is called the coma. Only the brightest develop evident tails.

Bright comets show two distinct types of tail: the gas tail and the dust tail. The gas tail is blown from the comet's head by the force of the solar wind. This means that, contrary to what you might expect, this tail does not necessarily follow the comet. As it heads back out towards the depths of the solar system, the comet travels tail-first.

The second tail is formed of the dust that is ejected from the comet's head. It tends

A CCD photo of a comet discovered with a robot telescope called NEAT in 2001.

to curve as the tiny particles are spread back along the comet's track, to disperse eventually along its orbit. You can read more about these dust particles in the next section.

The gas tail typically shows as blue in photographs, while the dust tail shows as red. This difference was clearly seen in the pictures of Hale-Bopp in 1997, although the colors are often very subtle. Amateur astronomers often sketch comets, noting how condensed the coma is and whether it has a bright central point. If there are tails, careful observation may reveal the delicate structure within as the gas streams are shaped by the solar wind. Bright comets can also be fine targets for photographers.

Some amateurs also search for new comets by sweeping the skies with giant binoculars or telescopes, a task which requires great dedication and endless patience.

WHAT IS A COMET?

Unlike the planets, comets travel in extremely elongated orbits that can bring them from the far realms of the solar system, only to be flung around the Sun and hurled back out into the depths of space. Despite their sometimes spectacular appearance, with tails that can stretch far across the sky, they are relatively insubstantial members of the solar system.

NASA Jet Propulsion Laboratory (NASA-JPL)

An artist's impression of Deep Impact probe at Comet Tempel 1

Comets are important because they are believed to contain pristine material older than the Earth, from the earliest days of the solar system. Scientists believe comets may have delivered the water that makes up Earth's oceans – and possibly even the organic material that sparked life itself.

Astronomers believe that comets with orbital periods of just a few hundred years come from the Kuiper Belt of frozen bodies near Pluto. But those that swoop in just once, or once every few thousand years, come from a swarm of billions of comet called the Oort Cloud which is predicted to lie around a light year from the Sun.

The heart of a comet is a frozen mass of rock and ice, usually no bigger than a mountain, that appears as little more than a blob of light when deep in space. But as it approaches the Sun, its frozen core begins to warm and wake up. A huge ball of gas expands to give the comet its hazy coma. Violent jets of gas and dust may erupt from the frozen core, called the nucleus, spewing the material that forms the tails.

Space probes now provide us with a wealth of information about comets. There have been a number of flybys since Giotto sped past Halley's Comet on its last return. Most spectacular was Deep Impact, when NASA deliberately fired a missile at a comet called Tempel 1 in July 2005. The resulting explosion, with the force of 4.5 tons of TNT, caused a brilliant flare visible 83 million miles away on Earth.

NASA's Stardust mission was the first to visit a comet and then return samples to Earth. The probe collected gas and dust surrounding the head of Comet Wild 2 in 2004, then flew by Earth, dropping this capsule into the Utah Desert in 2006.

NASA

Another US spacecraft, called Stardust, flew through the coma of Wild 2 and then sent a capsule containing samples of its dust to a soft landing back on Earth in January 2006.

METEORS

Spend more than a few minutes studying a clear dark sky and you will undoubtedly see one of nature's natural fireworks, a meteor.

NASA

A solitary Perseid meteor is captured in this image.

Often known as shooting or falling stars, meteors are simply pieces of cosmic debris blazing to a fiery death as they vaporize about 60mi/100km above the Earth.

We now know that most of this debris is the dust shed by comets as they cross the interplanetary space lanes. Some is from long-lost comets which we can no longer identify. Other displays may be linked to comets appearing in our skies today.

What might seem a bright streak is usually caused by just a tiny speck, no bigger than a grain of sand. As its zips through our atmosphere at up to 45mi/70km per second, it ionizes the air around it, causing the brilliant glow. Sometimes this glow will produce a long-lasting ghostly train for several seconds.

Technically, the particle itself is a meteoroid and the streak in the sky is a meteor. Meteoroids from comets are almost invariably destroyed by their blaze of glory. Objects termed meteorites are stones that have survived a fall to Earth and are more likely to be linked to the asteroids. A space rock big enough to reach the ground will produce a fireball in the sky.

Meteors may appear at random, in any part of the sky and at any time. However, there are particular periods in the year when we can predict a higher level of meteor activity. These are dates when, each year, the Earth crosses the orbit of a stream of dust left by a comet. The result is what called a meteor shower. The word "shower" is something of an exaggeration because you will rarely see more than one or two a minute. The number will depend not only on how much dust is entering the atmosphere but also on how dark the sky is and whether there is bright moonlight, for example.

Meteors not linked to showers are called sporadics. They are distinguished by the fact that they appear to radiate from a

Leo Stachowicz

Several meteors, some very faint, can be seen bursting across the sky in the last big Leonid meteor storm in 1999.

particular point in the sky. No matter in which part of the sky you see the meteor, trace back its path and it will cross that point. Meteors which appear to have shorter paths will seem to be closer to the radiant because they are heading more directly towards you.

It's all down to perspective. The meteors are flying parallel to each other as they stream into the atmosphere, but their paths, when traced back, converge on their radiant just as the parallel lanes of a long highway appear to converge in the distance.

Meteors not linked to showers are called sporadics. They are distinguished by the fact that they appear to radiate from a particular point in the sky. No matter in which part of the sky you see the meteor, trace back its path and it will cross that point. Meteors which appear to have shorter paths will seem to be closer to the radiant because they are heading more directly towards you.

It's all down to perspective. The meteors are flying parallel to each other as they stream into the atmosphere, but their paths, when traced back, converge on their radiant just as the parallel lanes of a long highway appear to converge in the distance.

Paul Sutherland

A brilliant fireball bursts from the constellation of Leo during the Leonid storm of 1999.

Individual showers are commonly named after the constellation in which the radiant appears to lie. So the strong shower that occurs every August and appears to radiate from the direction of Perseus is called the Perseid meteor shower, or simply the Perseids. Similarly, a major December shower radiating from Gemini is known as the Geminids. Some shower names even specify a bright star close to their radiants, such as the Delta Aquarids or Kappa Cygnids.

It's not only the brightness of the sky during a meteor shower that affects the numbers seen. Many radiants don't rise above the horizon until after midnight, and the higher the radiant is in the sky, the more meteors will be seen. Also, as we get closer to dawn, the part of the Earth where the observer is situated is likely to be turning into the direction from which the meteors come. The combined speeds of the rotating Earth and the traveling meteor particle make any meteor travel faster and burn brighter.

Meteor observation is an ideal project for the stargazer who's starting out, because it's a fun activity to share with friends but can also be of genuine scientific value.

You will need a watch, a notebook, a red light and a writing implement. A voice recorder will help you to make your notes without taking your eyes off the sky. Find a spot well away from streetlights, sit for an hour or so at a time steadily watching one particular patch of sky, say half-way between the horizon and the zenith.

When a meteor appears, quickly note the time, estimate the meteor's approximate brightness compared to the stars, its color, relative speed (such as fast, medium or slow) and features, such as whether it left a train. Note, also, whether the meteor was a shower member or a sporadic. Observe the sky conditions such as the presence of haze, cloud or moonlight and the brightness of the faintest stars overhead. Collectively these are called the limiting magnitude.

Your observations could be very useful to astronomical organizations and professional meteor scientists when combined with other members' records.

Don't expect to see the number of meteors quoted for any shower's maximum rate. This is usually a figure applied in ideal conditions and with the shower's radiant directly overhead, and is called the Zenithal Hourly Rate, or ZHR.

There are very rare occasions, called meteor storms, when observers witness great numbers of meteors. The storms happen when the Earth passes through a dense clump of particles in the stream's orbit. The Leonids generally reveal just a handful of meteors at maximum in November, but many thousands an hour may be seen at intervals of around 33 years. The last spectacular display was in 1999.

The following is a selection of the main showers of the year, as compiled by the International Meteor Organization. Those radiating from constellations in the northern sky are best seen from the northern hemisphere and those from southern constellations from the southern hemisphere.

SHOWER	WHEN VISIBLE	DATE OF MAXIMUM	ZHR
Quadrantids	Jan 01 – Jan 05	Jan 04	120
Lyrids	Apr 16 – Apr 25	Apr 22	18
Eta-Aquarids	Apr 19 – May 28	May 06	60
South Delta-Aquarids	Jul 12 – Aug 19	Jul 28	20
Perseids	Jul 17 – Aug 24	Aug 13	100
Orionids	Oct 02 – Nov 07	Oct 21	23
Southern Taurids	Oct 01 – Nov 25	Nov 05	5
Northern Taurids	Oct 01 – Nov 25	Nov 12	5
Leonids	Nov 10 – Nov 23	Nov 18	15+
Puppid/Velids	Dec 01 – Dec 15	Dec 07	10
Geminids	Dec 07 – Dec 17	Dec 14	120
Ursids	Dec 17 – Dec 26	Dec 23	10

THE AURORA AND OTHER SKYGLOWS

One of the brightest flares ever seen on the Sun, the first of a swift string of fiery eruptions, exploded into view on September 7, 2005. Three days later, the dramatic blasts made their effects felt on the Earth.

A tidal wave of highly charged particles buffeted the magnetic field which surrounds our planet, producing a major space weather storm.

This magnetosphere acted as a defensive shield, protecting us from being bombarded by massive doses of deadly radiation. But it also set the heavens ablaze, producing a brilliant and colorful light show in the night sky.

This phenomenon was a spectacular example of the aurora, a sky glow which occurs fairly frequently at high latitudes around the north and south magnetic poles. It is popularly known as the Northern or Southern Lights, depending on which hemisphere you live in, or the aurora borealis and aurora australis in scientific terms. It becomes a much rarer happening the further one travels from those poles. The storm of September 2005 was so powerful, that the aurora was seen as far south as Arizona and the Mediterranean.

Most aurorae occur in the shape of pulsating or rippling glows, but there is a range of other forms which appear, including arcs and rays. The bigger storms create the classic curtains which fill the entire sky.

A unique view of the aurora, as seen from above by astronauts orbiting the Earth aboard the International Space Station.

When observing, try to move away from streetlights and find a clear, dark sky to obtain the best display. The pulsations are subtle and moonlight may drown them. A great display can make for some spectacular photos; put your camera on a tripod and open the shutter for several seconds.

Because aurorae occur as a direct result of disturbances on the Sun, activity tends to be more frequent when the Sun is at the most active stage of its 11-year cycle. It remains unpredictable, though, and dramatic shows have been witnessed close to solar minimum.

Space scientists endeavor to learn more about the link between solar eruptions and aurorae because major storms threaten communications, power grids and satellite electronics and astronauts' lives.

ZODIACAL LIGHT

There are other glows in the sky worth observing for if you're lucky enough to have clear, dark skies and if moonlight is not a problem. They are not related to the aurora and are, instead, caused by dust spread through the solar system.

There are tiny, scattered specks of dust which combine to reflect the Sun's light back at us. This dust lies in the same plane as the planets' orbits, which passes through the zodiac, and is therefore known as the Zodiacal Light.

The glow appears particularly concentrated approaching the Sun and produces a ghostly cone in the sky before dawn or after sunset. It is best seen at times of the year when the ecliptic stands highest in the sky. Under ideal skies, such as in the tropics, it may be mistaken for the remains of twilight.

Even harder to spot is the Gegenschein, a large but ultra-faint glow found on the opposite side of the sky to the Sun. The clearest, darkest skies are necessary to see this phenomenon, which is again due to sunlight being reflected by distant dust.

JAXA

A classic view of a spectacular aurora, producing dancing curtains of light in the skies above a wintry landscape at a far northern latitude. This natural light show was sparked by the arrival of energetic particles from a storm on the Sun as they collided with the Earth's magnetic field.

BEYOND THE SOLAR SYSTEM

The magnitude of space is difficult to grasp: Pluto lies so far away from Earth that its light takes around five and a half hours to reach us.

A sense of the enormity of the universe is gained when you consider that one would travel for four and a half light-years through space before reaching the nearest star to the Sun. This distance, too, becomes insignificant against the scale of the Milky Way. Our home galaxy is made up of 200 billion or more stars within a pinwheel-shaped disk that stretches as much as 100,000 light years from one side to the other.

Of course, it doesn't end there. The Milky Way is just one of billions of galaxies, each filled with billions of stars, filling a visible universe more than 90 billion light years wide. There is still much uncertainty about the true nature of the universe and whether it is part of a host of universes with other, as yet undiscovered dimensions. Let us look at some of the wonders of the universe that we know about.

THE STARS

Every star we see when we look up at the clear night sky is part of our own galaxy, the Milky Way. And although even the brightest appears as merely a pinprick of light, all of them are suns similar to our own. And the 2,000 or so visible to the naked eye are a fraction of the many billions in the galaxy.

NASA, ESA and H. Bond (STScI)

Light from an outburst of the variable star V838 Monocerotis echoes from a cloud of surrounding gas in a view by the Hubble Space Telescope.

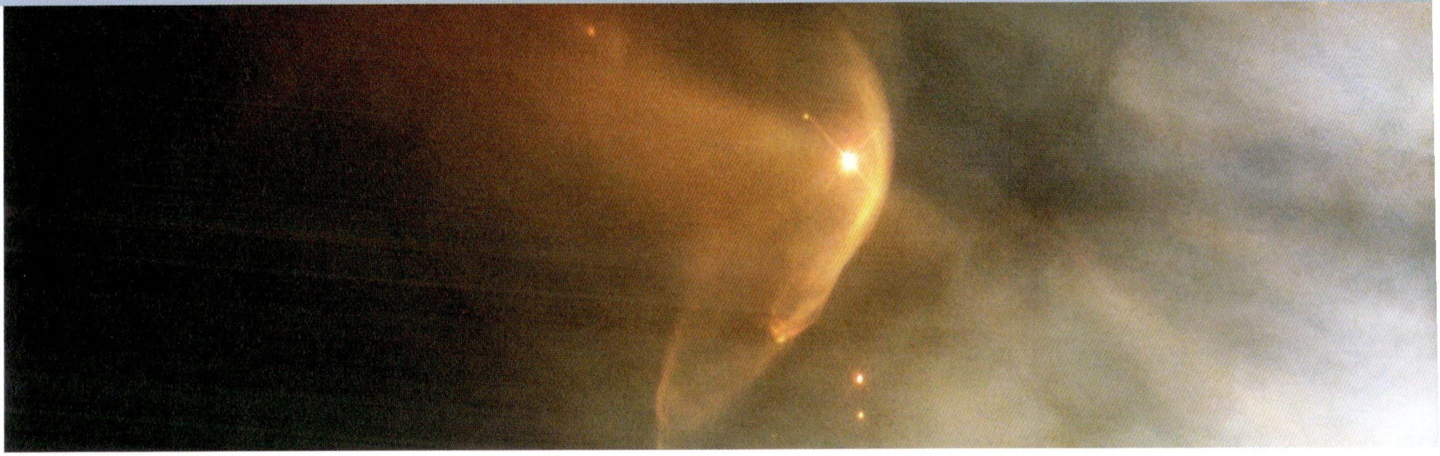

NASA Jet Propulsion Laboratory (NASA-JPL)

Astronomers using the Hubble have found a bow shock around a very young star in the Orion Nebula.

Stars come in many different shapes, sizes, colors and brightnesses, and these often indicate the stage they have reached in their own evolution.

Stars are born within huge swirling clouds of gas and dust. We can see the process happening today inside so-called celestial nurseries such as the famous Great Orion Nebula. A spinning disk of material condenses until a star forms at its center and shines by turning hydrogen into helium in a nuclear furnace. As the rest of the debris collects in orbit around the new star, other bodies, such as planets, are created.

Some stars are blue, condensed and super hot. Others nearing the end of their lives have become bloated red giants swollen hugely in size. Our Sun is middle-aged and will eventually meet such a fate itself, when it grows to a size including the orbit of Mars. By that time it will have had a life of around nine billion years. Eventually it will throw off a shell of material, and became what is called a planetary nebula.

Not all stars meet this relatively gentle demise. Some become so large and bright they explode as a supernova, making them – for a short while – as brilliant as all the other stars in a galaxy combined.

Stars are rated according to color and temperature. These basic "spectral types", beginning with the hottest, are O, B, A, F, G, K and M, with numbered subdivisions. Use the mnemonic Oh Be A Fine Girl, Kiss Me! The Sun is a G2 star on this scale.

NASA, ESA and the Hubble Heritage

Hubble shot of the tattered remains of a star which exploded as a supernova in Cassiopeia.

NASA Johnson Space Center – Earth

Hot blue stars have a much shorter lifespan.

It is remarkable that we can tell so much about stars. These days astronomers gauge their distances, sizes, temperatures at which they burn, whether they have planets and even what the atmospheres some of those planets contain. This has been arrived at by assembling the pieces of a puzzle scientists began to put together thousands of years ago.

Eratosthenes, the Greek scholar who lived around 200 years before Christ, set the ball rolling by defining the first measurement of the size of the Earth (he was also way ahead of his time in believing it to be round). He did so by measuring the height of the Sun in the sky from two locations about 500mi/ 800km apart in what is now Egypt.

Other Greek scientists, including Aristarchus, measured the distance of the Moon by observing and calculating angles during eclipses of the Moon and Sun. They went on to make a first stab at the Sun's distance and size too, but with less success. However, these first steps allowed successive astronomers to build on and refine their work, allowing us gradually to know the size and scale of the solar system.

Stars are a lot further away than anything else in the solar system, as calculated by ingenious astronomers who worked out their distances too. They began with stars which were relatively close.

Friedrich Bessel was first in 1838, when he accurately measured the distance to 61 Cygni. The same year, other astronomers gauged how far away Vega and Alpha Centauri are. They did so by using a technique called parallax, which you can use yourself very easily. Hold a finger up in front of your face, close one eye and note where the finger appears against the background. Now, without moving your finger, view with the other eye instead. Your finger will appear to have shifted.

Parallax showed how the nearby stars seemed to shift position against distant background stars. The astronomers made observations when the Earth was on opposite sides of the Sun in its orbit, equivalent to putting our eyes a very long way apart.

Another breakthrough in the 19th century came with the invention of a device called the Spectroscope. Attached to a telescope this split simple star light into its rainbow of colors, like a prism. Through this spectrum could be seen a pattern of bright and dark lines, a bit like the barcodes we now use today. These are the "fingerprints" of different elements or materials, such as sodium, inside the stars. So in a flash, quite literally, we could tell what individual stars were made of.

The position of the lines for the various elements remained the same relative to each other. However, the pattern shifted its position along the spectrum of colors according to whether the star was traveling toward us or away from us, and at what speed.

This phenomenon, called the Doppler Effect, is similar to that which changes the pitch of a siren on an emergency vehicle depending on whether it is approaching us or receding. In astronomy, it is called the Red Shift, indicating that an object is moving away while a Blue Shift is coming toward us.

The stars do not all shine in as stable a way as the Sun. Many vary hugely in brightness over a relatively short timescale. One type of variable star, called a Cepheid, changes in a particularly precise way. What's more, astronomers found that the time it takes to vary, called its period, was directly linked to the star's actual luminosity.

A Hubble image of the Crab Nebula, a six light year wide remnant of a supernova that was seen to explode in 1054.

NASA

This was a gift to astronomers. By comparing the apparent brightness of a Cepheid to its period, they could determine the distance. When giant telescopes detected Cepheids in other nearby galaxies, we could estimate distances for those, too.

Distances to the other planets are expressed in kilometers or miles that can unwieldy. It is around 250,000mi/ 385,000km to the Moon, for example, and approximately 93 million mi/ 150 million km to the Sun. Astronomers had to find more useful scales to describe such vast measurements to the stars.

One standard chosen was the Earth-Sun distance itself, which is termed one Astronomical Unit (AU). Another is the lightyear – not, as many seem to think, a measurement of time but the distance that light travels in one year at the velocity of 186,282mi/299,792km a second in a vacuum. A further popular unit used by professional scientists is called the parsec, which equals 3.26 light years. The Sun is a solitary star, but many more double stars exist than single ones, and there are plenty of other systems containing three or more suns. Many of these double or multiple star systems are wide enough apart for us to view their separate stars through the telescope as they orbit each other. Others are too close to split.

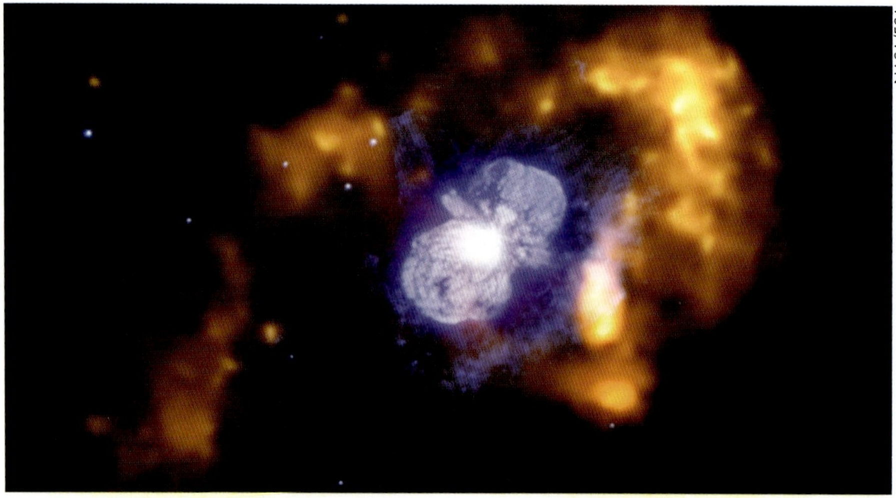
NASA/ESA

A huge, billowing pair of gas and dust clouds are captured in this stunning NASA Hubble Space Telescope image of the massive star Eta Carinae.

If the stars are orbiting edge on to our line of sight, eclipses occur and the starlight fades and then brightens again at regular intervals. These form another class of variable star, bright examples being Algol in Perseus and Beta Lyrae, both of which can be followed with the naked eye.

There are a number of different types of variable star, many of which are a lot less predictable than the Cepheids or eclipsing variables – and amateur astronomers can make a valuable contribution to science by monitoring them. The most spectacular type of variable star is the nova, a faint star which has suddenly undergone a huge, but non-destructive, explosion, temporarily becoming perhaps 10,000 times brighter.

The apparent brightness of stars is quoted by a measure called its magnitude. The brightest objects have negative magnitudes and each full magnitude is around two and a half times brighter than the next. The brightest stars in the sky are around

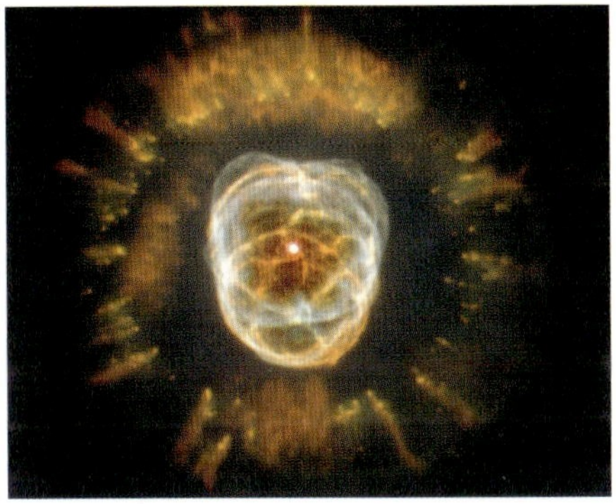
NASA/ESA/Andrew Fruchter (STScl)

The Eskimo Nebula resembles a human face in a hood in this photo from Hubble. It is really a double shell of material ejected from a star that was once like the Sun but has died and become a planetary nebula. The Eskimo lies 5000 light years away in Gemini.

magnitude 1. The faintest visible with the naked eye in a dark sky is about magnitude 6. The Sun has a magnitude of -27. Stars are also given a second brightness rating, termed their absolute magnitude, which describes how they would really compare if they were all at a standard distance of 10 parsecs (32.6 light years).

The stars are not fixed in space but are moving through space. This change is generally only perceptible over many thousands of years, but it means the patterns in the sky will change with time. The Sun is moving too, traveling at around 19mi/30km per second towards the bright star Vega.

The patterns we can see have been interpreted in different ways by civilizations around the world. Today there are officially 88 termed constellations, whose boundaries have been officially drawn by the International Astronomical Union.

We still call many of the brighter stars by names given them by Arabian astronomers many hundreds of years ago. And although there are modern, advanced catalogs, we also use the system started in 1603 of using the Greek alphabet to label the brighter stars, with the early letters usually, but not always, issued in order of brightness. Other stars have numbers from various other catalogs.

Stars are not arranged evenly across the sky. On a clear, dark night away from streetlights, it's not difficult to see the Milky Way stretching across the sky but our galaxy is widely spread but relatively thin.

The hazy band that we see is where stars are densest because we are looking edge-on through towards the center.

Though the term Milky Way was originally thought up to describe the band in the sky, we now use it to describe the galaxy itself. Determining the galaxy's shape is extremely difficult, but we know that the Milky Way is a spiral galaxy with arms of stars spreading outwards. The Sun is about two-thirds of the way out along one of these arms.

Away from light pollution, our own home galaxy, the Milky Way, can be seen as a glowing band with dark lanes of dust.

The age of the Milky Way has been estimated to be around 13.6 billion years – almost as old as the universe itself.

CLUSTERS, NEBULAE & GALAXIES

Medialab/ESA

Point a pair of binoculars at the sky and it is relatively easy to detect that there are more than just stars and planets in the heavens. Many slightly fuzzy objects will catch your eye, especially if you sweep along areas of the Milky Way.

Closer inspection can reveal these blurred patches to be collections of faint stars. Others may continue to look fuzzy no matter how much you try to magnify them. These are the clusters and nebulae that are mainly to be found in our own galaxy and the myriad of other galaxies ranged across the universe.

For many years following the invention of the telescope, very little if anything was known about the true nature of most of these objects. Surprisingly, it was not until well into the 20th century that astronomers realized that some were other galaxies of stars outside our own Milky Way.

Astronomers decided early on that they served to confuse observation projects. The most famous index of the universe's indistinct inhabitants was drawn up by a French astronomer who was in the business of searching for comets sweeping the solar system.

Charles Messier became frustrated when attempting to identify comets so, with the help of colleague Pierre Méchain, he drew up an 18th century catalog of the blurred patches and their positions. In this way, comet-hunters had a reference guide to help them discount the imposters. There are 110 objects in Messier's list.

Today, Messier is better known for his famous catalog than for any of his comet discoveries. Amateur astronomers in particular still refer to the brightest clusters, nebulae and galaxies by their Messier or M numbers.

Later catalogues covered the vast number of objects Messier failed to include. The important ones for amateur observers include the New General Catalog of Nebulae and Clusters of Stars (NGC) of 1888 and its subsequent Index Catalog supplements (IC).

Europe's Gaia satellite will map a billion stars in the Milky Way after it launches in 2011.

ESA

The Milky Way stretching from Carina on the left to Orion on the right. Our satellite galaxy the Large Magellanic Cloud is seen lower left.

ESA/Hubble

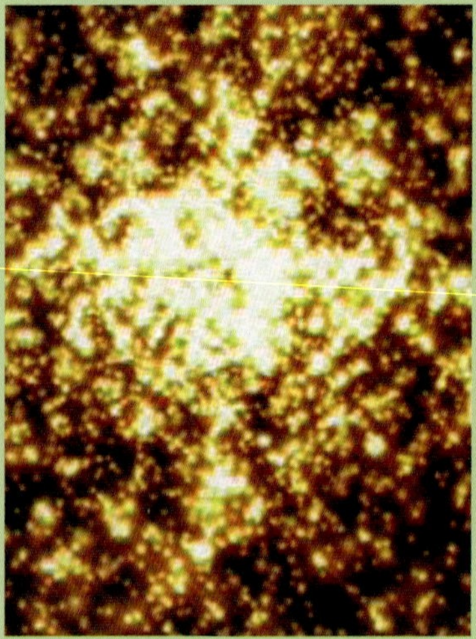

Globular clusters are dense, spherical concentrations of many thousands, or sometimes millions, of stars and can often be found forming a wide halo around a galaxy. They are among the oldest objects found in the universe.

ESA ©2005 MPS for OSIRIS Team

This view of Mars (visible towards the top of the image) and of the Milky Way was taken by the OSRIS camera on board the Rosetta spaceprobe on December 3 2006.

OPEN CLUSTERS

Some of the objects in Messier's catalog are clearly not comets. The naked eye, for example, can tell that M45, the Pleiades or Seven Sisters, in Taurus is a collection of stars. Many other open clusters are further away and look more condensed and fuzzy through binoculars.

Some are much more spread out. The Hyades is another cluster in Taurus which does not have a Messier number because it forms a large and distinct V shape in the sky. More than 1,000 open clusters are known to exist.

GLOBULAR CLUSTERS

If open clusters are scattered villages of stars, globular clusters are truly cosmic cities. These are huge, spherical concentrations of close-packed stars usually found in a wide halo around the galaxy. They are some of the oldest objects in the universe and many contain more than a million stars. They can resemble the contents of an overturned sugar bowl and telescopes will often help pick out individual stars. Bright globular clusters include M13 in Hercules for northern observers and Omega Centauri for the southern hemisphere.

ESA/NASA and Albert Zijlstra

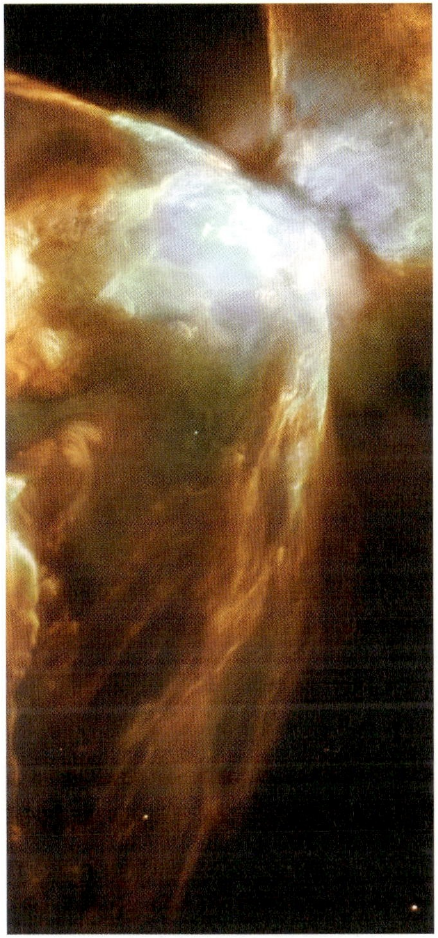

NEBULAE

Some fuzzy patches will remain unclear no matter how much you magnify them, because they are simply clouds of gas and dust. Mostly hydrogen, this gas may be a stellar birthplace, as in M42, the Orion Nebula. But it may also be the remains of a star's death in a catastrophic explosion. M1, the Crab Nebula in Taurus, is the tangled remains of just such a supernova that was seen to flare in 1054. So too is the Veil Nebula, the strands of gas from a much older blast.

Some gas clouds are known as emission nebulae because stars within them excite the gas and make it glow. Reflection nebulae are those that shine simply because they bounce back the light of nearby stars. A further type is the dark nebula, which makes itself visible as a silhouette obscuring bright regions behind it. The Coalsack in Crux and the Horsehead Nebula in Orion are examples.

Planetary nebulae are bright shells of gas thrown off by stars in their dying days. They were named for their shape and are totally unrelated to the planets, so the term can be misleading. Because the gas shell appears more concentrated at the edges, due to a line-of-sight effect, the spherical shell can look more like a ring. A classic case is M57, known as the Ring Nebula, in Lyra. A telescope may show the faint central star that shed its shell.

Beautiful images from the Hubble of the Butterfly Nebula in Scorpius, above, and Horsehead Nebula in Orion, right.

GALAXIES

Ask someone to imagine a galaxy and they will probably produce a picture of a swirling spiral, with millions of stars sweeping away from its heart. This classic shape was first observed in the mid-19th century by the Third Earl of Rosse, using a telescope at Birr Castle, Ireland, (then the largest instrument in the world). Their real nature as vast collections of stars was then still unknown, so they were called spiral nebulae.

The Milky Way is a spiral galaxy. So too is our biggest neighbor, M31 in Andromeda, 2.5 million light years away, although it is hard to tell on first viewing as we are seeing it at an oblique angle. Other spirals, such as M51 and M101, are viewed from above, so their swirling patterns are clear. Still more, like NGC 891, which is also in Andromeda, are seen edge-on. They appear long and thin and the spiral pattern is completely hidden, but what is evident is the thicker bulge such galaxies have at their centers.

A Hubble view of the magnificent spiral galaxy NGC 4603, the most distant galaxy in which a special class of pulsating stars called Cepheid variables have been found.

Such galaxies can be so huge that they contain many billions and sometimes even trillions of stars. Astronomers are finding that many, including the Milky Way, also contain a supermassive black hole at their heart, steadily devouring stars and other matter which swirls into its clutches.

Spiral galaxies vary in how tightly wound their arms are, and many also feature an elongated bar from which the arms coil. Our own galaxy is an example of a barred spiral.

Though spiral galaxies are common, they are not the only form a galaxy can take. So-called elliptical galaxies are conglomerations of stars which have oval forms but no structure within them. Irregular galaxies, more formless still, are believed to result from collisions, or close approaches, of two separate galaxies, or close approaches.

Some galaxies are described as being active because they have intensely hot, bright centers sending out enormous amounts of energy. These violent reactions are probably driven by the effects of the black holes at their centers. Powerful sources called quasars, which look like stars but emit as much energy as hordes of galaxies, are extreme examples of active galaxies.

Galaxies also have satellites of their own. The Milky Way has a number, including two irregular dwarf galaxies known as the Magellanic Clouds. Together with these, plus M31 and a number of others, the Milky Way is part of the so-called Local Group of galaxies.

This is not unusual. Most galaxies tend to collect together in clusters, which range in size from a few to many thousands. One notable large grouping is the Virgo Cluster, 60 million light years distant.

Observations of all galaxies outside our own Local Group reveal that they display a red shift when viewed through a spectroscope. This shows they are moving away from us and is key evidence that the universe is expanding following the Big Bang around 14 billion years ago.

VIEWING THE STARS

The stars shine all around us, in all directions. Which ones we see in our own sky depends on just where we live.

As we explained earlier, there are stars in the southern sky people living in northern latitudes never see, because they lie too far south. Inhabitants of the southern hemisphere cannot observe some of the stars of the northern hemisphere for the same reason. How much you see of the other hemisphere's stars depends on the latitude at which you live.

It is impossible to produce tailored sky maps for any particular night. The view changes from place to place. But we have found a three-stage solution.

First, we will present two maps, one showing the bright stars of the northern half of the celestial sphere and one displaying those of the southern half. This is like separating the two halves of a globe and then printing each as a flat circular map. These two hemispheres, each bounded by the celestial equator, contain all 88 constellations, numbered in their alphabetical order along the bottom of the two pages.

If you live anywhere other than the areas around the North and South Poles, you will see, at some time during the year, the stars of your hemisphere plus a certain number of stars in the other hemisphere. If you live on the Equator, you will be lucky enough to see all the constellations in both hemispheres at some stage.

Our approach is also to create a few windows onto the sky. These are collections of star patterns, distinct during the late evening at different seasons in each hemisphere. We have also included a window for each of the areas of sky around the celestial poles, featuring constellations that you may either see every night or, if you live in the other hemisphere, never see at all.

The winter, spring, summer and autumn windows change due to the way, described earlier, that the stars appear to shift their positions in the sky, rising four minutes earlier every night. Because the Earth is turning, you will see more stars rising as the night wears on. Stay up into the early hours and you will even get a sneak preview of the next season's sky window.

The images shown here were all taken by Nik Szymanek with a CCD camera. The colors will not be visible to the naked eye.

M8 in Sagittarius

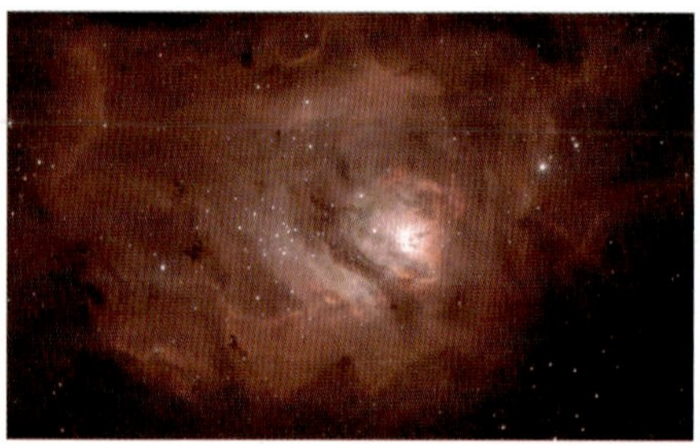

M16 in Serpens

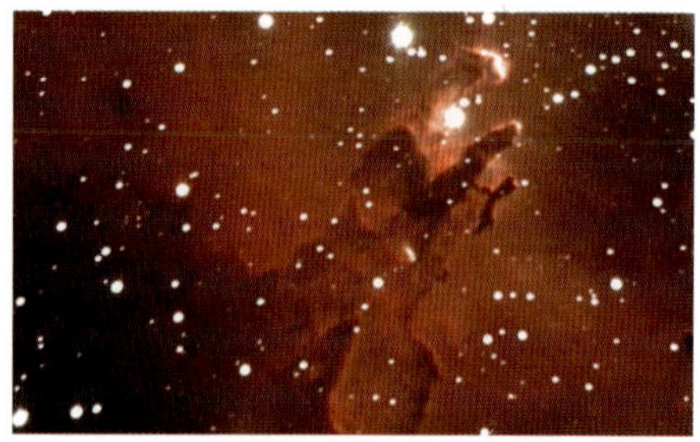

We are also presenting a rundown of all 88 of the constellations in the sky, including mentions of particularly interesting objects which you can observe within them, using binoculars or a small telescope. Many of these star patterns are fairly inconsequential, so we have picked 30 of the most prominent or interesting to illustrate with individual star maps.

You can still locate the others by using the two hemisphere charts, and if you want to see them all in detail, you could buy a dedicated star atlas or planetarium-type program for your computer.

Another useful tool is a star disk commonly called a Planisphere. You need to buy one that has been made for your home's approximate latitude. You then simply turn it so that its oval window shows you the night sky as it appears for you at any time of the night on any date of the year.

The individual constellation maps in our book are drawn with north at the top. Depending on where you live or the time of night, you might see them the other way up or lying on their side.

The maps are marked with symbols to indicate objects mentioned in the text, whether stars, nebulae or star clusters.

All our targets are visible in amateur instruments if you pick a clear, dark night and are away from city lights.

M31 in Andromeda

Orion Nebula M42 in Orion

THE GREEK ALPHABET

The brighter stars in each constellation are usually indicated by a Greek letter. This table will help you match each Greek letter with its English spelling as used in the text:

α –	Alpha	ν –	Nu
β –	Beta	ξ –	Xi
γ –	Gamma	ο –	Omicron
δ –	Delta	π –	Pi
ε –	Epsilon	ρ –	Rho
ζ –	Zeta	σ –	Sigma
η –	Eta	τ –	Tau
θ –	Theta	υ –	Upsilon
ι –	Iota	φ –	Phi
κ –	Kappa	χ –	Chi
λ –	Lambda	ψ –	Psi
μ –	Mu	ω –	Omega

NORTHERN HEMISPHERE

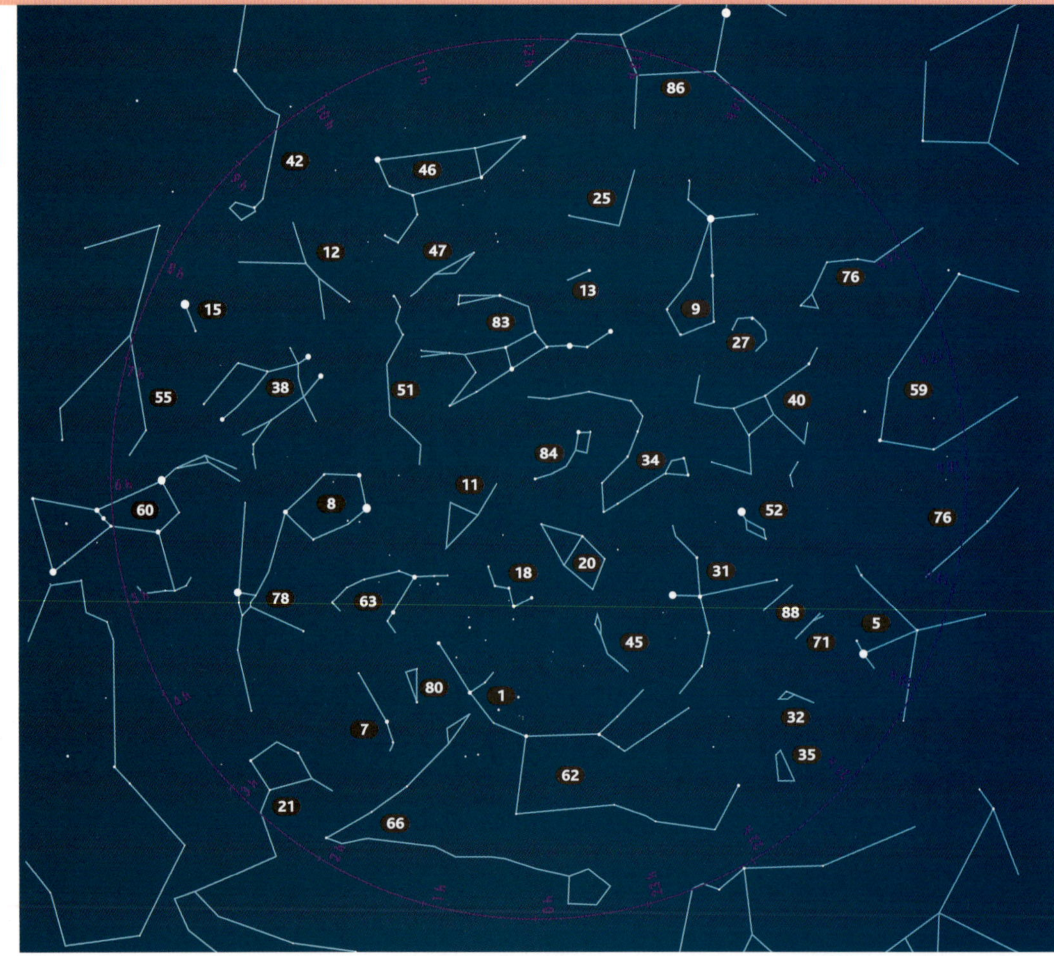

The 88 Constellations (numbered for charts).

1. Andromeda 2. Antlia 3. Apus 4. Aquarius 5. Aquila 6. Ara 7. Aries 8. Auriga 9. Boötes 10. Caelum 11. Camelopardalis 12. Cancer 13. Canes Venatici
Columba 25. Coma Berenices 26. Corona Australis 27. Corona Borealis 28. Corvus 29. Crater 30. Crux 31. Cygnus 32. Delphinus 33. Dorado 34. Draco
Minor 48. Lepus 49. Libra 50. Lupus 51. Lynx 52. Lyra 53. Mensa 54. Microscopium 55. Monoceros 56. Musca 57. Norma 58. Octans 59. Ophiuchus
Sagittarius 73. Scorpius 74. Sculptor 75. Scutum 76. Serpens 77. Sextans 78. Taurus 79. Telescopium 80. Triangulum 81. Triangulum Australe

SOUTHERN HEMISPHERE

14. Canis Major 15. Canis Minor 16. Capricornus 17. Carina 18. Cassiopeia 19. Centaurus 20. Cepheus 21. Cetus 22. Chamaeleon 23. Circinus 24.
35. Equuleus 36. Eridanus 37. Fornax 38. Gemini 39. Grus 40. Hercules 41. Horologium 42. Hydra 43. Hydrus 44. Indus 45. Lacerta 46. Leo 47. Leo
60. Orion 61. Pavo 62. Pegasus 63. Perseus 64. Phoenix 65. Pictor 66. Pisces 67. Piscis Austrinus 68. Puppis 69. Pyxis 70. Reticulum 71. Sagitta 72.
82. Tucana 83. Ursa Major 84. Ursa Minor 85. Vela 86. Virgo 87. Volans 88. Vulpecula

WINTER SKY WINDOW DECEMBER TO FEBRUARY

THE VIEW

This window on the sky shows the general view looking south from the northern hemisphere. The bottom of the map approximates to your horizon and the constellation of Auriga lies more or less overhead during winter evenings. Winter is a good time to enjoy astronomy because the nights are long. As long as you wrap up warm, there are plenty of fine sights to enjoy.

WHAT TO SEE

The view south at this time is dominated by the magnificent constellation of Orion the hunter. And you can use this prominent constellation to help find other sky patterns.

Orion is easy to spot thanks to its line of three bright stars that make up the hunter's belt.

Above them, two bright stars mark Orion's shoulders, and below the belt, two others represent his knees. The top left star is Betelgeuse, a red supergiant. The color is fairly obvious to the eye.

Betelgeuse is 800 times the diameter of the Sun and 40,000 times brighter. It is considered a candidate for a supernova that will one day flare brilliantly in the sky before collapsing into a black hole. Betelgeuse lies 420 light years away.

The star at bottom right of Orion is Rigel, a hot blue superstar. Rigel is 60,000 times brighter than the Sun but nearly twice as far away as Betelgeuse, at a distance of 800 light years.

Follow the line of Orion's belt down to the left. The bright twinkling star is Sirius, the dog star, the brightest star in the night sky.

Sirius's brilliance is due entirely to the fact that it lies only eight light years away from Earth. It would look considerably fainter if it was as far away as Betelgeuse or Rigel.

Look above Sirius and to the left of Orion to find Procyon, a prominent star in an indistinct constellation called Canis Minor. Sirius, Procyon and Betelgeuse make up a clear Winter Triangle.

Look above Procyon to find two bright stars close together in the constellation of Gemini. These are the twins Castor and Pollux. The upper twin is Castor and the lower is Pollux, viewed from the north.

Gemini is also the constellation from which one of the year's major meteor showers appears to radiate. Watch a clear, dark sky around December 13 and you may well see one or two bright meteors streaking across the heavens.

We return to Orion's belt to find our next major constellation. Continue the line of three stars to the upper right and you come to a bright orange/red star called Aldebaran. This marks the eye of Taurus the Bull. It sits at one end of a large "V" shape of stars which form the Hyades star cluster. Aldebaran is not actually part of the cluster; it simply lies between the cluster and us.

SPRING SKY WINDOW MARCH TO MAY

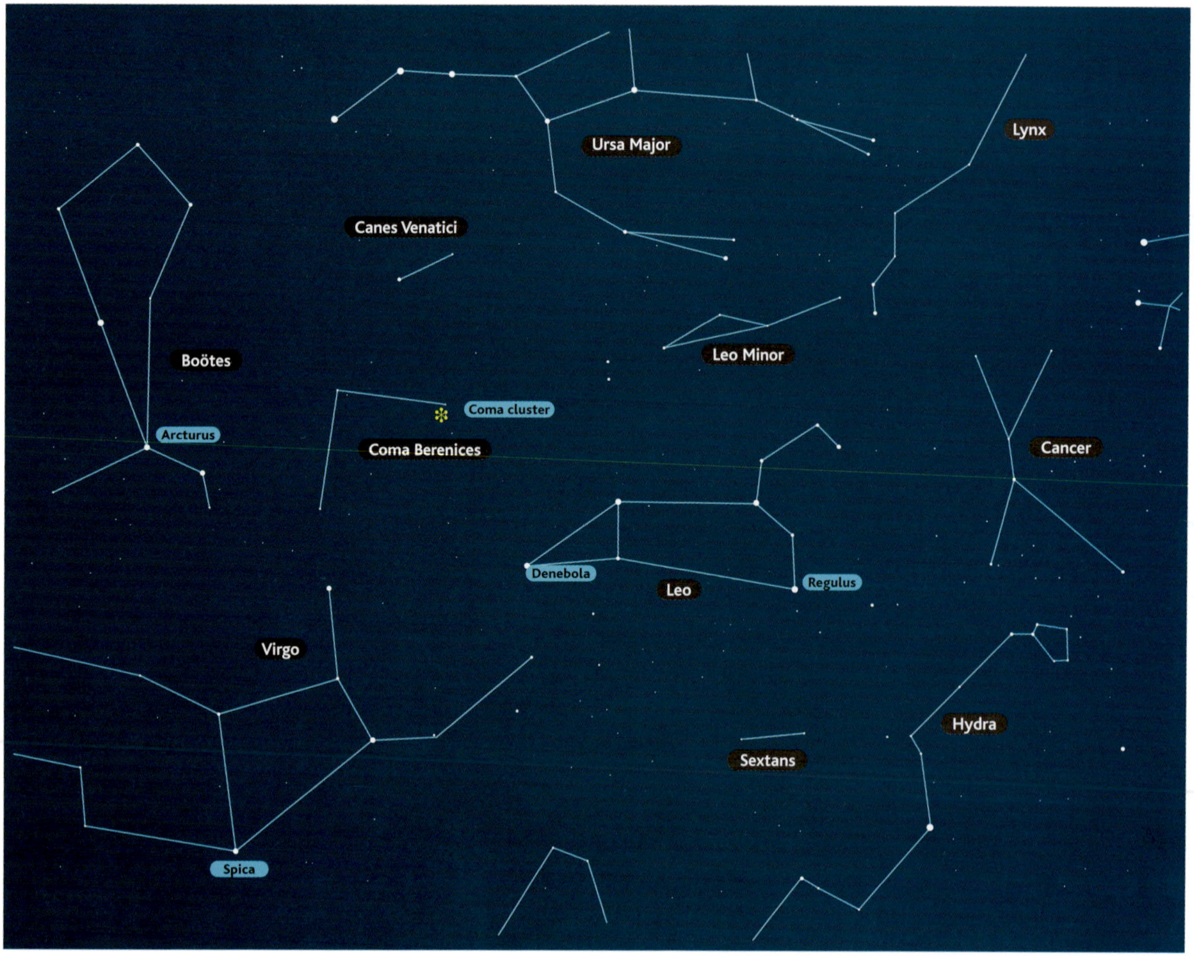

THE VIEW

This shows the general view looking south from the northern hemisphere which in spring, in the south, is dominated by Leo.

The bottom of the map approximates to your horizon and the constellation of Ursa Major lies roughly overhead during spring evenings.

WHAT TO SEE

Spring evening skies are dominated in the south by the Zodiacal constellation of Leo, the lion.

The head of the lion, resembling a giant question mark written backwards in the sky, is easy to spot. At the base of this hook is Regulus, the brightest star in Leo. This regal name, which literally means King Star, was awarded because the planets pass close by during their orbits of the Sun.

One passing through in 2008 and 2009 will be the bright ringed world Saturn, which will make Leo look as if it has gained an extra star.

Regulus is 150 times brighter than our Sun and 80 light years away. To its left, the triangle of stars which make up the haunches of the lion and his tail is marked by a star called Denebola.

Almost overhead is the Plough, a saucepan shape of seven stars within the constellation of Ursa Major. Some people call it the Big Dipper because it resembles a spoon.

Follow the curve of the spoon's handle down to the left until you come to Arcturus, the fourth brightest star in the sky. Arcturus, which is about 40 light years from Earth, is a red giant, nearing the end of its life.

Arcturus is the main star in the constellation of Boötes the Herdsman. Above it, you will see the kite-shape of stars that make up this figure.

Look between Boötes and Leo to find a less distinct grouping of faint stars called Coma Berenices. This is worth seeking out because it contains a cascade of faint stars that are part of a star cluster called Coma.

You will need clear, dark skies to see them and they will appear more distinct if you look slightly away and view them out of the corner of your eye. This is a technique called averted vision and uses the fact that the human eye's receptors are more sensitive away from the center.

Continue the curved line that took you from the Plough to Arcturus and you will come to another bright star, Spica. This is a super-luminous star, shining 14,000 times brighter than the Sun.

Spica is the brightest star in Virgo and lies 260 light years away from Earth. Virgo is another constellation of the Zodiac and Saturn moves into it in 2010 and 2011.

Virgo is famous for being home to a vast cluster of galaxies that lies an average distance of 60 million light years away from us. The cluster is so extensive that our own local group of galaxies, including the Milky Way and M31 in Andromeda, are actually related to it.

SUMMER SKY WINDOW JUNE TO AUGUST

THE VIEW

This window on the sky shows the general view looking south from the northern hemisphere in summer, when skies become darker much later in the evening and the nights are short.

WHAT TO SEE

When night does fall in the summer in the northern hemisphere three bright stars forming a prominent triangle are among the first to appear in the fading light.

These are Altair, Deneb and Vega, the brightest stars in Aquila, Cygnus and Lyra respectively. The unofficial pattern that they form is called the Summer Triangle. At top right in the triangle is Vega, the brightest of the three, largely because it is very close by astronomical standards – only 25 light years away.

Left of Vega is a genuinely brilliant star, Deneb. Although it appears fainter, it is really shining 70,000 times brighter than the Sun, but from a distance of 1,800 light years.

The third star of the triangle, Altair, is below the other two and is another whose brightness is mainly due to its distance. Altair is only ten times brighter than the Sun, but it lies even closer to us than Vega, being just 16 light years away. Two slightly fainter stars, one on either side of Altair, make it easy to identify.

Return to Deneb and look at a pattern of other stars which stretch from it into the Summer Triangle. These form the shape of a cross and represent the body of the flying swan that is the constellation of Cygnus. Deneb is at the tail end and the opposite end of the cross marks the bird's long neck. The middle struts indicate the swan's wings.

Because of its distinct shape, Cygnus is sometimes also known as the Northern Cross.

A couple of small but attractive groupings can also be found nearby. Below Cygnus, Sagitta resembles the Archer's arrow being shot into heaven. And to the left of Altair, you can see a tiny diamond of stars, with another star underneath. This is Delphinus the Dolphin, so named because it is as if it were leaping out of the sea.

Look to the right of Vega to identify another of the characters of the sky, the legendary hero Hercules. Although the stars that mark his body are not terribly bright, they form a distinctive enough pattern.

Find the two stars defining the right hand side of Hercules' torso. About a third of the way between them, from he top, can be seen one of the finest globular star clusters in the sky, M13. If there are really clear, dark skies, you might just be able to see it with the naked eye. Binoculars will show it as a fuzzy glow and it takes a telescope to display it as it really is – a tightly condensed ball of stars.

There are around one million stars packed together in this cluster, which lies about 25,000 light years away.

During 2008 and 2009, the great planet Jupiter will be low in the south during summer. If you are watching the area during the first couple of weeks in August in both years, you may catch a number of shooting stars. They are most likely to be members of the Perseid meteor shower, which peaks around August 12, although there are other showers active during the summer too.

AUTUMN SKY WINDOW SEPTEMBER TO NOVEMBER

THE VIEW

This window on the sky shows the general view looking south from the northern hemisphere in autumn. The bottom of the map approximates to your horizon and the 'W' shape of Cassiopeia should be overhead.

WHAT TO SEE

For northern observers, nights draw out once more at this time, presenting the chance to start observing the sky earlier in the evening.

As it darkens, you will see the stars of Cygnus, now flying further to the west. To their left, in an otherwise fairly barren region of the sky, you should be able to make out a giant square of four stars.

None is particularly bright, but this shape, dubbed the Great Square of Pegasus, is a distinctive one, although the top left star is actually borrowed from neighboring constellation Andromeda.

From the bottom right star in the square, more stars stretch to make the neck and head of Pegasus, the winged horse, revealing that it is actually flying upside down.

Return to the top left star in the square, and look for a line of stars stretching away to the upper left. These mark Andromeda (The Princess).

Two stars along, another pair of stars branch off upwards. Look here for the closest giant galaxy outside our own Milky Way, known as M31 or the Great Andromeda Galaxy.

M31 is fairly easy to spot with the naked eye as a large hazy blob, if you have a clear, dark sky and stand away from streetlights. But as it lies an incredible distance of 2.5 million light years away, it is probably the furthest object that most of us will see with our eyes alone. Its light that we see today left the galaxy before Man inhabited the Earth.

Binoculars or a small telescope will show the fuzzy, elongated blur of the galaxy more clearly. Below Andromeda is a small triangle of stars called, fittingly, Triangulum.

In this constellation lies the galaxy M33, which binoculars will pick out in clear skies.

Legend has it that Andromeda was rescued from a sea monster, which still lurks nearby in the sky. Cetus, also known as the Whale, can be found by following a line from the top right star in the square of Pegasus through the bottom left star.

Between Pegasus and Cetus is a long V-pattern of stars representing Pisces, the two fish of the Zodiac. A bright new "star" will travel through this faint star pattern between 2010 and 2012 – the giant planet Jupiter.

Return to Andromeda and extend its main line of stars away from Pegasus and you will reach another celestial hero – Perseus.

Above Andromeda, and roughly overhead on autumn evenings, is the "W" shape of Cassiopeia. Look between Perseus and the W with binoculars and you will spot two attractive concentrations of stars. These form the famous Double Cluster, NGC 884 and NGC 869.

These lie around 8,000 light years away. Through a small telescope they look like collections of sparkling jewels.

SKY WINDOW ALL YEAR STARS

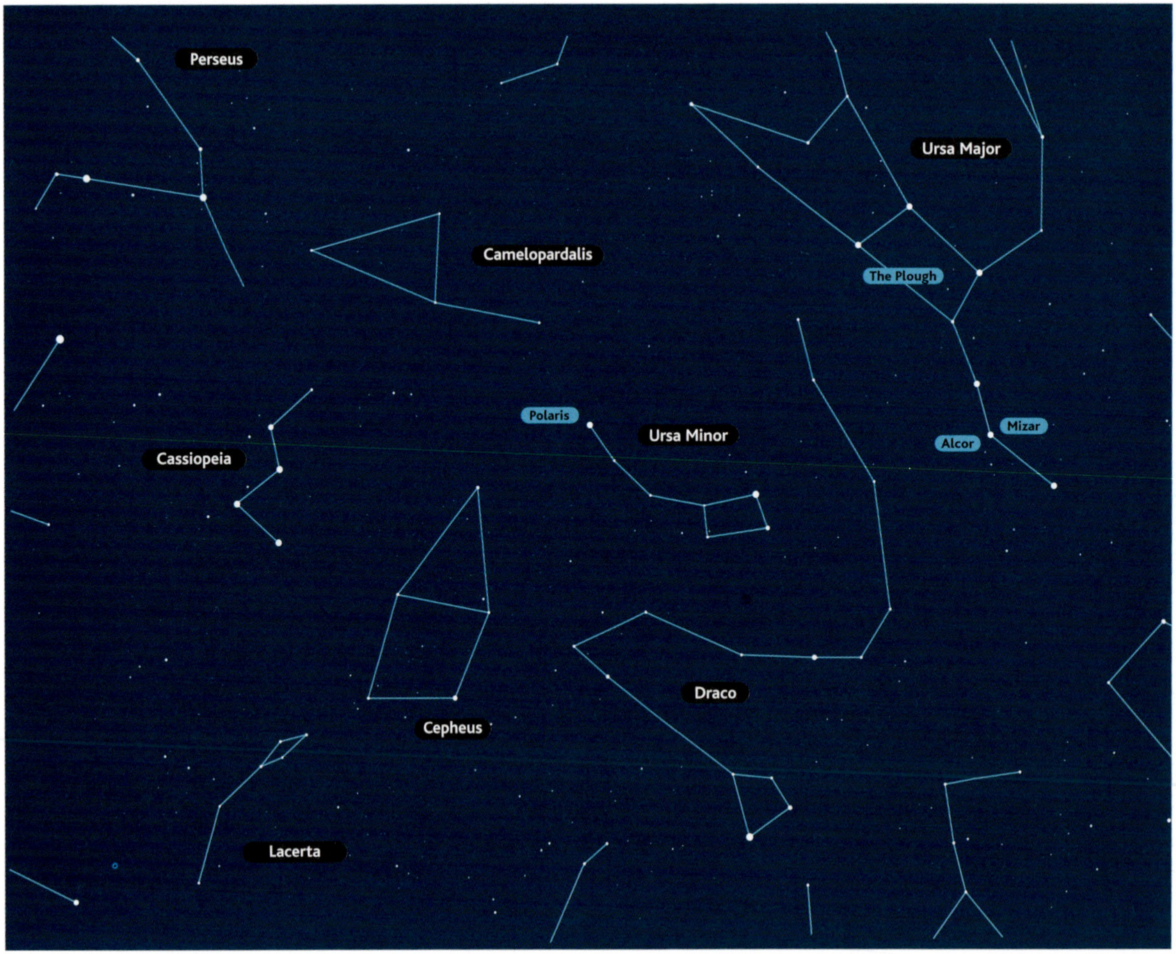

THE VIEW

Previous sky windows have shown us the views looking south at different seasons of the year. For our final window for the northern hemisphere, you need to turn and face in the opposite direction, due north.

WHAT TO SEE

When you look north, you see the patterns of stars that lie close to the North Celestial Pole. Helpfully, this point in the sky is marked by a fairly bright star called Polaris.

Throughout the night and, indeed, throughout the year, the other constellations in our window appear to wheel around Polaris as the Earth rotates. But those stars closer to Polaris than the horizon never set and remain visible at any time. They are described as circumpolar.

This means that, whatever season it is, the patterns on view in this direction remain the same, although their position changes, just like the hands of a clock.

How many stars are circumpolar depends on the latitude at which you live. The view here shows these northern stars as they appear on a mid-evening in spring.

The well-known pattern of the Plough, or Big Dipper, in Ursa Major, the Great Bear, is climbing in the sky to the right, with its top two stars, dubbed the Pointers, doing just that – pointing to Polaris in Ursa Minor.

The stars of Ursa Minor itself, sometimes dubbed the Little Dipper, curve away from Polaris toward the handle of the Plough.

Look to the other side of Polaris from the Plough and you will find the distinctive "W" shape of Cassiopeia, the queen. In this view, Cassiopeia is seen on its side and slowly sinking, like the hands of a clock running backwards. This view revolves, counterclockwise around Polaris as the night wears on.

If you view this direction on a summer evening, the Plough will lie at the top of the map, virtually overhead, while Cassiopeia will resemble that "W" low above the northern horizon.

On autumn evenings, the Plough will be descending again on the left hand side of the sky window with Cassiopeia rising on the right side. And at the same time in winter, it will be the Plough that is low in the north and Cassiopeia that lies overhead.

Look at the second star from the end of the handle of the Plough with the naked eye and you will see that it has another close by.

The brighter star is called Mizar and the fainter is Alcor. A telescope shows that Mizar is a close double star itself.

Between Ursa Major and Ursa Minor, a straggly line of stars forms the tail of Draco, the dragon. Follow the meandering line to locate the diamond shape marking the dragon's head.

Look between the head of Draco and Cassiopeia and you will find Cepheus, a constellation representing Cassiopeia's husband, the King. The house-like shape is not bright but it is not too difficult to make out.

SUMMER SKY WINDOW DECEMBER TO FEBRUARY

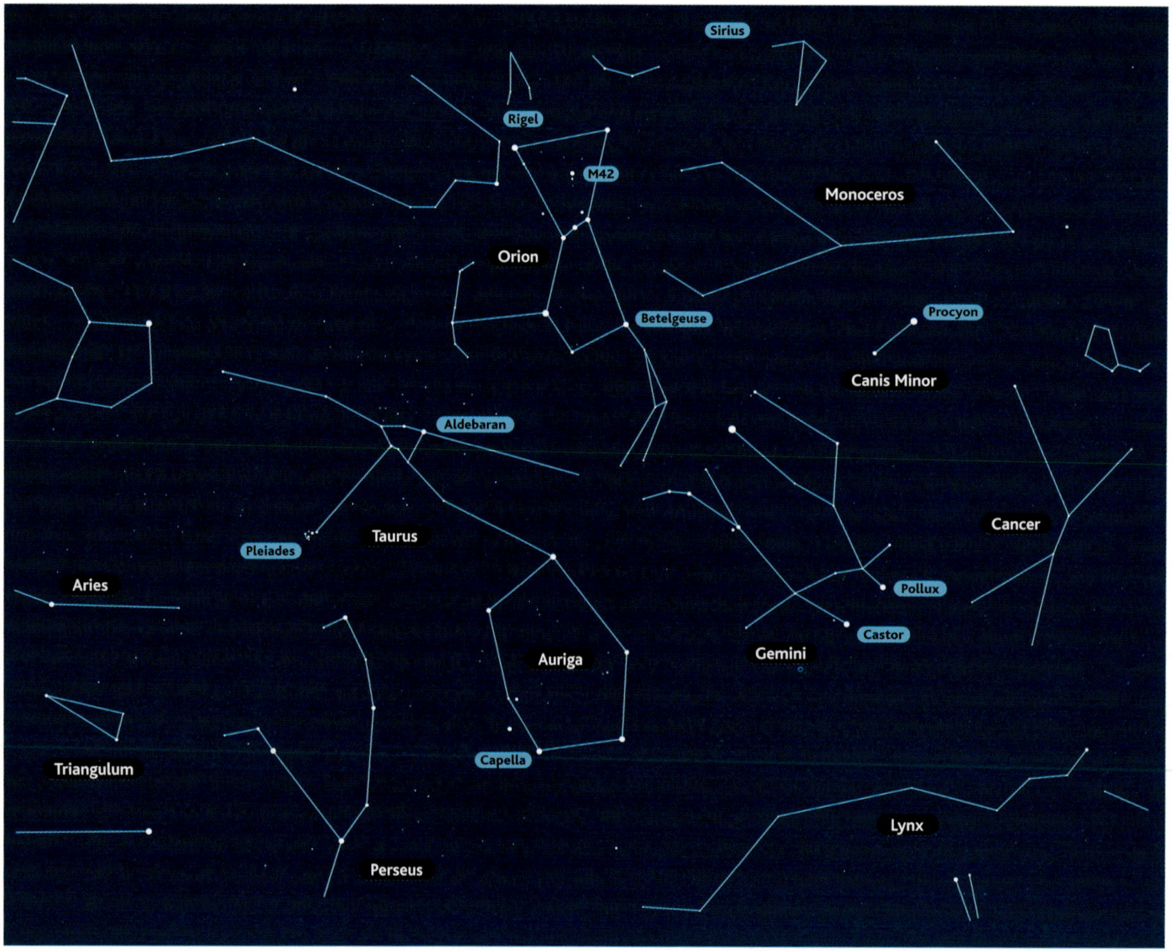

THE VIEW

This window on the sky shows the general view looking north from the southern hemisphere. The bottom of the map approximates to your horizon.

To help get your bearings, use a use a compass to find north or stand with the direction of sunset, in the west to your left. For example, changing south to north and right to left.

WHAT TO SEE

The view south at this time is dominated by the magnificent constellation of Orion the hunter. You can use this prominent constellation to help find other sky patterns.

Orion is easy to spot thanks to its line of the three bright stars that make up the hunter's belt. But from the southern hemisphere, the hunter is standing upside down.

Below the belt, two bright stars mark Orion's shoulders, and above it, two others represent his knees. The bottom right star is Betelgeuse, a red supergiant whose color is fairly obvious to the eye.

Betelgeuse is 800 times the diameter of the Sun and 40,000 times brighter. Lying 420 light years away, it is considered a candidate for a supernova which will one day flare brilliantly in the sky before collapsing into a black hole.

The star at top left is Rigel, a hot blue superstar. Rigel is 60,000 times brighter than the Sun but nearly twice as far away as Betelgeuse, at a distance of 800 light years.

Follow the line of Orion's belt up to the right. The bright twinkling star is the brightest star in our night sky: Sirius, the dog star. Sirius's great brilliance is due entirely to the fact that it lies only eight light years away from Earth. It would look considerably fainter if you put it as far away as Betelgeuse or Rigel.

Look below Sirius and to the right of Orion to find the next bright star in our sky window. This is Procyon, a prominent star in an indistinct constellation called Canis Minor. Sirius, Procyon and Betelgeuse make up a clear triangle.

Look below Procyon to find two bright stars close together in the constellation of Gemini. These are the twins Castor and Pollux. The lower twin is Castor and the upper is Pollux, viewed from the south.

Gemini is also the constellation from which one of the year's major meteor showers appears to radiate. Watch a clear dark sky around December 13 and you may see one or two bright meteors streaking across the heavens.

We return to Orion's belt to find our next major constellation. Continue the line of three stars down to the lower left and you will soon come to a bright orange/red star called Aldebaran, which marks the eye of Taurus the bull. You can see that it sits at one end of a large "V" shape of stars, which form the Hyades star cluster. Aldebaran is not really part of the cluster; it simply lies between the cluster and us.

Continue the line from Orion's belt through Aldebaran and you come to another pretty little cluster of stars, which the poet Tennyson compared to "a swarm of fireflies". These are the Pleiades, popularly known as the Seven Sisters because a keen-sighted observer can see seven with the naked eye.

Most people will be lucky to spot six, but a telescope will reveal hundreds of stars in this cluster.

Low in the sky you might see a very bright yellow star, Capella, in the constellation of Auriga the chariot driver. Capella is the 11th brightest star in the sky and lies 42 light years away. Its light actually shines from a pair of stars so close together that the naked eye cannot separate them.

AUTUMN SKY WINDOW MARCH TO MAY

THE VIEW

This shows the general view looking north from the southern hemisphere. The bottom of the map approximates to your horizon.

To help get your bearings, use a use a compass to find north or stand with the direction of sunset, in the west to your left. For example, changing south to north and right to left.

WHAT TO SEE

Spring evening skies are dominated in the north by the Zodiacal constellation of Leo, the lion.

The head of the lion is easy to spot, resembling as it does a giant upside-down question mark written backwards in the sky. At the top of this hook is the brightest star in Leo, Regulus. This regal name, literally meaning King Star, was awarded because the planets pass close by during their orbits of the Sun.

One passing through in 2008 and 2009 is the bright ringed world Saturn, which will make Leo look as if it has gained an extra star.

Regulus is 150 times brighter than our Sun and 80 light years away. To its right, a triangle of stars makes up the haunches of the lion and the tail is marked by a star called Denebola.

Look further to the right and you will come to a bright star called Arcturus. This, the fourth brightest star in the sky, is a red giant, nearing the end of its life, about 40 light years from Earth.

Arcturus is the main star in the constellation of Boötes, the Herdsman. The kite-shape of stars that make up this figure can be seen stretching below it.

Look between Boötes and Leo to find a less distinct grouping of faint stars called Coma Berenices. It is worth seeking out because it contains a cascade of faint stars that are part of a star cluster called Coma.

You will need clear dark skies to see them and they will appear more distinct if you look slightly away and view them out of the corner of your eye. This is a technique called averted vision and uses the fact that the human eye's receptors are more sensitive away from the center.

> "Saturn will make Leo look like it has gained an extra star"

Look above Coma to find bright Spica, a super-luminous star, shining 14,000 times brighter than the Sun.

Spica is the brightest star in Virgo and lies 260 light years away from Earth. Virgo is another constellation of the Zodiac, and Saturn moves into it in 2010 and 2011.

Virgo is famous for being home to a vast cluster of galaxies that lies an average distance of 60 million light years away. The cluster is so extensive that our own local group of galaxies, including the Milky Way and M31 in Andromeda, are actually related to it.

WINTER SKY WINDOW JUNE TO AUGUST

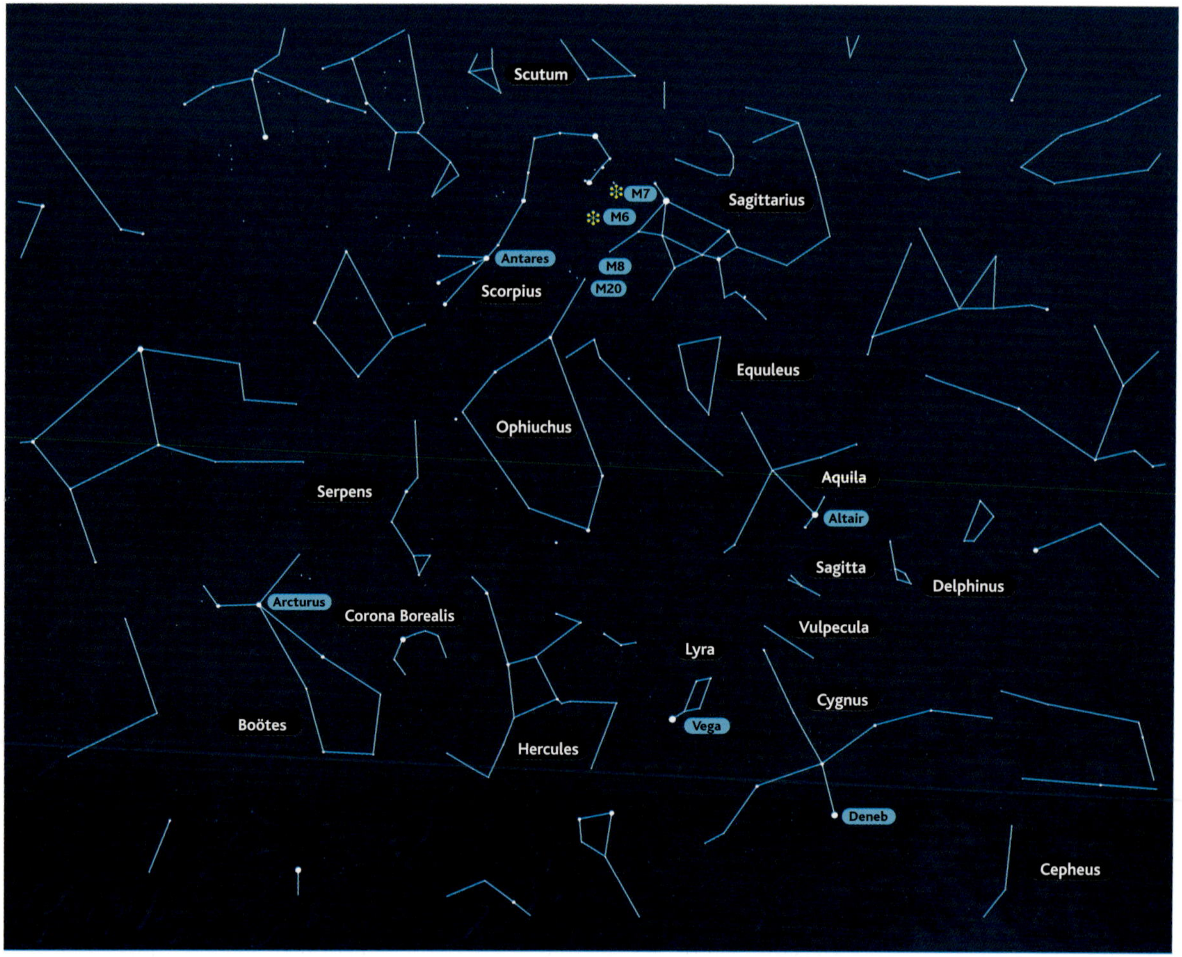

THE VIEW

This window on the sky shows the general view looking north from the southern hemisphere in winter, when longer nights offer up some of the finest sights.

WHAT TO SEE

Among the sights viewable during the longer nights of southern winter are the treasures of the Milky Way.

Look high in the sky to find the distinctive shape of Scorpius, the scorpion that legend has it killed Orion with its sting.

Its brightest star is the red giant Antares, whose name literally means rival of Mars. It was so named because its color means it can be confused for the Red Planet when Mars arrives close by on its journey through the Zodiac.

Follow the curve of the scorpion's body upwards and you can see the stars which represent its poisonous sting. Below Antares, more stars form the creature's claws.

Look to the right of Scorpius for another Zodiacal constellation, Sagittarius the Archer. You might find it easier to spot a more mundane image in these stars: the Teapot. Four stars form the pot, two stars to the right make his handle and another to the left completes his spout.

If there are dark skies, you will have the richest views of the Milky Way in Sagittarius, because you are looking towards the heart of the galaxy. The center itself is hidden by clouds of dust and gas, but we see stars densely packed.

Some of the greatest star clusters and nebulae are to be found in this region of the Milky Way, making it a delight to sweep with binoculars or a small telescope.

Below the teapot are two nebulae called M8 (the Lagoon), which is one of the brightest gas clouds in the sky, and M20 (the Trifid Nebula), which is somewhat dimmer.

Above these nebulae are two magnificent star clusters: M7 (called Ptolemy's Cluster) and, below and to its left, M6, the Butterfly Cluster. M6 and M7 each contain around 130 stars and are best seen through binoculars.

"Legend has it that Scorpius the Scorpion killed Orion with its sting"

Below Scorpius, a large, faint pattern of stars makes up Ophiuchus, the serpent holder. You can find the snake he carries in the two halves of Serpens on either side of him.

Below Ophiuchus, you may spot the mythical hero Hercules, with the brilliant star Vega low in the sky to the right. It is bright because it lies only 25 light years away.

During 2008 and 2009, Jupiter will be a prominent visitor to this sky window, standing high in the sky.

SPRING SKY WINDOW SEPTEMBER TO NOVEMBER

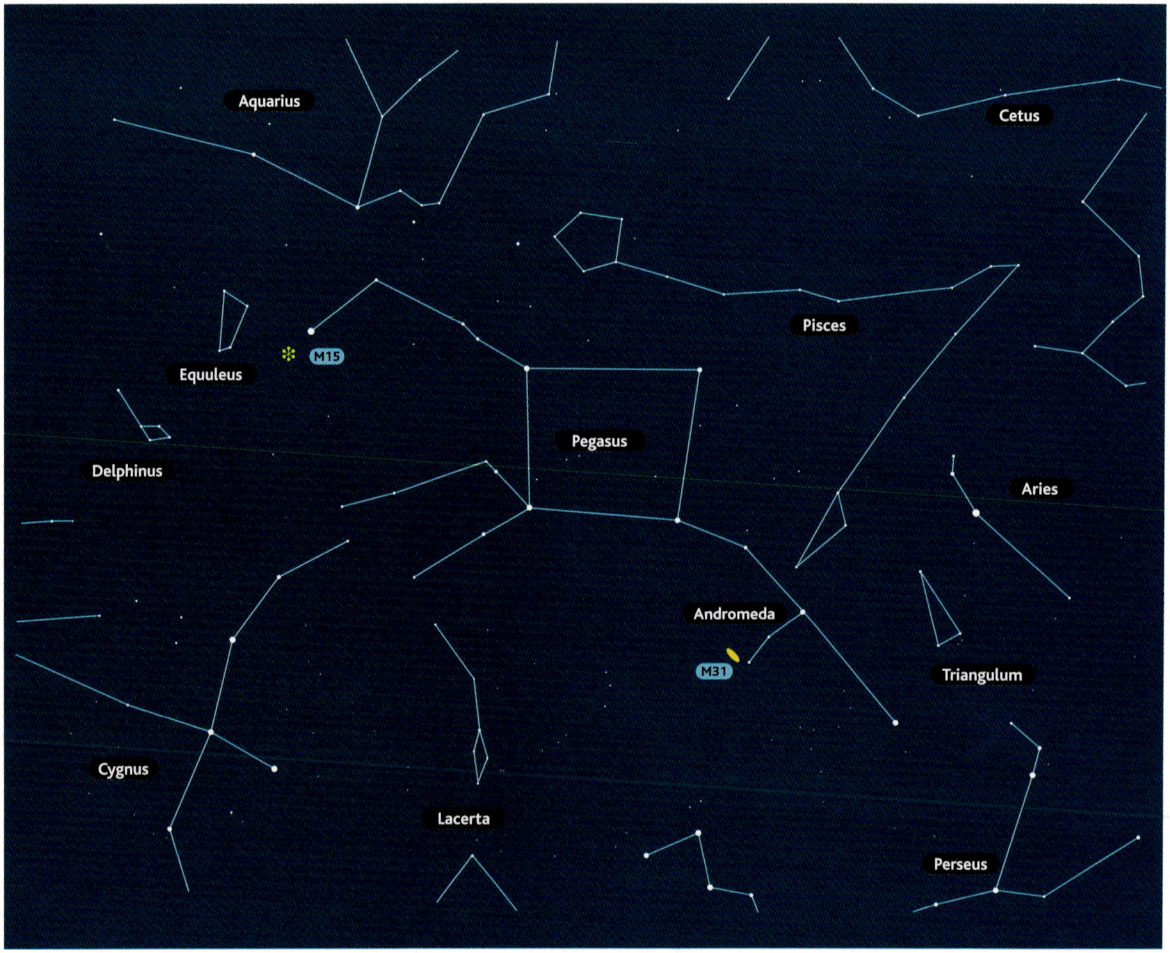

THE VIEW

This window on the sky shows the general view looking north from the southern hemisphere in spring. The bottom of the map approximates to your horizon and the view north is dominated by four stars.

WHAT TO SEE

The prominent square of four medium-bright stars is the famous Great Square of Pegasus, part of the mythological winged horse, and a constellation that southern observers will see the right way up.

The square forms the horse's body and a curved line of stars runs from top left to produce his head. More stars from the base of the square make up his front legs.

Just to the left of the head, binoculars will reveal what first appears as a rather fuzzy star. This is actually a fine globular cluster of tightly packed stars called M15, and makes an excellent target for small telescopes.

Technically, the star at bottom right of the Great Square does not belong to Pegasus at all. It has been borrowed from the neighboring constellation of Andromeda, the princess.

The stars of Andromeda stretch away to the lower right. Two bright stars along, another pair of stars branch off downwards. Look here to spot the closest giant galaxy outside our own Milky Way, known as M31 or the Great Andromeda Galaxy.

Although M31 does not get very high from southern locations, you may be able to spot it as a large hazy blob with the naked eye if you have a clear, dark sky and stand away from streetlights. Since it lies an incredible distance of 2.5 million light years away, it is probably the furthest object most of us will see with our eyes alone. As we know, the light that we see today from this galaxy left it before Man inhabited the Earth.

Binoculars or a small telescope will show the fuzzy, elongated blur of the galaxy more clearly.

Above Andromeda lies the compact triangle of stars called Triangulum. In this constellation another nearby spiral galaxy, M33, can be picked out in binoculars in clear skies.

Cetus, also known as the whale, can be found by following a line from the bottom left star in the Square of Pegasus through the top right star.

Between Pegasus and Cetus is a long "V" pattern of stars that represents Pisces, the two fish of the Zodiac. A bright new "star" will travel through this faint star pattern between 2010 and 2012 – the giant planet Jupiter.

Return to the head of Pegasus and look above it to find the stars of Zodiacal constellation Aquarius, the Water Carrier. To the left of Pegasus is an attractive, tiny diamond shape of stars: Delphinus, the dolphin. Another star running above the diamond is the dolphin's tail

None of the stars in this watery region of the sky is particularly bright but they will receive a particularly brilliant visitor when Jupiter passes through.

SKY WINDOW ALL YEAR STARS

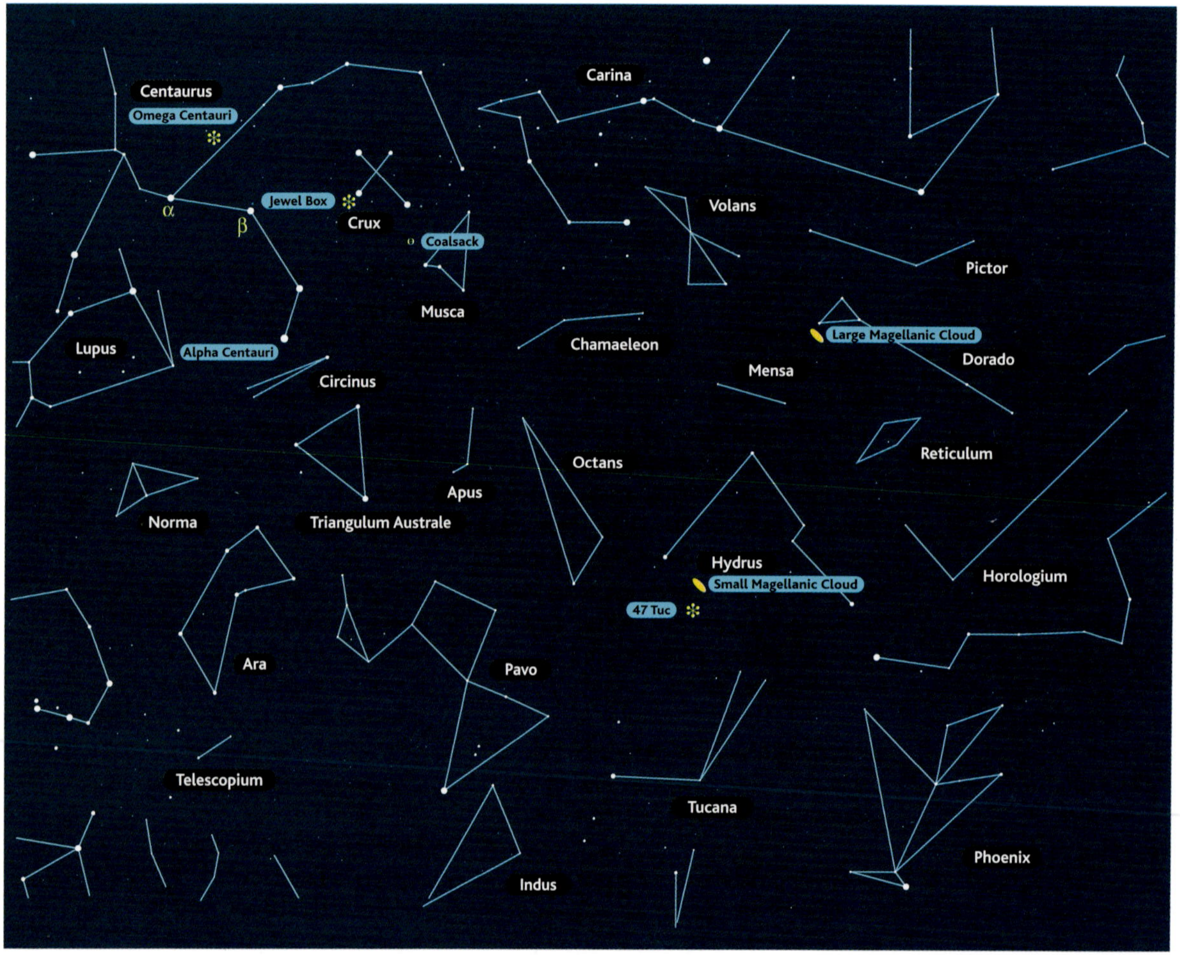

THE VIEW

Previous sky windows have shown us the views looking north at different seasons of the year. For our final window for the southern hemisphere, you need to turn and face in the opposite direction, due south.

WHAT TO SEE

When you look south, you see the patterns of stars that lie close to the South Celestial Pole. Unfortunately, there is no bright star to mark this point in the sky as there is for the northern pole, but we we can help you locate it.

Throughout the night and throughout the year, the other constellations in our window appear to wheel around the South Celestial Pole as the Earth rotates. But those stars closer to the pole than the horizon never set and remain visible at any time. They are said to be circumpolar.

The view here shows these southern stars as they appear on a mid-evening during autumn in the southern hemisphere.

The best known star sign is Crux, the Southern Cross, which is rising at this time as it circles the pole in a clockwise direction. Six months later at this time, Crux will be sinking low on the opposite side of the pole.

The point where the Celestial Pole lies is in Octans, just above the letter "t" in the word "Octans" in our sky window. One way to find it is to follow the long bar of the Southern Cross which points to it. Follow the bar by around four and a half times its length and you will be there.

Crux contains a cluster of stars called the Jewel Box plus a dark patch in the sky, which is really a cloud of dust called the Coalsack.

Below Crux at this time can be found two bright stars: Alpha and Beta in Centaurus. In fact they point to the Southern Cross and so can also help you to find it. Alpha is the star further from the cross and is part of the closest star system to us. Its small red dwarf companion, Proxima Centauri, is the nearest star after the Sun, and lies just 4.2 light years away.

Also in Centaurus, close to Crux, can be found Omega Centauri, the finest globular star cluster in the entire sky. A fuzzy glow to the naked eye, it appears as a grainy ball in binoculars. A small telescope shows countless stars packed together.

> "Find Octans by following the long bar of the Southern Cross"

On a clear, dark night, two wispy star clouds are visible in this window on the sky. These are the Magellanic Clouds. They are dwarf satellite galaxies of our own Milky Way, lying around 160,000 light years away and 75,000 light years apart.

The Magellanic Clouds form an equilateral triangle with the South Celestial Pole, offering another way to locate this.

Close to the Small Magellanic Cloud (SMC) can be found another spectacular globular cluster in Tucana, called 47 Tucanae or simply 47 Tuc. It appears as a fuzzy star with the naked eye and lies about 13,000 light years away.

ANTLIA

This is one of the "modern" constellations, lying too far south in the sky to have been noticed by the ancient civilizations of the north. Its name, awarded by French astronomer Nicolas Louis de Lacaille in 1751-52, means the Air Pump.

Antlia contains little of interest other than Zeta, a widely-spaced pair of 6th magnitude stars for binoculars, and NGC 3132, a bright planetary nebula for small telescopes.

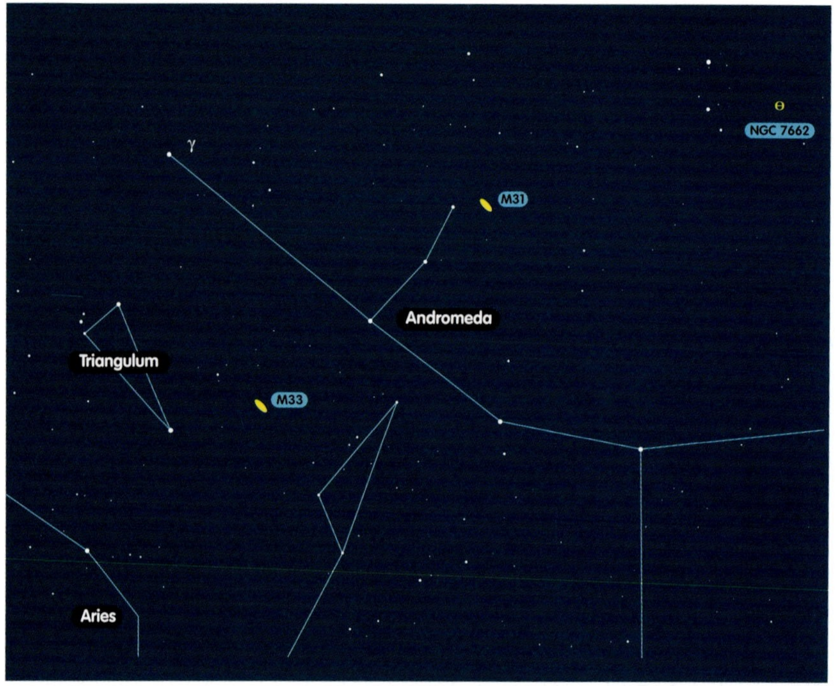

ANDROMEDA

This constellation is named after a legendary Ethiopian princess who was chained to the rocks and devoured by a sea monster.

As with so many star patterns, you need a vivid imagination to see her form. The brightest star in Andromeda, Alpheratz, was awarded to the constellation as recently as 1928, having previously been shared with a neighboring constellation, forming one corner of the Great Square of Pegasus.

Andromeda's greatest claim is as the home of our nearest spiral galaxy. Messier 31, sometimes wrongly termed the Andromeda Nebula, is a spiral of around a trillion stars, 2.5 million light-years away. The spiral is turned at an angle to us and is even visible to the naked eye in dark skies as an elongated blur. Binoculars will show it as a bright misty patch and amateur telescopes will pick out two of its smaller satellite galaxies: M32 and M110. A planetary nebula for small telescopes is NGC 7662.

The star Almech (Gamma Andromedae) shows as a beautiful double star in small telescopes, with contrasting orange and blue colors. Larger instruments will reveal a third companion.

APUS

The Bird of Paradise, a constellation identified in the 16th century, never flies high enough to rise above the horizon for most of the northern hemisphere. It offers little to see other than the double star Delta, a pair of 5th magnitude orange objects.

ARA

The constellation of the Altar is a compact southern grouping of faint stars. It contains NGC 6397, which is thought to be the closest globular cluster to the solar system, although it still lies 8,400 light-years away and, at magnitude 7.5, requires binoculars to be seen. NGC 6193 is an open cluster of stars for binoculars.

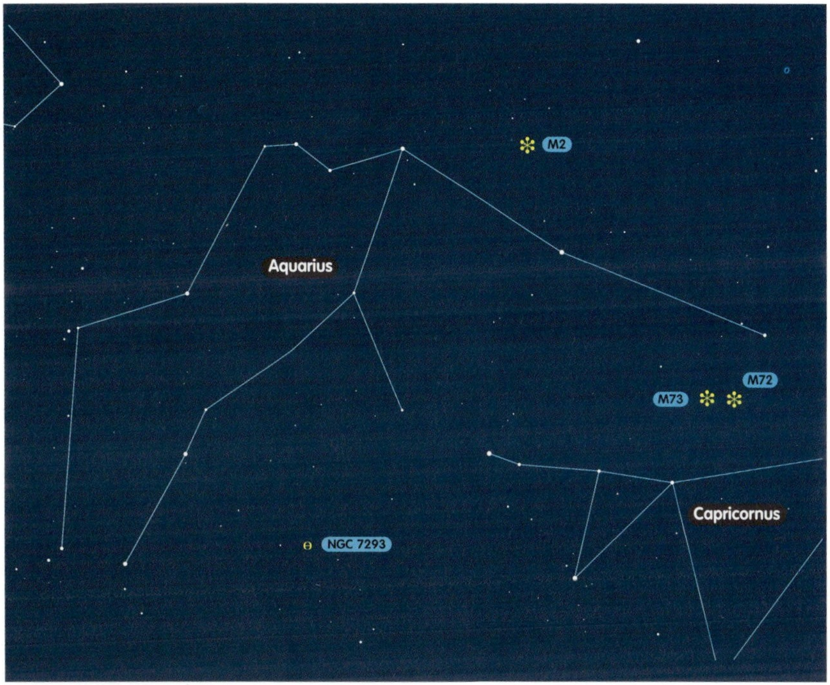

AQUARIUS

A classic constellation of the Zodiac, depicting the Water Carrier. The Sun passes through every February.

Several summer meteor showers appear to radiate from this area, notably the Eta and Delta Aquarids.

Aquarius is also where you will find the Helix Nebula or NGC 7293, the closest planetary nebula to Earth. Actually a shell of gas thrown off a star 700 light years away, the Helix is best seen in binoculars from southern latitudes, where it is higher in the sky. Space telescopes including Hubble have taken spectacular images which show it resembling a giant eye in the sky.

M2 is a globular cluster that may just be glimpsed with the naked eye. A fainter globular is M72, while M73 is simply a chance grouping of faint stars.

AQUILA

Another of several birds in the heavens, the Eagle is found easily thanks to the two attendant stars which sit either side of its brightest star, Altair. Altair also forms one point in another celestial pattern that, while not a proper constellation, is a well-known landmark in the sky: the Summer Triangle. The two other bright stars making up this feature are Deneb in Cygnus and Vega in Lyra.

Eta Aquilae is an interesting variable star of the Cepheid variety. Its brightness changes between magnitudes 3.5 and 4.3 in 7.177 days. Telescopic double stars include 15 Aquilae and 57 Aquilae.

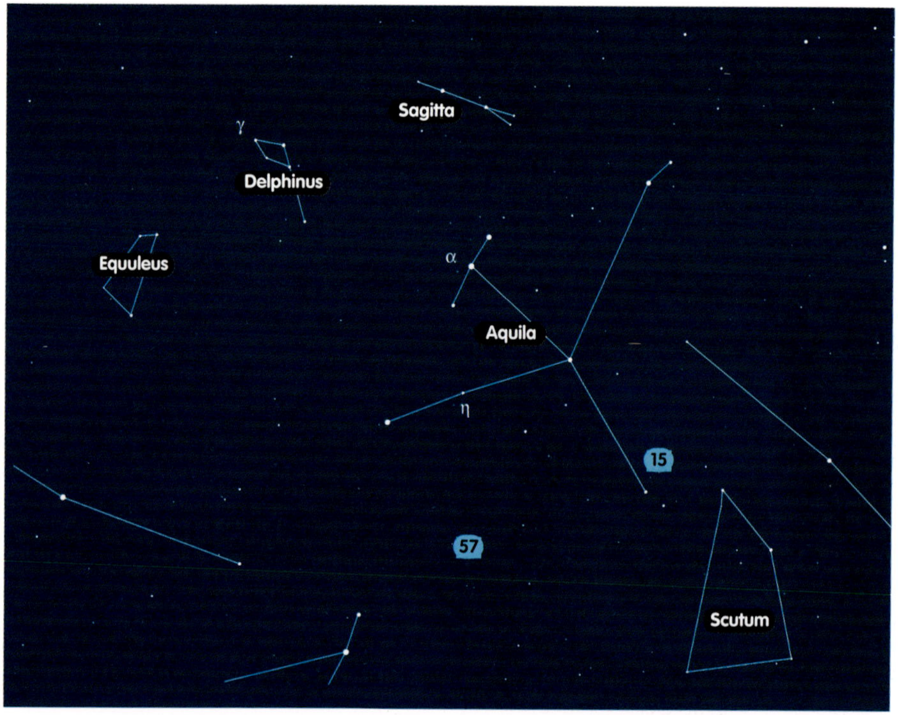

CAELUM

Created by Lacaille in the mid-18th century, the Sculptor's Chisel is a small, insignificant collection of faint stars in the southern sky. Gamma is a 5th and 8th magnitude double.

ARIES

The Ram shows as little more than a squashed triangle (as shown on the map on p124). One of these three stars, Gamma Arietis, was among the earliest double stars spotted in the sky, although you need a telescope to be aware of this. Lambda and Pi are two other pairs. The so-called "First Point of Aries", which is where the Sun appears to cross the Celestial Equator on its journey along the ecliptic, actually now lies in the neighboring constellation of Pisces and has done so since 27BC.

CAMELOPARDALIS

The far northern constellation of the Giraffe, stretches almost to the north celestial pole. It is largely unremarkable, however, there is a double star, Struve 1694, for small telescopes, with magnitudes of 5 and 6. Binoculars will show the cluster NGC 1502 and, with luck, the 9th magnitude spiral galaxy NGC 2403.

COLUMBA

Yet another celestial bird is the Dove. This is an obscure grouping.

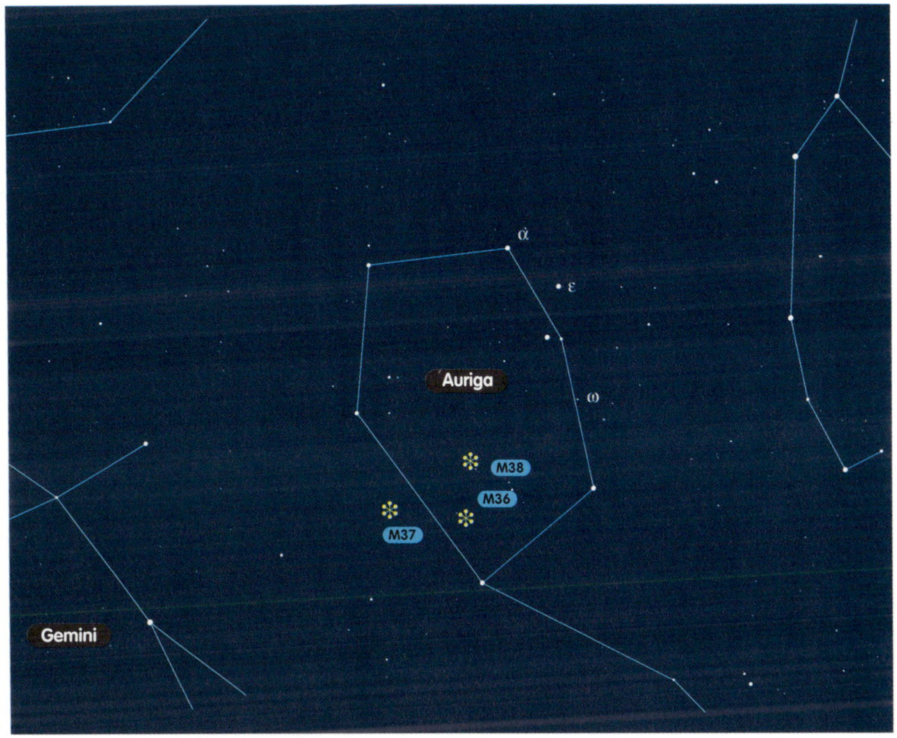

AURIGA

The Charioteer is like a large polygon, especially if you include a star that it once shared with its neighbor, Taurus, but which has now been determined to be Beta Tauri. Its brightest star, Capella, or Alpha Aurigae, is one of the most prominent in the sky. Close by, you will find a little triangle of stars dubbed the Kids. Auriga, is rich in star clusters and repays a sweep with binoculars. M36, M37 and M38 are all open clusters, with M37 the richest. Epsilon Aurigae is a particularly unusual star. Usually shining at magnitude 3, it undergoes a significant and regular fade every 27 years. The fades are thought to be due to an invisible companion, possibly a cloud of debris, orbiting and eclipsing the bright star. Each eclipse lasts around two years and the next is expected to begin in 2009. Omega is a double for telescopes. Its stars are 5th and 8th magnitudes.

CANES VENATICI

More easily known by its English name, the Hunting Dogs, this is a minor constellation that sits beneath the tail of the Great Bear (or handle of the Plough, if you see it as such).

Unremarkable in itself, the star pattern contains a number of interesting deep sky objects. Most notably is M51, the Whirlpool, which is one of the finest spiral galaxies in the sky. It played a vital role in our understanding of the universe when, in 1845, Lord Rosse first detected its spiral structure using his giant telescope – then the biggest in the world – at Birr Castle, Ireland.

M3 is a 6th magnitude globular cluster. M63, M94 and M106 are other spiral galaxies that may be glimpsed with binoculars.

CIRCINUS

The Compasses is another compact southern constellation created by Lacaille. It holds very little interest.

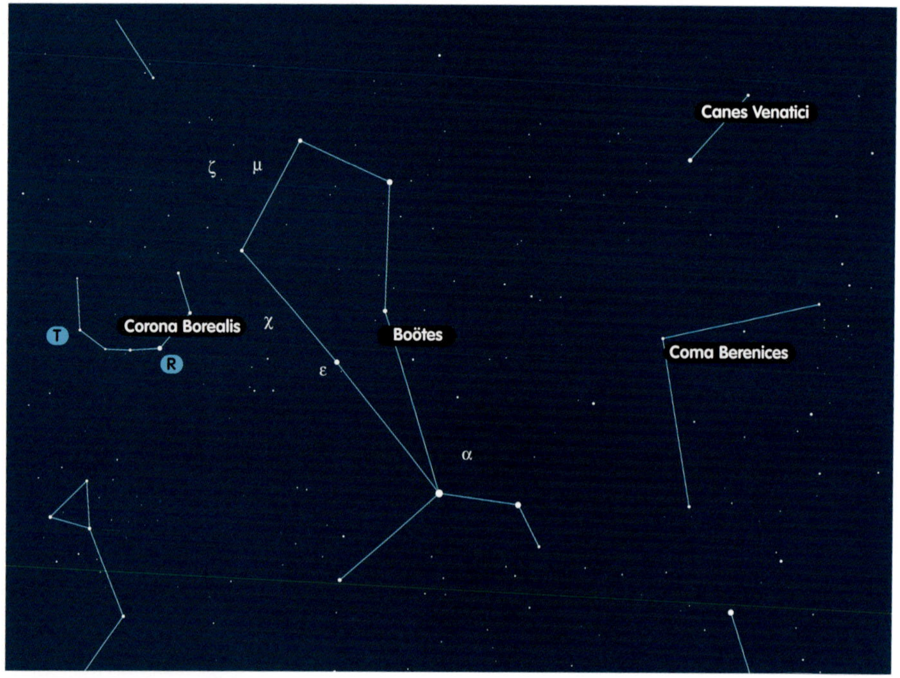

BOÖTES

Another celestial character is the Herdsman, sometimes called the Bear Driver because he stands close to the Great Bear, Ursa Major, in the heavens. Arcturus, or alpha Boötes, is another of the brightest stars in the sky. It can found easily, when it's above the horizon, by following the curve of the Great Bear's tail.The star Epsilon Boötes is seen to be a double star through a telescope, with the companions having contrasting orange and blue colors. No wonder its Latin nickname is Pulcherrima, meaning "most beautiful". Other doubles include Mu at magnitudes 4 and 7 and Xi at 5 and 7.

CANCER

The Crab is another celestial creature within the Zodiac. It forms a spidery shape of faint stars inside which a large blur is visible to the unaided eye on a clear dark night. Binoculars reveal this to be a cloud of stars, M44, which has been given the name of Praesepe, or the Beehive Cluster.

Galileo was first to see the individual stars, managing to count 36 using his telescope. Two double stars for small telescopes are Zeta and Iota.

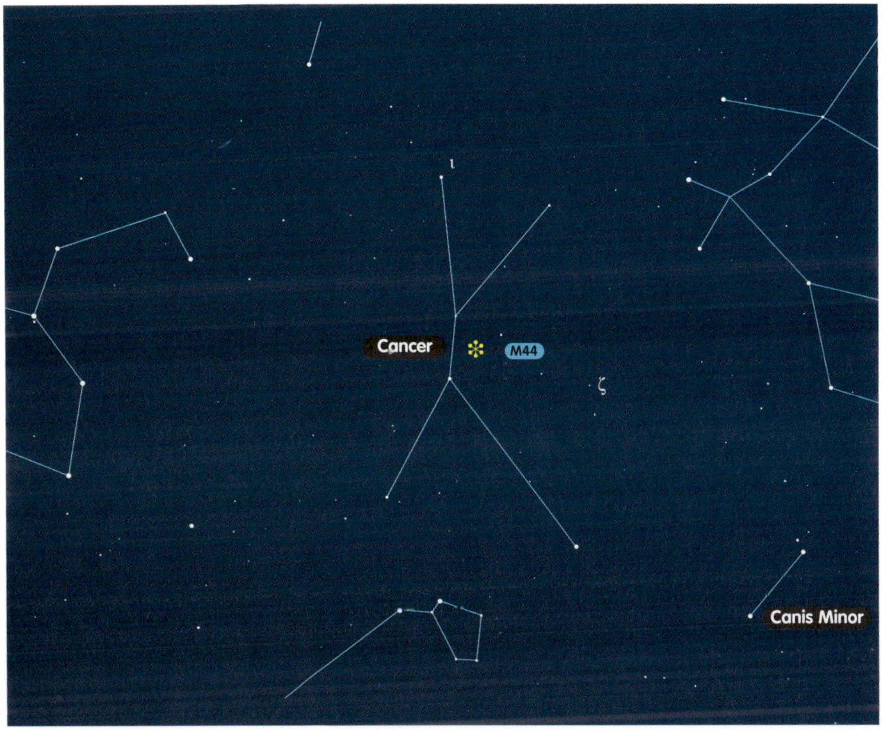

CHAMAELEON

The Chameleon is a small pattern close to the south celestial pole, invented in the late 16th century.

There are few special treats, but Delta is a pair of stars that are not really connected but lie in the same direction, and NGC 3195 is a planetary nebula.

CANIS MINOR

Not far from its big brother sits the Little Dog. It is notable only for being home to one of the brighter stars, Procyon. This star also helps make up an unofficial grouping in the sky, the Big G. It is formed by linking Capella, in Auriga, to Castor and Pollux in Gemini, then Procyon, Sirius in Canis Major, Rigel in Orion, Aldebaran in Taurus and back into Orion to meet Betelgeuse.

CANIS MAJOR

We are back to canines with the Big Dog, which sits faithfully at the feet of Orion the Hunter.

The constellation is recognized easily thanks to a number of bright stars, none more brilliant than Sirius (also known as Alpha), the brightest star in the sky. Sirius, also known as the Dog Star, appears bright largely because it lies so close to us, at a distance of just 8.6 light years, but in reality it is also burning 36 times brighter than the Sun.

M41 is an open cluster of stars that can be seen with the naked eye but looks superb in binoculars. Another is NGC 2362.

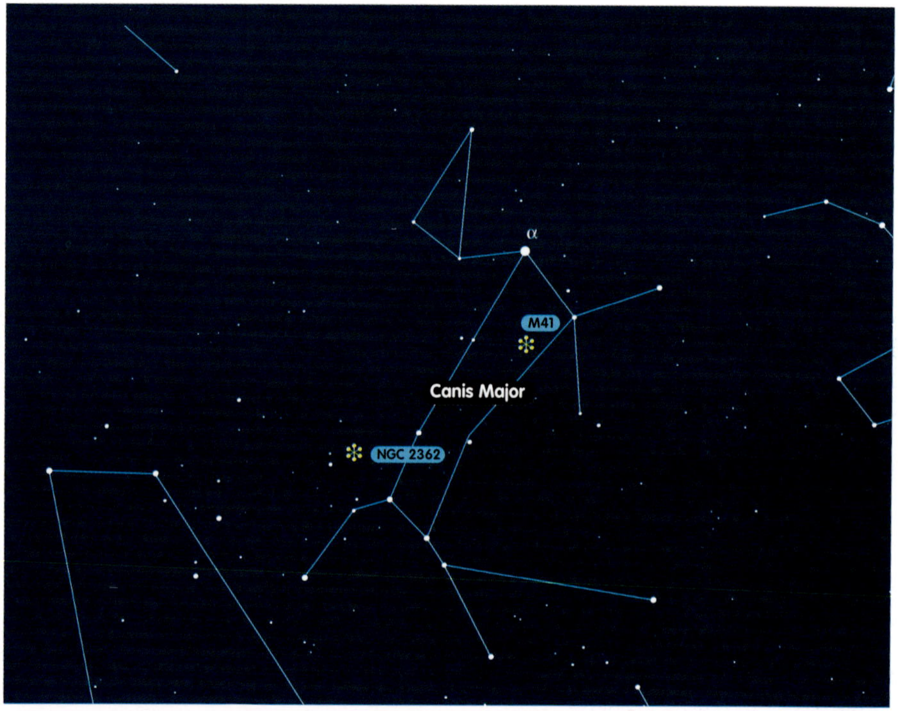

COMA BERENICES

Berenice's Hair contains a scattering of faint stars that appear as a "V" formation in binoculars. The constellation holds a lot of galaxies for amateur telescopes, part of the same cluster of galaxies that lies in the neighboring constellation of Virgo.

There are no fewer than eight members of Messier's famous catalog of deep sky objects in this tiny part of the sky. M53 is an 8th mag globular cluster for telescopes; M64 is a spiral known as the Black Eye galaxy because of the dark band of dust that crosses its center; other galaxies are M85, M88, M91, M98, M99 and M100.

A beautiful double star in the telescope is 24 Coma Berenicis, a 5th magnitude orange star with a 7th magnitude blue companion.

CAPRICORNUS

Another weird and wonderful animal is the sea goat, the smallest constellation of the Zodiac. Its pattern of stars, which more resembles a deep bowl or a laughing mouth. Its brightest star, Alpha Capricornus, is a double star that can be split with the naked eye alone. Third magnitude Beta has a 6th magnitude companion. Binoculars will show M30, an 8th magnitude globular cluster.

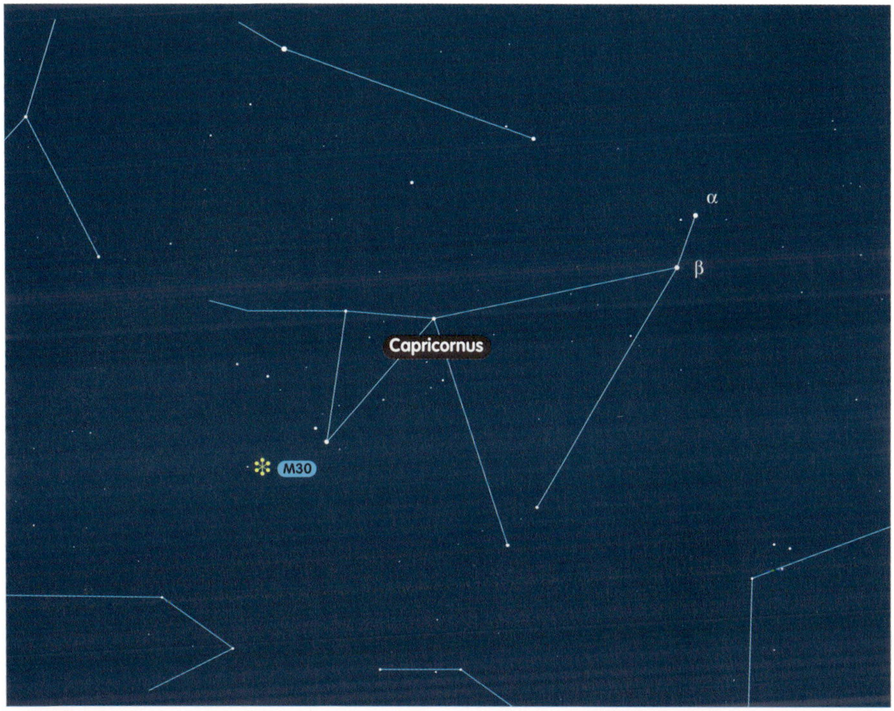

CORONA AUSTRALIS

The southern crown is a small and slightly less distinct replica of a similar crown in the northern sky (as shown on the map on p125). Gamma Coronae Australis is an attractive pair of 5th magnitude stars. A small instrument will show the globular cluster NGC 6541. Gamma, Kappa and Lambda are telescopic double stars.

CORONA BOREALIS

The northern crown is a compact and easily recognized circlet of stars with its brightest star set like a diadem (as shown on the map on p106). It is remarkable for having two variable stars which behave in exactly opposite ways. Amateurs keep an eye on R CrB, a 6th magnitude star visible in binoculars, because it suddenly dims at random intervals to as faint as 15th magnitude, when it is only visible in big telescopes. It is thought that this may be due to the star throwing off great clouds of soot that mask its light before they are blown away. T CrB is a faint 10th magnitude star that occasionally flares like a nova. It was first spotted at 2nd magnitude in 1866 and brightened again to 3rd magnitude in 1946. Keep an eye on Corona Borealis and you could be first to spot the next fade or flare by one of these stars. Fifth and 6th magnitude stars form the double Zeta.

CARINA

The name means the Keel because Carina used to be part of a vast and unwieldy constellation called Argo Navis, the ship sailed by Jason and the Argonauts in Greek legend. It is a grouping for the southern hemisphere. Its brightest star, Canopus or Alpha Carinae, appears as the second most brilliant in our skies, with only Sirius being brighter. Strangely, Carina is also home to Eta Carinae, a nova-like star embedded in a naked eye nebula. On occasions, it becomes thousands of times brighter than its usual 4th magnitude. In 1843 it briefly toppled Canopus from the No 2 spot. The Hubble Space Telescope revealed a bow tie-shaped cloud of debris ejected from Eta. A bright open cluster of stars is IC 2602. Others visible in binoculars are NGC 2602. Others visible in binoculars are NGC 2516 and NGC 3532.

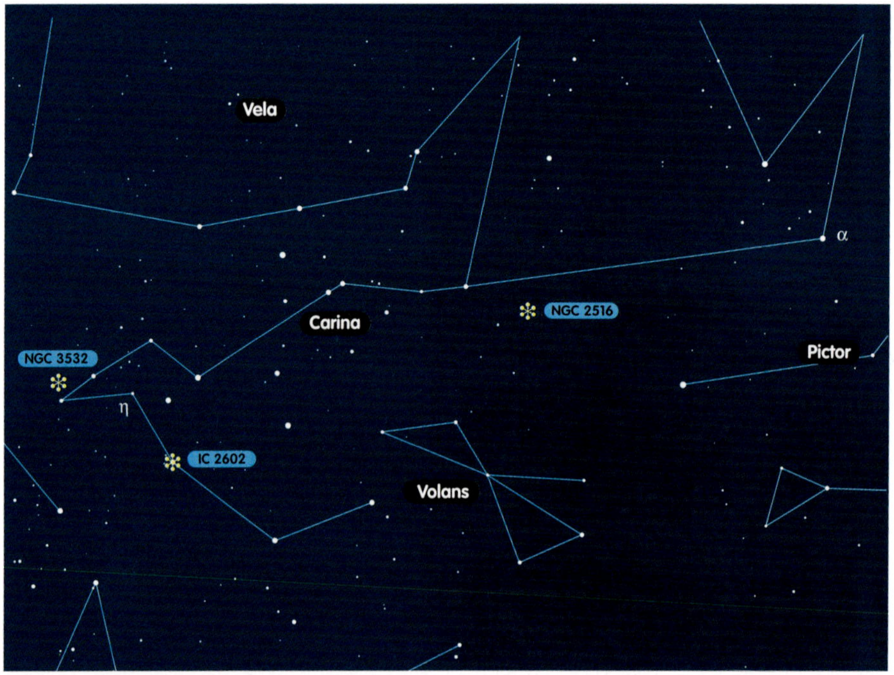

CRUX

The Southern Cross is another small patch of sky, but this time one of great interest to observers (as shown on the map on p112). It is also one of the best-known constellations, featuring on the flags of a number of countries in the southern hemisphere, including Australia and New Zealand. It lies so far south that it cannot be seen from most of the northern hemisphere. Gamma and Alpha Crucis act as pointers to the South Celestial Pole, although there is no bright star to mark its actual location. Alpha is a fine double star through a small telescope, and both stars are bright. Crux lies in the Milky Way, but close to Beta appears a large dark patch known as the Coal Sack. This is an invisible nebula that only makes its presence known to us by hiding the richness of stars that lie beyond it. Another prize that Crux holds is possibly the most beautiful star cluster in the sky, NGC 4755, or the Jewel Box.

CASSIOPEIA

The Queen in the Chair is one of the most easily recognizable star patterns in the northern sky, resembling a "W" or "M", depending on which way up it is when you view it. A compact group, that is a circumpolar constellation for much of the northern hemisphere, meaning it never sinks below the horizon. Conversely, it never rises from parts of the globe south of a -44 degree latitude. Cassiopeia lies more or less on the opposite side of the Pole Star to Ursa Major, so one will be high in the sky when the other is low over the horizon. It is a delightful part of the sky to sweep over with binoculars, being rich with stars of the Milky Way. M52 and M103 are two 7th magnitude open clusters of stars. Other pretty collections, which Messier seems to have missed, are NGC 663 and NGC 7789. The star at the center, Gamma Cassiopeiae, is a peculiar variable star prone to eruptions. It has been brightening slowly and erratically over recent decades to magnitude 2.2. Keep an eye on it: it's thought it could suddenly flare in brightness at any time. In 1572, a supernova also flared in Cassiopeia, becoming for a few months as bright as Venus. RZ Cassiopeiae is an eclipsing binary that fades from 6.4 to 7.8.

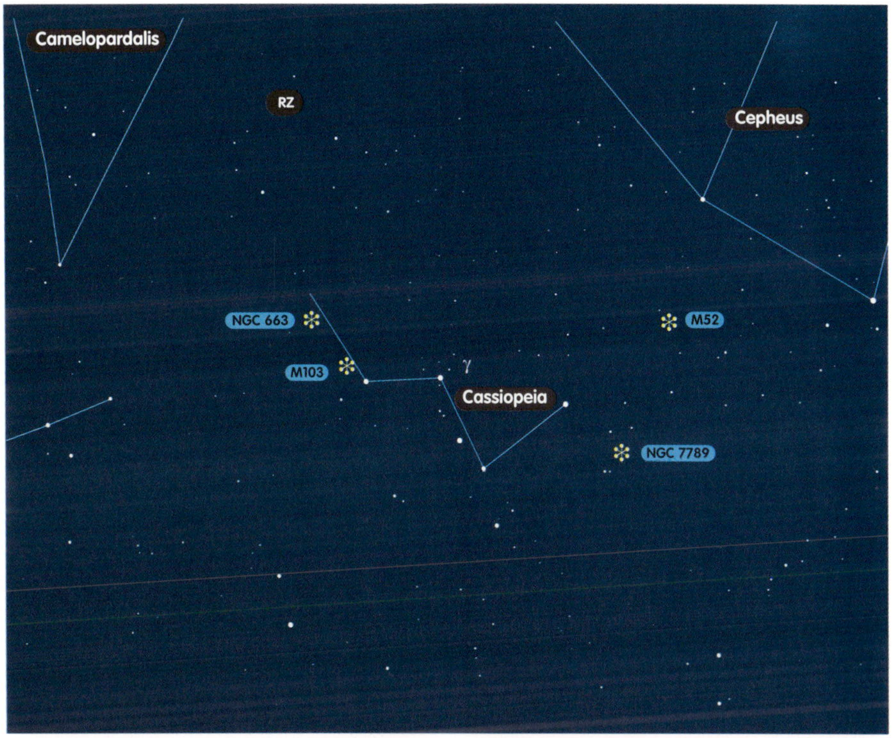

CORVUS

One more bird in the celestial aviary is the Crow, which is a tight and conspicuous pattern. A small telescope will reveal that 3rd-magnitude star Delta has a faint, 8th magnitude companion.

CRATER

This Crater represents the Cup in the heavens. There is little reason to go to this constellation as there is very little to see.

DELPHINUS

The Dolphin of the Sky is a very compact and recognizable group that looks a bit like a kite (as shown on the map on p104). It hit the astronomical headlines in 1967 when one of the most interesting novae, or exploding stars, of the 20th century flared there. There is little today of particular interest, however, although Gamma is a double star with 4th and 5th magnitude components which may be split in small telescopes.

EQUULEUS

The Baby Horse, or Foal, is also one of the smallest constellations (as shown on the map on p104). Gamma, an easy double star for binocular observers, has companions of magnitudes 4.5 and 6.

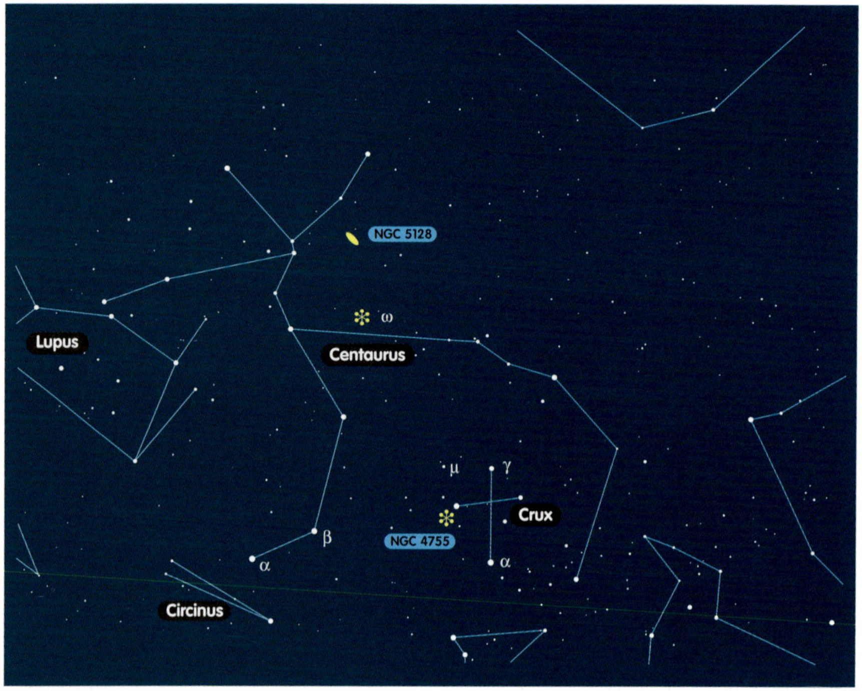

CENTAURUS

Half man, half horse, the Centaur rides deep in the southern sky. It sprawls over a large area and, includes two bright stars close together: Alpha and Beta Centauri. Alpha's claim to fame is that it is the closest star to the Sun, which helps explain why it is the third brightest star in the night sky. It is really a triple star system. Small instruments will show Alpha as two bright stars, but there is also a faint orbiting companion, Proxima Centauri, which is the nearest to us in the group. Centaurus is also where you will find the finest globular cluster in the entire sky. Despite the single star's label of Omega Centauri, it is a cloud of millions of closely-packed stars. A bright blur seen with the naked eye by southern observers, covering a larger area of the sky than the Full Moon, but binoculars and telescopes will show its full glory. Some astronomers believe Omega to be the remains of a dwarf galaxy that was absorbed by our own Milky Way. A fuzzy 7th magnitude patch visible in binoculars is a powerful broadcaster for radio telescopes. Centaurus A, also known as NGC 5128, is thought to be two colliding galaxies.

DORADO

The Swordfish is a southern constellation created in the 16th century. It is interesting as it contains a bright companion galaxy to the Milky Way within its borders. The Large Magellanic Cloud can be clearly seen as a bright blur in dark skies but lies around 180,000 light years away. Within the LMC is a remarkable nebula called the Tarantula, because it resembles a spider in photos. It looks like a fuzzy star to the naked eye. The closest supernova in recent times was spotted in the LMC in 1987. Beta is a bright Cepheid variable.

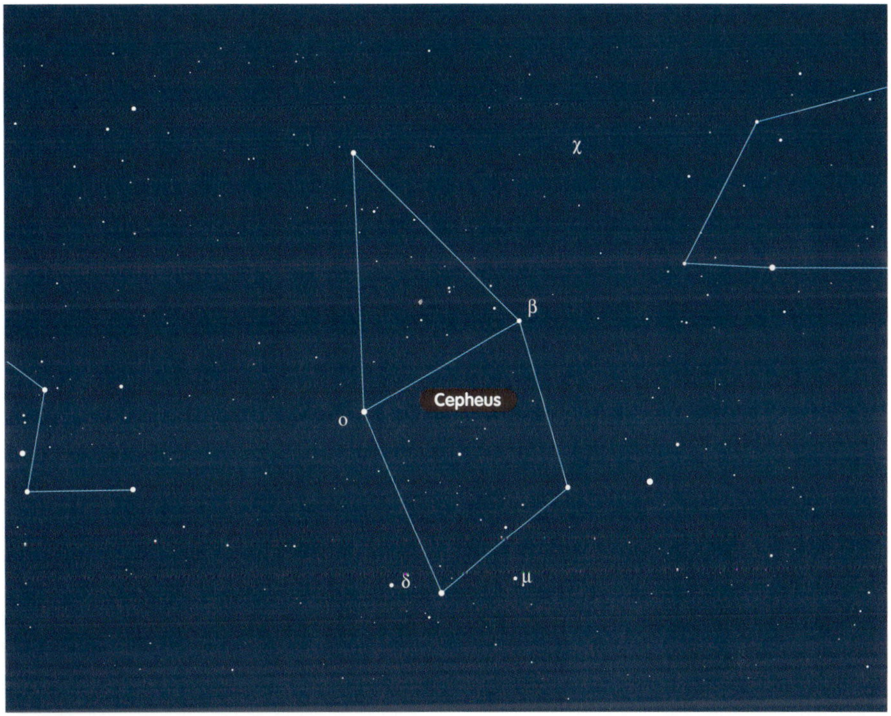

CEPHEUS

In legend, the King of Ethiopia was Cassiopeia's spouse. This constellation, bordering Cassiopeia and close to the north celestial pole, is inconspicuous because its stars are not particularly bright. However, it's not difficult to make out a house shape, and it contains some interesting stars. Perhaps the most important is Delta Cephei, which gave its name to a special type of variable star which helped give us a sense of scale in the universe. These Cepheids vary in a very regular way, and it was discovered that the time it takes one to complete one cycle or variation is directly related to its luminosity. By comparing the apparent magnitude to the real brightness, it was therefore possible to determine how far away they are. Delta Cephei's brightness varies between 3.4 and 4.3 magnitude in 5.366 days. Another naked eye variable star in Cepheus is Mu Cephei, nicknamed the Garnet Star because it is one of the reddest stars known. Binoculars will bring out this red giant's color and will help to monitor the irregular pattern of changes in brightness, ranging from 3.6 to 5.1 magnitude. U Cephei is an eclipsing variable fading from 6.6 to 9.3. Interesting double stars are Beta, Delta, Xi and Omicron.

DRACO

We are back in the northern hemisphere for this snake-like pattern named the Dragon. The four stars that form the beast's head are not difficult to find, but it is out of reach for much of the southern hemisphere.

Nu Draconis is a splendid double star in binoculars, both stars being white and of 5th magnitude. Other interesting multiple-star targets are the doubles Omicron and Psi, plus the triple systems 16-17 and 40-41.

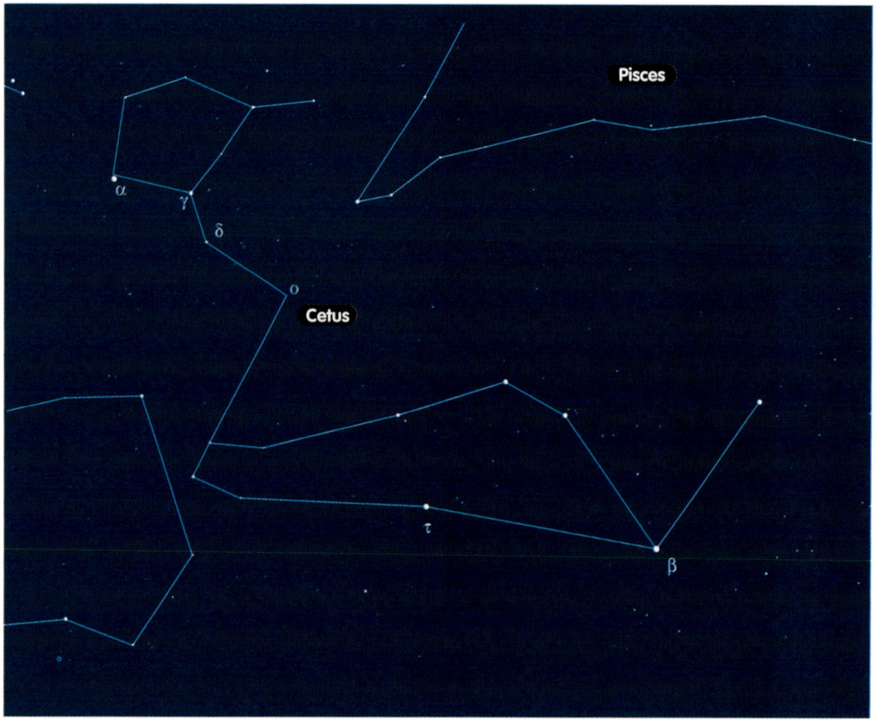

CETUS

It's not impossible to see the shape of a whale in the Sea Monster, although traditionally its head was supposed to be the tail and vice versa. The bright star Beta makes a very fine whale's snout and a little close pattern of stars below Aries form a realistic tail. Three of these stars – Alpha, Gamma and Delta – also form a pattern very like Aries, so be careful you don't mistake them. Cetus contains two stars of particular interest. The first is Omicron Ceti, which has the nickname Mira, meaning "the wonderful", as it undergoes an extreme change in brightness every year. Usually its range is from 3rd or 4th magnitude at its brightest, to between 8th and 10th at its faintest, in a period of 331 days. But sometimes it becomes really bright, as in March 2007 when it reached 2.2 magnitude. The second, Tau Ceti is a star only moderately bright in the whale's belly. But it is interesting because it is similar to our Sun, if slightly smaller, and lies just 11.68 light years away from us. To the disappointment of professional astronomers, no planets have yet been detected, although we know it is surrounded by a disk of dust and debris. Alpha and Gamma Ceti are double stars.

CYGNUS

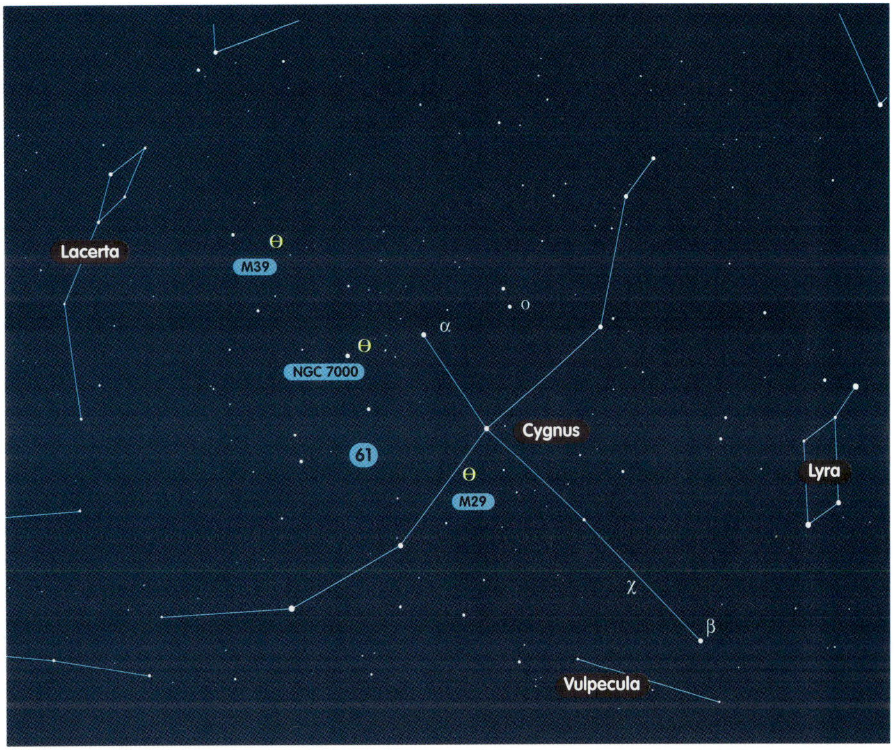

The Swan is often known as the Northern Cross. It is far bigger than its southern rival and for once it's not difficult to imagine this as a bird in flight with a long neck and outstretched wings. It lies in the Milky Way and, as a result, contains a lot within its boundaries that will appeal to the astronomer. Cygnus's brightest star, Alpha Cygni (also known as Deneb) is one of the galaxy's most luminous stars. It is one of the three bright stars which make up the unofficial pattern of the Summer Triangle. At the other end of the longer bar of the cross is Beta Cygni, otherwise known as Albireo. This is one of the most beautiful double stars in the sky, with a bright 3rd magnitude yellow star joined by a 5th magnitude blue companion. The contrasting colors are splendid to see, even in binoculars. Fourth magnitude Omicron has a 5th magnitude companion. One of Cygnus's fainter naked eye stars, 61 Cygni, is another binary system and is interesting because it is one of the closest stars to our own Sun, lying just 11 light years away. It has the distinction of being the first star to have its distance measured by parallax. This technique involves observing a close star's position against distant background stars from points on opposite sides of the Earth's orbit, a long enough baseline to reveal a tiny but detectable difference. It is believed that 61 Cygni might be a star that has planets. Chi Cygni is a long period variable star, like Mira. It can reach 4th magnitude at brightest but becomes as faint as 12th magnitude with a period of 407 days. Professional astronomers are interested in an intense source of X-rays called Cygnus X-1. This is thought to be a black hole, the first to be identified. Binoculars will reveal a bright patch close to Deneb that has been dubbed North America Nebula, because its shape vaguely resembles that continent. In truly clear and dark conditions, it may be seen with the naked eye.

FORNAX

There is little to see in this constellation of the southern sky. The brightest star, Alpha, can only manage 4th magnitude but those with a decent telescope may appreciate its 6th magnitude partner.

GRUS

The Crane is yet another bird let loose in the heavens, but its flight is one for southern observers. There are two double stars visible with the naked eye. Delta Gruis is a pair of 4th magnitude stars and Mu has two stars of 5th magnitude.

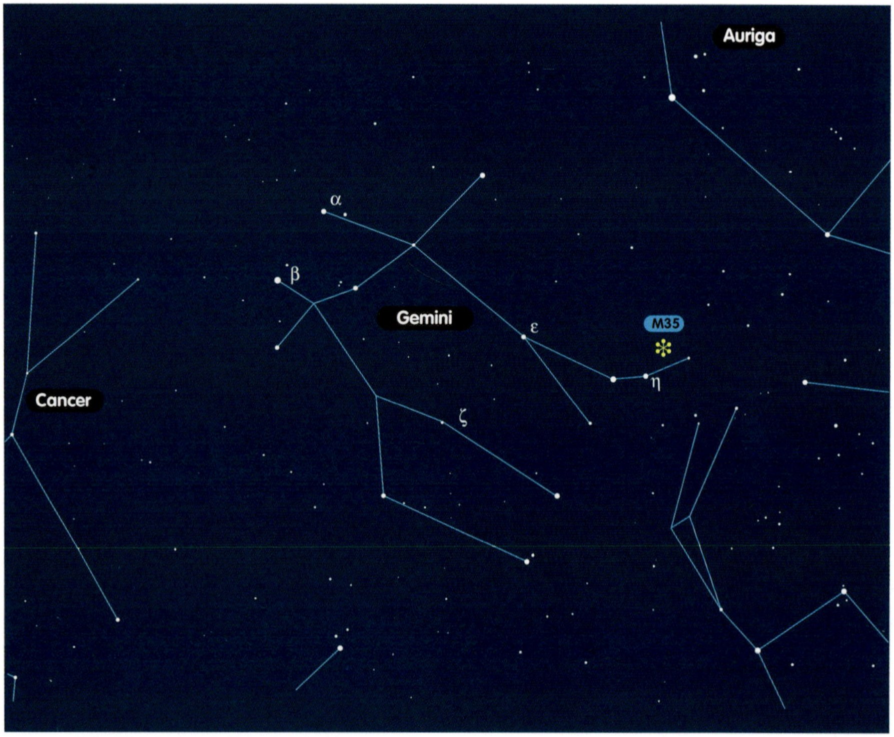

GEMINI

The Twins are part of the Zodiac and, with two strikingly bright stars called Castor (also known as Alpha) and Pollux (also known as Beta), offer a variety of interesting objects to observe. The two main stars also form part of the Big G described earlier. A small telescope will show magnitude 1.6 Castor as a close pair of bright stars of 2nd and 3rd magnitude. There are actually six stars in Castor's system. Eta Geminorum is a particularly interesting bright variable. Usually its brightness ranges from around 3.1 to 3.5, but the star is also eclipsed by an invisible companion just over every eight years, so that it can dim to around magnitude 3.9. Another variable star is Zeta Gem, which varies by only four tenths of a magnitude in 10.2 days. A fine sight in binoculars is the fuzzy patch that is the star cluster M35. A telescope will reveal the stars within it. Gemini is also the source of the radiant of one of the year's strongest meteor showers. The Geminids might be better known if they did not occur in midwinter for northern latitudes. A night's viewing could be rewarded by the sight of several bright meteors in a matter of minutes.

HERCULES

The hero of Greek legend stands proud with his club held high in this prominent northern constellation. Hercules's torso is drawn fairly clearly by four stars. Between the two at top right, Eta and Theta, can be found a bright blur that is M13, the finest globular cluster in the northern sky. It contains around 300,000 stars and is easy to pick out in binoculars and any telescope. M92 is another globular cluster for binoculars in Hercules, that is rather unfairly overlooked because of its brighter rival. Alpha Herculis is a naked eye variable star. This red giant's brightness ranges between magnitudes 3 and 4 in a fairly unpredictable fashion. Double stars include Rho, Kappa and 95 Herculis.

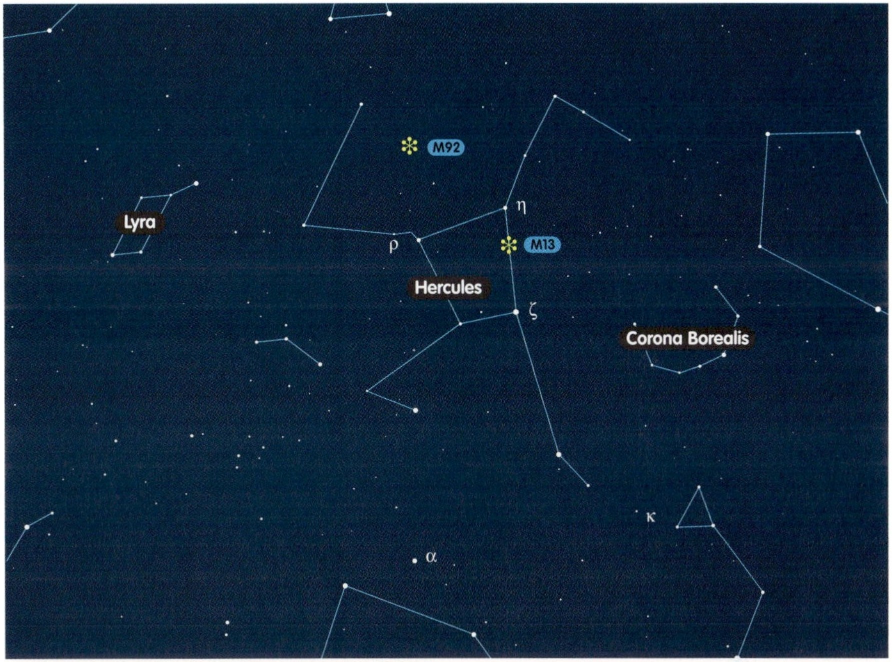

HOROLOGIUM

The Pendulum Clock is a relatively modern constellation created in the southern sky by Lacaille in the 18th century. Binocular users may watch the red semi-regular variable TW Horologii change its brightness between magnitudes 5 and 6. A telescope will be needed to follow R Horologii through its 400-day cycle.

HYDRA

The Water Snake is an inconspicuous constellation that is also the largest in the sky. Only its brightest star, Alphard, is brighter than magnitude 3. The constellation contains three Messier objects: M48 is a cluster of around 80 stars that can be seen in binoculars; M68 is a small globular cluster of 8th magnitude; and M83 is a fine spiral galaxy viewed in all its glory from above. Look, too, for the planetary nebula NGC 3242. Small telescopes will show the double stars 27 Hydrae, 54 Hydrae and I Hydrae.

LEO

This is a constellation that resembles the lion it represents. A backward question mark represents the head and a triangle of stars the haunches of the king of the jungle. Leo is part of the Zodiac through which the Sun travels.There are several galaxies including the spirals M65 and M66 for small telescopes. Fainter spirals are M95 and M96. M105 is a faint elliptical galaxy that is challenging to find. An interesting variable star is R Leonis, which fades from 5th to 10th magnitude with a period of around 310 days.

Double star observers may enjoy spotting Gamma, which shows 2nd and 3rd magnitude companions in a telescope. Zeta is revealed to be three unrelated stars in the same line of sight when checked out with binoculars. Orange star Tau Leonis is visible in binoculars, showing a 5th magnitude star with a 7th magnitude companion. Leo is also home of the Leonid meteor shower which has produced some spectacular storms in the past.

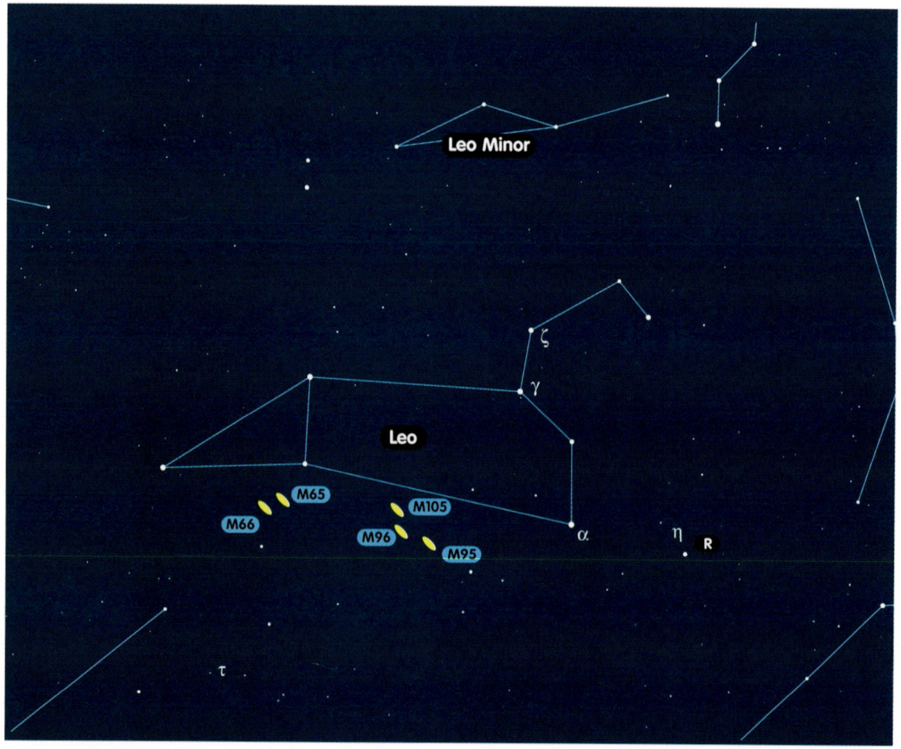

LEO MINOR

The Lion Cub sits above its mighty adult relative, . Unfortunately, there is nothing of interest to view within this small grouping.

INDUS

This constellation was created in the late 16th century to represent the American Indian. There is little to observe save for the double star Theta Indi, which may be split by small telescopes into 5th and 7th magnitude companions.

HYDRUS

There is a second southern Water Snake in the heavens. The only target within it of minor interest is the double star Pi Hydrae, two 5th magnitude stars that may be viewed with binoculars or even the naked eye.

LYRA

The Lyre, an ancient form of the harp, is a striking little pattern that is easy to locate. A major reason is that its main star, Vega (Alpha), is one of the brightest in the sky. It is the brightest, too, of the three stars that make up the Summer Triangle, together with Deneb in Cygnus and Altair in Aquila. Delta is a double star. A magnitude 6 blue star is accompanied by a red giant star that fluctuates between magnitudes 4 and 5.

Epsilon is the best-known multiple star system in the heavens. The keen-sighted will spot two 5th magnitude stars close together, but a telescope will reveal each to be formed of two stars.

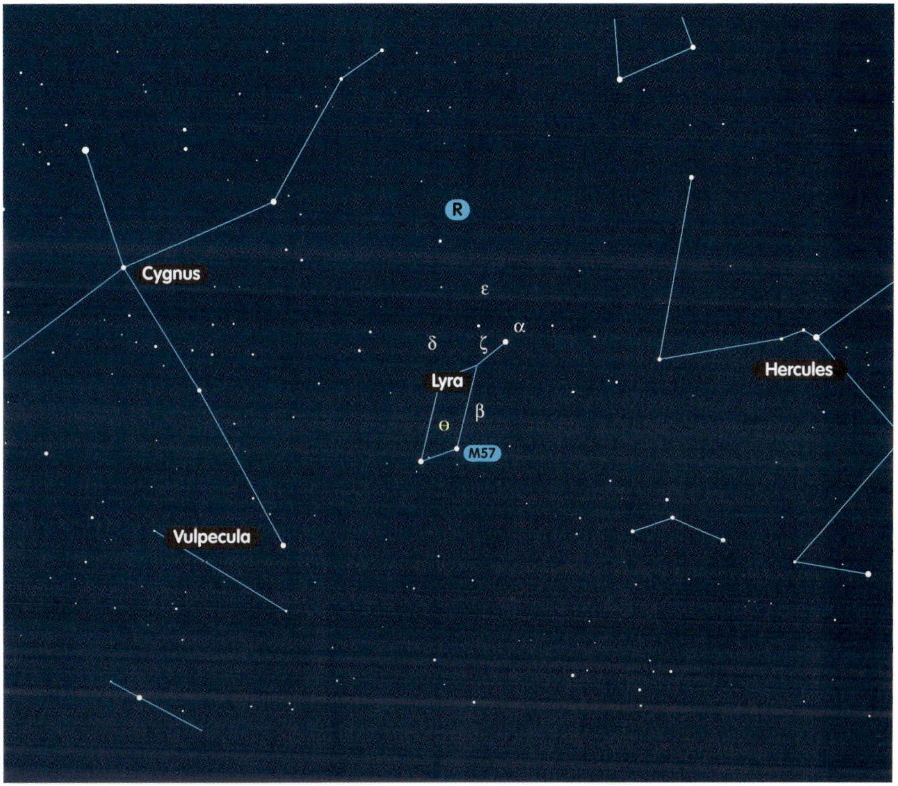

Look at Zeta in binoculars to find another double, this time with components of magnitudes 4 and 6. Beta Lyrae is the best-known member of a class of variable star, the bright eclipsing variables. Both components of this system are bright and they orbit each other so closely that they are egg-shaped and almost touching. This results in a constant brightness exchange as the stars dance around each other, varying between magnitude 3.4 and 4.3 in a little under 13 days. You won't be able to see these two stars individually, but a small telescope will reveal another 8th magnitude blue companion plus two other 9th magnitude stars close by R Lyrae is a semi-regular variable that fluctuates between 3.9 and 5.

There is a further challenge in Lyra – the famous Ring Nebula, M57. This is easy enough to locate, midway between the lower two stars in Lyra's diamond, but you need transparent skies and a powerful telescope to make out very much.The radiant of the Lyrids, a meteor show active in April, lies in this constellation.

ERIDANUS

Fittingly for a constellation named the River, this star grouping meanders a long way across the sky from its "source" Alpha, a bright star that lies too far south to be seen from many northern countries.

The other end of this cosmic waterway is right up alongside the stars of Orion and visible throughout the world.

Epsilon Eridani, clearly visible at magnitude 3.7, is another star of great interest to those hunting for planets, as it lies only 10.7 light years away and is of a similar type to the Sun. Star Trek fans will recognize it as Mr Spock's home star, around which Vulcan supposedly revolved. Small telescopes will split the double stars Theta and 32 Eridani. Also look for the 9th magnitude planetary nebula NGC 1535.

LACERTA

The Lizard is one of the sky's least interesting constellations. It lacks anything worth viewing for an observer with only a small telescope.

LIBRA

The Scales are a constellation of the Zodiac. Alpha, a 3rd magnitude star with a 5th magnitude companion, rejoices in the splendid name Zubenelgenubi.

Iota Librae can be seen through a telescope to have three companions. Some say Beta Librae looks decidedly green – you should check for yourself. Delta Librae is an Algol-type eclipsing binary star with a range from 4.8 to 5.9.

LUPUS

Another member of the celestial menagerie is the Wolf. Telescopes will be needed to tackle its horde of double stars: Epsilon Lupi (mags 3 and 9), Kappa (4 and 6), Mu (4 and 7), Xi (5 and 6) and Pi (a 5th magnitude pair).

Binoculars will show the large star cluster NGC 5822.

LEPUS

The Hare is found directly beneath the feet of Orion the Hunter. It is not striking but there are treasures to be found. Gamma Leporis is an easy binocular double star with a yellow 4th magnitude star and an orange 6th magnitude companion.

Another interesting star is the variable R Leporis, a deeply red star that fades from 6th to 10th magnitude with a cycle of 430 days. It is nicknamed Hind's Crimson star after a 19th century observer who noted its intense hue.

Small telescopes will reveal M79, an 8th magnitude globular cluster. Nearby is a group of five stars in one system that form the cluster NGC 2017.

LYNX

The Lynx is the most inconspicuous constellation. Small telescopes will reveal that 5 Lyncis is an orange star of 5th magnitude with an 8th mag partner.

12 Lyncis is a bluish star, also of 5th magnitude, with companions of 6th and 8th magnitude.

ORION

The Hunter is perhaps the best known of the constellations, and because he stands across the Celestial Equator, he can be seen from all parts of the world.

Orion contains some fascinating objects for the amateur astronomer. Alpha Orionis, or Betelgeuse, on the Hunter's left shoulder, is a red giant star, 427 light years away, that varies erratically in brightness between magnitude 0.4 and 1.3. Some believe it could be on the verge of becoming a supernova within the next 1,000 years. If it does, it will be bright enough to be seen in daylight for several months.

Beta Orionis, or Rigel, is a brilliant, blue-white star shining at magnitude 0.1 – compare its color with that of Betelgeuse. It is also a luminous supergiant nearly 48,000 times brighter than our Sun and lying 900 light years away. Double stars include Delta (mags 2 and 7), Zeta (2 and 4), Iota (3 and 7), Lambda (4 and 6) and Sigma (4 and 7). Theta is actually a wide and complex pair of stars that can be found in.

Orion's most famous feature – the Great Orion Nebula, a bright celestial nursery of

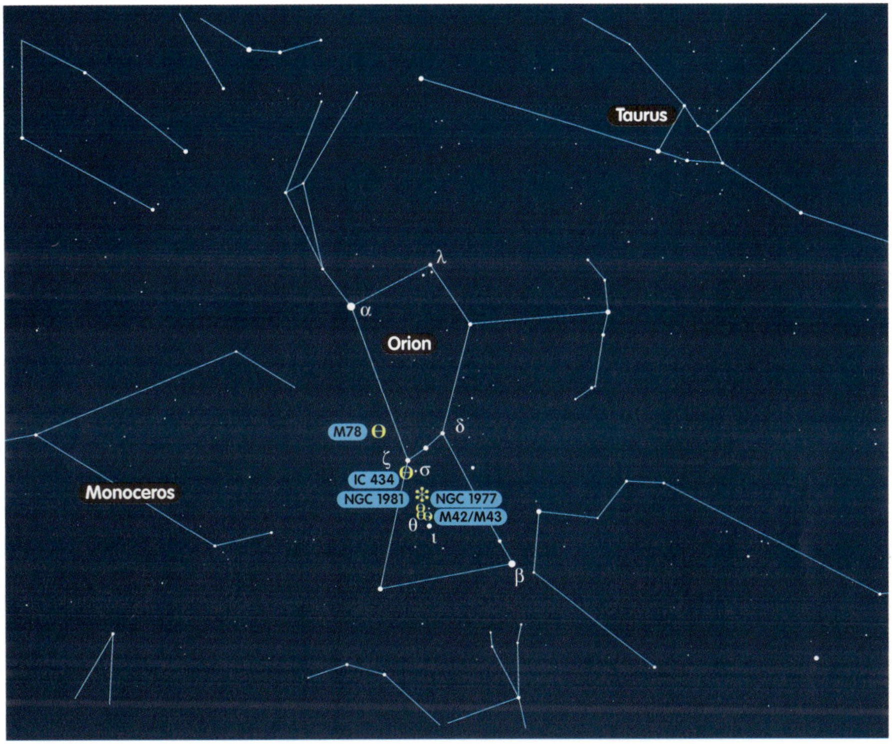

newborn stars and one of the outstanding sights in the sky. Theta1 is a pattern of four of these infant stars that are illuminating the nebula, which was given two labels by Messier, M42 and M43, for its two brighter regions. Fainter stars may be seen in larger telescopes. More wisps of nebulosity, labeled NGC 1977, can be seen just to the north in small telescopes. Another nebula, IC 434, close to Zeta Orionis, is famed for a dark silhouette that resembles a chess piece. However, the Horsehead Nebula is virtually impossible to spot in amateur telescopes. For binoculars, there is an open star cluster NGC 1981. The Orionids are a strong meteor shower visible in October that are the product of debris from Halley's Comet.

PEGASUS

The Winged Horse is mainly seen as an easily recognized Great Square rather than an animal, although the four stars of that square include one that was awarded in the last century to neighboring Andromeda.

The bright magnitude 2 star Epsilon Pegasi has a 9th magnitude star visible in small telescopes. A variable star worth watching is Beta Pegasi, which fluctuates erratically between magnitudes 2 and 3.

Binoculars or a small telescope are enough to spot the splendid 6th magnitude globular cluster M15.

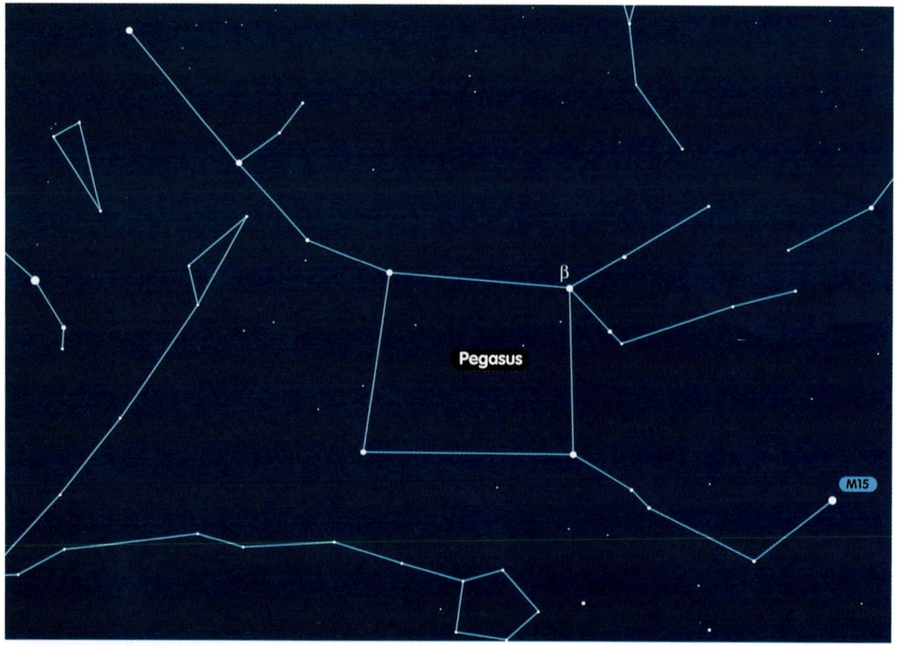

OCTANS

You can't get further south than the Octant. Invented by Lacaille, it is the constellation containing and centered on the South Celestial Pole. There is no bright Pole Star to mark it, unlike Polaris in the north, but the faint mag 5.5 star Sigma is actually closer to its pole than is its northern equivalent. The only other object of interest is Lambda Octantis, a double star with 5th magnitude yellow and 8th magnitude white companions.

OPHIUCHUS

The Serpent Bearer straddles the Celestial Equator. It is rich with deep sky gems, containing seven objects from Messier's catalog. M9, M10, M12, M14, M19, M62 and M107 are all globular clusters for binoculars or small telescopes. An open cluster for binoculars, lying close to Beta Ophiuchi, is IC 4665. The most interesting object in Ophiuchus is Barnard's Star, which a small telescope will show shining at magnitude 9.5. Lying a little under six light years from us, its motion across the sky is easily detectable over a relatively short time.

PICTOR

The Painter's Easel is, unfortunately, an empty canvas when it comes to targets for the amateur astronomer.

PHOENIX

The Phoenix is the most unusual of the birds flying the heavens, being the one that rose from the ashes.

A challenge for small telescopes is the close pair of 4th magnitude stars Beta Phoenicis. Another double, Zeta, is a 4th magnitude eclipsing binary with an 8th magnitude companion.

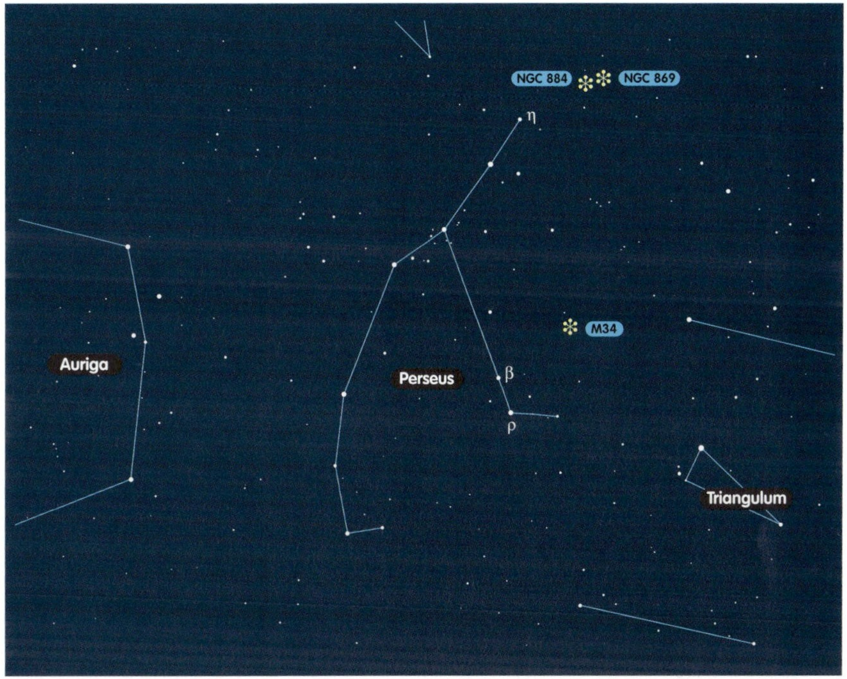

PERSEUS

The Greek hero of legend is another of the sky's characters. It lies in the Milky Way and is a constellation with many interesting objects. Check out Eta Persei, with a small telescope, to discern an orange 4th magnitude star with a blue 9th magnitude companion. There are two interesting variable stars in Perseus, both visible with the naked eye and coincidentally lying close together. Beta Persei is Algol, the prototype of the dark eclipsing variables. These are twin stars, one small and bright, one large and dim, close together and orbiting in our line of sight. When the dark star passes in front of the bright one, the light from the combined pair fades from 2.2 to 3.5. The eclipses happen every two days, 21 hours.

Rho Persei is a totally different type, a red giant, semi-regular variable, with a range from magnitude 3.3 to 4. The jewels in Perseus's crown are its famous Double Cluster, NGC 869 and NGC 884. Binoculars are enough to show these rich concentrations of stars, but in small telescopes they sparkle like diamonds.

Another bright cluster is M34. The Perseid meteor shower in August is one of the strongest for northern hemisphere observers, with a rate of 100 an hour under ideal conditions.

PISCES

A forked pattern represents the two Fishes, an inconspicuous but important constellation in the Zodiac because it contains the point where the Ecliptic crosses the Celestial Equator. This is the point where the Sun passes at the time of the vernal equinox in March.

Easy double stars in small telescopes are Zeta Piscium (magnitudes 5 and 6), Rho (both 5th magnitude) and Psi1 (both 5th magnitude). A bright binocular variable is TX Piscium, a red giant that varies from 5th to 6th magnitude. M74, an unimpressive faint blur in small telescopes, shows itself as a fine spiral galaxy in professional photographs.

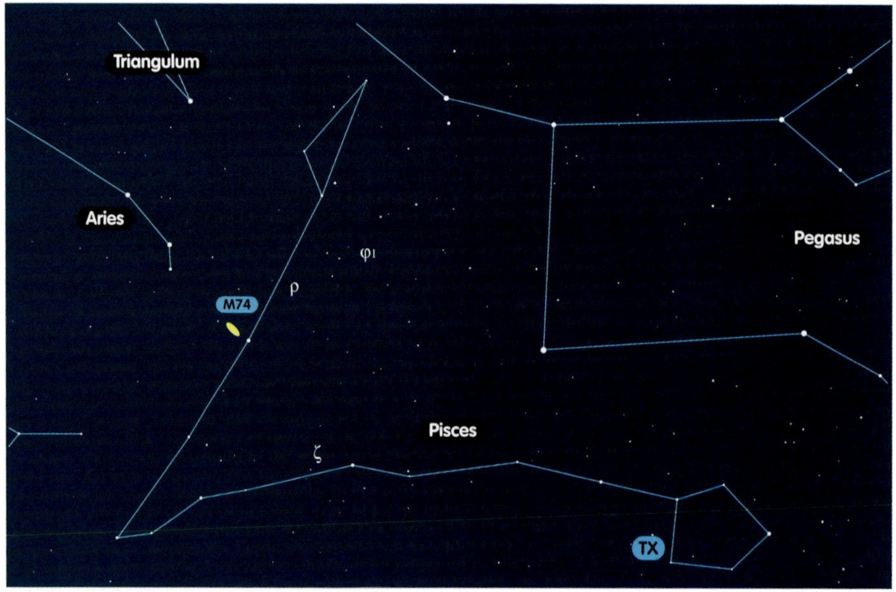

PISCIS AUSTRINUS

Another fish swims among the southern stars. Though hardly prominent, it does have one very bright star, 1st magnitude Fomalhaut. Small telescopes will separate the 4th magnitude star Beta from an 8th magnitude star close by.

PUPPIS

This represents the stern of the former huge constellation of Argo Navis. It lies in the Milky Way and its attractive offerings include the double stars Xi Puppis, a 3rd magnitude yellow star with an orange 5th magnitude companion, and k Puppis, twin 4th magnitude stars.

Two variable stars are L2 Puppis, a red giant varying between magnitudes 3 and 6, and V Puppis, an eclip-sing binary rang-ing between magnitudes 4.5 and 5.1. Fine star clusters for binoculars are M47 and NGC 2451.

SCULPTOR

The Sculptor is in the southern sky . An interesting star for binocular users is the red giant R Sculptoris, with a range from magnitude 5.8 to 7.7. There are two galaxies for small telescopes: the edge-on spiral NGC 55 and NGC 253.

SAGITTARIUS

The Zodiacal constellation of the Archer actually looks like a teapot. It's a treasure trove of interesting objects for observers.

For double star observers, there is Beta Sagitarii, two stars that can be split by the naked eye. The more northerly star has a 7th magnitude partner. Two Cepheid variables are W Sagittarii, with a magnitude range from 4.3 and 5, plus X Sagittarii, fluctuating between magnitude 4.3 and 4.9.

There are no less than 15 Messier deep sky objects in Sagittarius. M8 is the Lagoon Nebula, a large, naked eye gas cloud shining at 5th magnitude. It contains a cluster of stars, NGC 6530, that can be viewed in binoculars.

Another blur for binoculars is the nebula M17. M18 is an 8th magnitude open cluster. M20 is the Trifid Nebula, a gas cloud with dark, dusty patterns that can only be made out with large amateur telescopes. M21 is a star cluster that lies in the same region. M22, M28, M54, M55, M69, M70 and M75 are globular clusters of magnitude 6.5, 8.5, 8.5, 7, 9, 9 and 9.5. M23 and M25 are bright open clusters while M24 is a dense cloud of stars in the Milky Way.

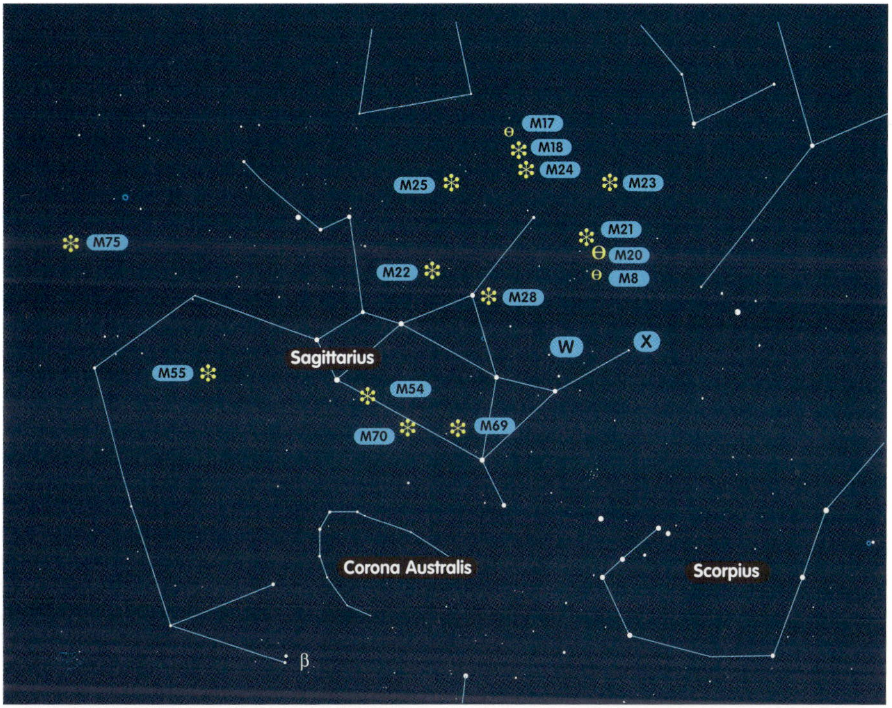

PYXIS

A further part of the defunct Argo Navis, that offers little of interest for amateur astronomers.

At rare intervals, a 14th magnitude star, T Pyxidis, flares like a nova to around 6th magnitude.

RETICULUM

The Net is another tiny and obscure southern constellation. Binoculars will clearly show Zeta Reticuli, a pair of yellow, 5th magnitude stars.

SCORPIUS

Also in the Zodiac is the Scorpion. The curve of its stars make it closely resemble the creature that it represents, right down to the sting in the tail. Its brightest star, Antares (Alpha), has a name that translates as "the Rival of Mars", because its red color compares with that planet when it passes through the area. With a large enough telescope, you might spot Antares' blue 6th magnitude companion. Scorpius is another Zodiacal treasure chest, although its position favors more southerly observers. Beta Scorpii is a good double star target for small telescopes, with 3rd and 5th magnitude companions. Zeta is a 4th and 5th magnitude pair that can be split with the naked eye, but the stars are not really related. Also unrelated are the two stars marking Omega. Mu shows two bluish stars of 3rd and 4th magnitude.

Turn a small telescope on Xi to find a system of four stars, of magnitudes 4, 7, 7 and 8. Keep an eye on Delta up near the Scorpion's head, because it unexpectedly brightened by around half a magnitude in recent years. This is thought to be due to eruptions of gas from the star.

There are four objects from Messier's catalog: M4 and M80 are globular clusters for binoculars or small telescopes, while M6 and M7 are fine open star clusters.

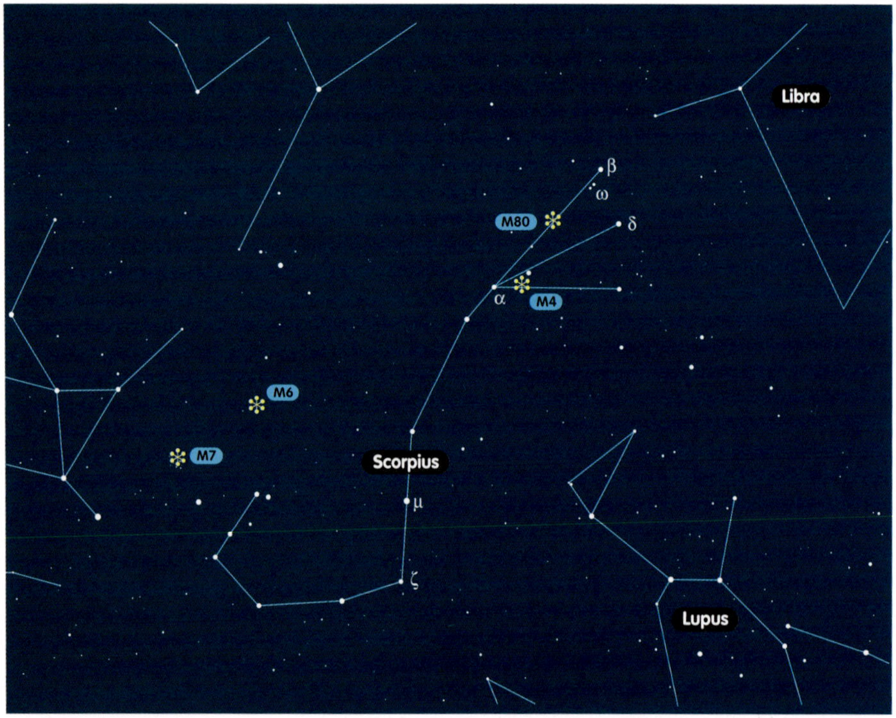

SCUTUM

The Shield is a tiny but rewarding constellation close to the Celestial Equator. The Milky Way passes through it, presenting some fine sweeping for binoculars. R Scuti is a yellow giant variable star that may be followed in brightness between 5th and 8th magnitudes.

M11 is a splendid scattering of stars for small telescopes and even binoculars, with the nickname the Wild Duck Cluster. M26 is a less spectacular open cluster.

MICROSCOPIUM

The Microscope is another in conspicuous southern constellation, created in the 18th century by Lacaille. It is devoid of interest.

PAVO

Another bird, the Peacock, looks a lot less dazzling than its real-life cousin in this constellation of the far south. Variable star observers can follow Kappa Pavonis, which ranges between mag 3.9 and 4.8 in just over nine days. There is also a 7th magnitude globular cluster, NGC 6752, visible in binoculars.

MENSA

The Table Mountain, a "modern" 18th century constellation, lies to the far south. There is little to see in this grouping of stars, although it does include a small part of the Large Magellanic Cloud, a satellite galaxy of our Milky Way.

MUSCA

The Fly buzzes far in the southern sky and Crux is its neighbor. Telescopes reveal that the bluish, 3rd magnitude star Beta Muscae is formed of two close 4th magnitude companions.Theta is another double with 5th and 7th magnitude components.

NORMA

The Set Square has two true double stars, Epsilon and Iota Normae, for telescopes. Each comprises a 5th magnitude star with an 8th magnitude companion. Gamma appears double and is easy to split with the naked eye, but the 4th and 5th magnitude yellow stars are really not connected.

Binoculars will show one large star cluster, NGC 6087. It is formed from more than 30 stars including a Cepheid variable, S Normae, shining at around 6th magnitude.

MONOCEROS

The unicorn lies pinned between two heavenly dogs – Canis Major and Canis Minor – and straddles the Celestial Equator. It is not easy to spot, with attention being grabbed by its neighbors, including Gemini and Orion.

Despite its feeble appearance, there is much to see within it. Stars with partners include the fine Beta Monocerotis, a group of three bluish suns of 4th, 5th and 6th magnitude. Binoculars show that 4th-magnitude Delta appears to have a companion a magnitude fainter, but they just happen to lie closely in line.

For another genuine double, check out Epsilon, where a yellow 4th magnitude star contrasts with a blue 7th magnitude star. Binoculars will also bring into view a number of star clusters, including M50, NGC 2232, NGC 2244 and NGC 2264. The infant stars of NGC 2244 are surrounded by the remnants of their birth, the gas of the Rosette Nebula. A bright but unrelated star, 12 Monocerotis, lies in front of the cluster. One of the stars in the cluster NGC 2264 is an irregular variable star with a range between magnitudes 4 and 5.

TAURUS

The Bull is a prominent constellation of the Zodiac, pictured making a charge at neighbor Orion. It contains two striking star clusters, the Hyades and the Pleiades. The Hyades are spread out in a "V" shape that represents the Bull's head. The constellation's brightest star, 1st magnitude Aldebaran (Alpha), appears at one end of this "V" but is really at half the distance of the cluster which lies 150 light years away from us. Nearby M45, the Pleiades, is the most spectacular open cluster in the heavens. It was nicknamed the Seven Sisters – see how many you can count with the naked eye – but telescopes will reveal dozens more stars. Long-exposure photos show the young stars embedded in wisps of nebulosity. Double stars for binoculars include Theta (3rd and 4th magnitude) in the Hyades, Kappa (4th and 5th) and Sigma (both 5th). An interesting variable star is Lambda, an eclipsing binary with a cycle between magnitudes 3.4 and 4.1. Also in Taurus is the first object in Messier's catalog, M1, the remains of a supernova blast in 1054. It is nicknamed the Crab Nebula from the shape of its filaments of gas, but small telescopes will reveal only a tiny hazy patch.

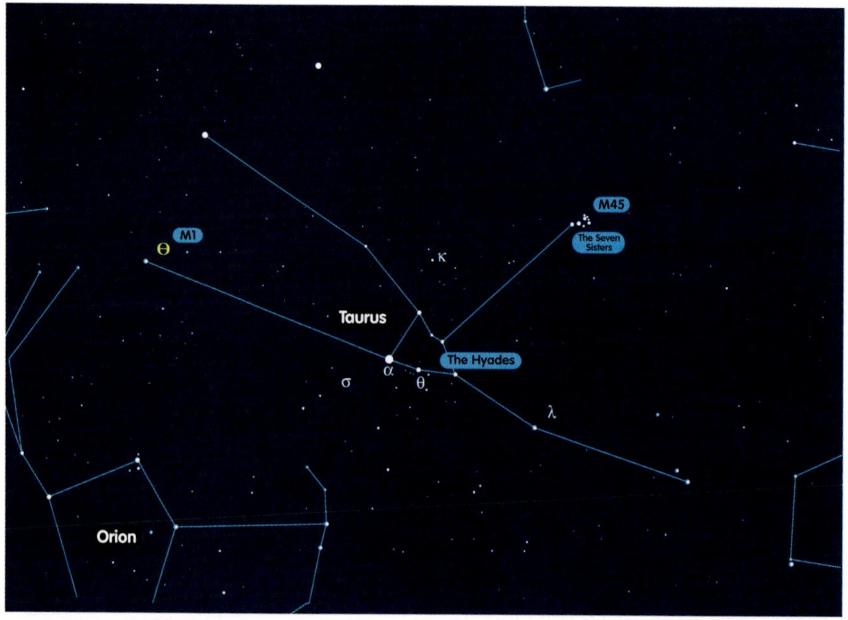

TELESCOPIUM

The Triangle is a compact group between Andromeda and Aries (as shown on the map on p102). It holds one treasure, M33, nicknamed the Pinwheel Galaxy. This is a large and faint member of our local group of galaxies, which can make it a challenge to find in telescopes. However, if the sky is clear and dark, it may be seen with the naked eye.

TRIANGULUM

Disappointingly for a pattern named after the telescope, there is nothing worth viewing in this southern group created by Lacaille.

URSA MAJOR

The Great Bear is one of the best-known constellations, with its seven main stars also dubbed the Plough and the Big Dipper.

Bayer generally awarded Greek letters to stars in order of brightness, but obviously found that too much trouble here and, instead, gave the first seven in the order they lined up. Alpha and Beta Ursae Majoris are also known as the Pointers, because they indicate the direction of the Pole Star. Zeta, also known as Mizar, can be seen with keen eyes to have a 4th magnitude companion, Alcor. Small telescopes will reveal a 4th magnitude star between them. Although you can't separate them, both Mizar and Alcor have been found to be close binary stars too.

There are some great galaxies for observers. M81 and M82 are a close pair in binoculars, one a spiral and one cigar-shaped. M101 is seen as a face-on spiral in photos. M108 and M109 are two fainter spirals. M97 is the Owl Nebula, a planetary nebula for telescopes. Ursa Major is also the source of the Ursids, a meteor shower visible in late December.

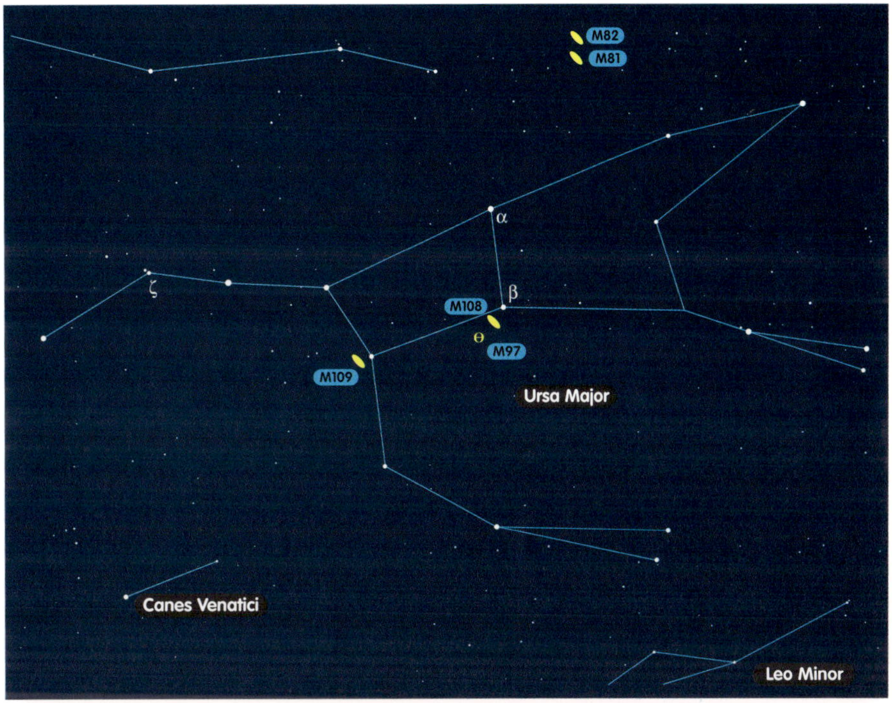

TUCANA

The Toucan would not be very interesting if it was not for the presence of a bright satellite galaxy called the Small Magellanic Cloud and 47 Tucanae, the second best globular cluster in the sky. This can be seen with the naked eye. Sadly, both are hidden from much of the northern hemisphere.

The Small Magellanic Cloud lies 200,000 light years away and contains hundreds of millions of stars. It appears as a bright patch of mist to the naked eye but is fascinating to sweep with binoculars. Beta Tucanae is a 4th and 5th magnitude double star in binoculars, but a telescope reveals that the brighter star has actually two components.

URSA MINOR

The Little Bear wraps itself around the North Celestial Pole. Second magnitude Alpha Ursae Minoris, known as Polaris or the Pole Star, actually lies a degree from the Pole. It has a 9th magnitude companion in small telescopes.

Gamma is 3rd magnitude but keen eyes will spot a 5th magnitude star close by. They are not related.

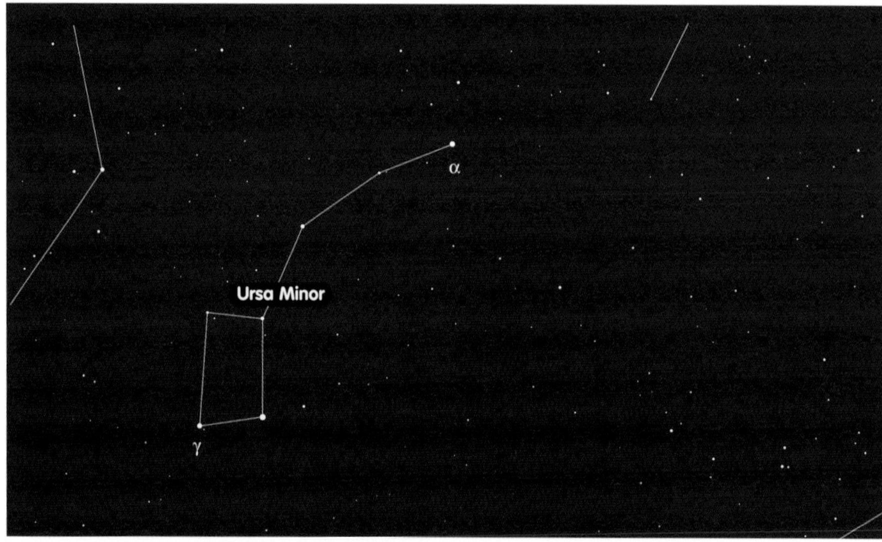

SERPENS

The Serpent is the only constellation to come in two sections: a head (Serpens Caput) and tail (Serpens Cauda) on either side of Ophiuchus. They are still considered a single constellation.

Bright double stars are Delta Serpentis and Theta, each with 4th and 5th magnitude components. For star clusters, turn your binoculars on Tau Serpentis and M16, which clear skies may reveal is embedded in a cloud of gas. This is the Eagle Nebula, famous for the finger-like Pillars of Creation pictured by the Hubble. M5 is a superb globular cluster that is almost a rival for M13 in Hercules in the northern sky.

SAGITTA

The Arrow is a tiny star grouping within the Milky Way. Turn a small telescope on the 5th magnitude star Zeta Sagittae to spot a 9th magnitude companion. M71 is a 7th magnitude star cluster that may be picked out in binoculars.

SEXTANS

The Sextant is a small and feeble 17th-century constellation. There is very little of interest here.

TRIANGULUM AUSTRALE

The Southern Triangle. There is not a lot to spot but use binoculars to view NGC 6025, an open cluster.

VIRGO

The virgin of the Zodiac is not a terribly prominent shape, although it has one bright, 1st magnitude star, Spica (also known as Alpha).

The Autumnal Equinox lies in Virgo, marking the point where the Ecliptic again crosses the Celestial Equator. Virgo's main prize is a huge cluster of distant galaxies around 65 million light-years away. M49, M58, M59, M60, M61, M84, M86, M87, M89 and M90 are brighter members of the cluster, which may be spotted in small telescopes. Another famous galaxy, M104, lies somewhat closer and is nicknamed the Sombrero as it resembles the hat.

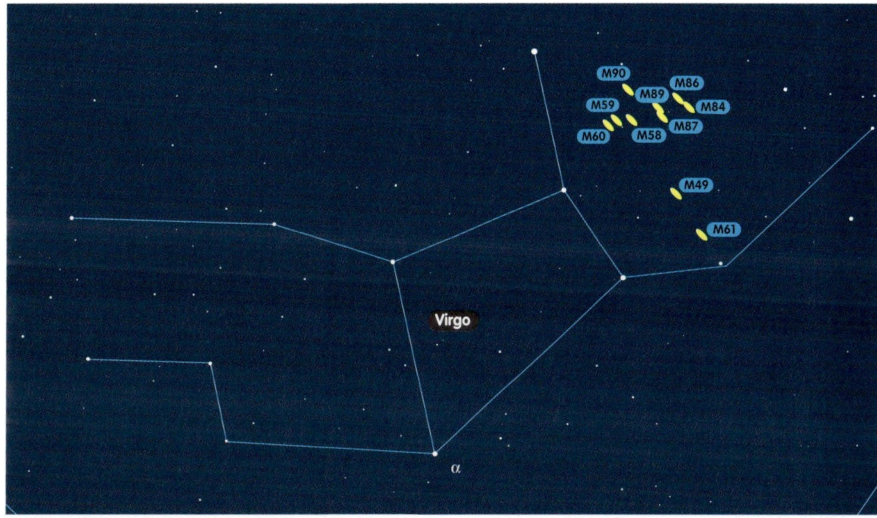

VOLANS

The Flying Fish is a faint and a far southern grouping. Gamma Volantis is a 4th magnitude white star with a 6th magnitude yellow companion.

VELA

The sail is the final part of the old broken-up sailing ship Argo Navis in the southern sky. Binoculars will split Gamma Velorum into a 2nd and 4th magnitude pair. Telescopes reveal two more 9th and 10th magnitude stars in the system.

The Milky Way runs through Vela and offers two binocular star clusters: IC 2391 and NGC 2547.

VULPECULA

The last of the constellations is small and faint but has some interesting inhabitants. Alpha Vulpeculae is a 4th magnitude red star. Binoculars show an unrelated 6th magnitude star close by.

A fun asterism is the Coathanger, a pattern of stars that looks just like that household item. Vulpecula is also home to M27, the Dumbbell, which is said to be the easiest planetary nebula to make out in the sky.

EQUIPMENT NEEDED TO BE AN ASTRONOMER

Astronomers do not need to pay out on a lot of expensive gear to get started. The truth is that you don't need any equipment to enjoy observing the sky, apart from your eyes.

Although you will not be able to obtain close-up views of the Moon and planets, there is plenty more to see. It can be very helpful to get to know your way around the sky and learn how it changes before stepping up a gear and mastering a piece of optical equipment. Take time to learn the different star patterns, or constellations.

Start with the easy ones such as the Great Bear, or Orion, then use these as signposts to help locate other constellations nearby. The more you learn, the more quickly you will fill in the gaps to complete the celestial jigsaw. The human brain is good at making out patterns, and it will not be long before the stars appear not as random points of light scattered across the sky but as instantly recognizable shapes. You will note, as ancient man did, that they return to greet you at particular times of the year. Such familiarity was vital for our ancestors in helping them know when to plant crops, for example. For today's astronomer, it is a welcome connection with the natural rhythm of the calendar.

Learning the constellations is also a solid grounding for when you finally use a telescope and have to decide where in the sky to point it.

NAKED EYE ASTRONOMY

What sort of astronomy can you carry out with your eyes alone? You have taken your time and learned the star patterns, so where to look?

As the sky darkens you can make key observations about the elementary effects of the Earth's rotation and journey around the Sun. Did you know that, on a perfectly clear day, you can look towards the opposite horizon and watch the Earth's own shadow rising in the sky? This appears as a red-tinged, deep mauve band that lifts slowly and expands across the sky as dusk deepens, bringing the natural darkness of night. Staying with sunsets – and sunrises – note how the position of these phenomena along the horizon varies depending on the time of year.

In northern latitudes, where midsummer occurs in June, the tilt of our axis in space means the Sun rises around the north-eastern point on the horizon, rises to a high point in the sky at local noon, then sets to the north-west. In midwinter, note how the Sun rises in the south-east, struggles to get very high in the sky at all, then slinks back below the horizon in the south-west. For southern hemisphere observers, of course, these midsummer and midwinter dates are reversed.

Paul Sutherland

Comet Hale-Bopp over Stonehenge – you don't need a powerful telescope to witness incredible sights in the night sky.

While the Sun is in the sky, you can check for naked eye sunspots: those darker regions of solar activity which occasionally become big enough to be seen with the eyes alone. Only attempt to look if you have a suitable filter, such as the special specs handed out for eclipse viewing (make sure they are completely undamaged), or a number-14 welder's glass.

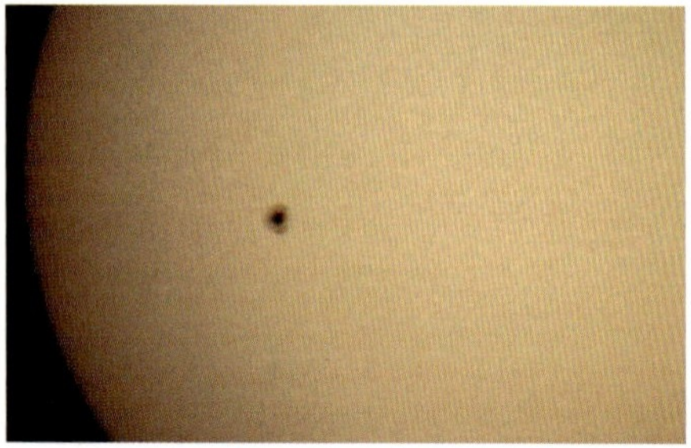

Paul Sutherland

A naked eye sunspot.

Anthony Ayiomamitis

The lunar seas of the moon can be seen with the naked eye as shown by this moonrise over Temple of Poseidon near Athens.

Do NOT attempt to use old film negatives or underexposed slides as they are not safe and will not protect your eyes. If you do see a naked eye sunspot, then you can watch it from day to day and, if it survives long enough, note how the Sun is rotating on its axis.

As the sky darkens, watch the other celestial bodies appear. The Moon may already have been visible in the daytime sky, but it will become a lot more obvious as it shines against a darker backdrop. You will not be able to see any crater detail with just your eyes, but you could note the shapes of the lunar seas – the maria – and note brighter and darker regions.

If you catch the Moon shortly after First Quarter, you can actually see a lunar mountain range, the Apennines, curving down the dark terminator that divides the shadowed part of the moon from the side in sunlight.

After the Moon, the next objects to appear will be the brighter planets. If Mercury is at a favorable elongation, look for its star-like point low towards the horizon. Brilliant Venus will reveal itself first, being the third brightest object in the sky. Indeed, if you know just where to look and have very clear blue skies, Venus can be seen in broad daylight. It may take a while to locate but, once you have found it, you will wonder how you ever missed it.

A good way to achieve this is to use a planetarium program on your computer to note when the crescent Moon lies near Venus. Then find the Moon in the daytime sky and use it as a guide to your target. Try this only when Venus is further from the Sun, around the time of elongation, and obscure the Sun behind a building or tree so that its glare does not hinder you.

As the brighter stars start to show themselves, so too will the other bright planets – Jupiter, Saturn and Mars – assuming that they are above the horizon. Note their distinctive colors and see how their light appears steady. The stars twinkle, because they are distant pinpricks of light whose brightness is distorted by the atmosphere.

An interesting project is to note the slowly-changing position of the planets against the starry background. If you plot their paths, you will see how they stick close to the ecliptic, that imaginary line through the zodiac, and see how the superior planets appear to perform their little loops in the sky as the Earth overtakes them in its orbit each year. These are fun projects, which you can also produce astronomical observations adding to scientific knowledge.

The meteor showers the Earth encounters every year are by no means predictable. Just by sitting for an hour or more assiduously watching a patch of sky, you can keep a log of the number of meteor streaks which appear. By tracing their paths backwards, you will learn to distinguish between those that are shower members and the so-called sporadics appearing any time and at random.

The more time and the more nights you are willing to spend meteor-watching, the more valuable your observations become. When combined with results from other observers around the world, such monitoring helps professional astronomers to learn about the distribution of dust through the solar system and the make-up of the meteors' parent comets. If you join a major astronomical society, it will give you advice and be happy to add your results to those of others.

Another science ideally suited to naked eye observers is following the changing brightness of variable stars. A number are bright enough to be seen without optical aid. Some, such as Cepheids or eclipsing binaries like Algol in Perseus, undergo changes which can be forecast precisely. But others, notably the red giant stars, are far less predictable and tracking these provides useful data.

With practice an observer may estimate a variable star's brightness, or magnitude, with considerable accuracy by comparing it to other stars of known fixed brightness. Once again, combining one's observations with those of others add to the precision of the results.

As you watch the stars, you will sometimes spot a light moving slowly. This is more likely than not a satellite. Experience helps one distinguish these from aircraft, which usually show more than one light. Satellites high above us shine by reflected sunlight and can be seen slowly to fade as their orbits carry them into the Earth's shadow.

The big daddy of satellites is the International Space Station, which shines as a more and more brilliant star as astronauts add new sections to it.

You can use the internet to be notified of times when the ISS passes over your location.

As well as these predictable phenomena, unexpected events occasionally occur which will interest the naked eye observer, such as the appearance of a particularly bright comet or possibly a nova exploding to brilliance deep in the galaxy. These rare events are further evidence that the sky is always changing.

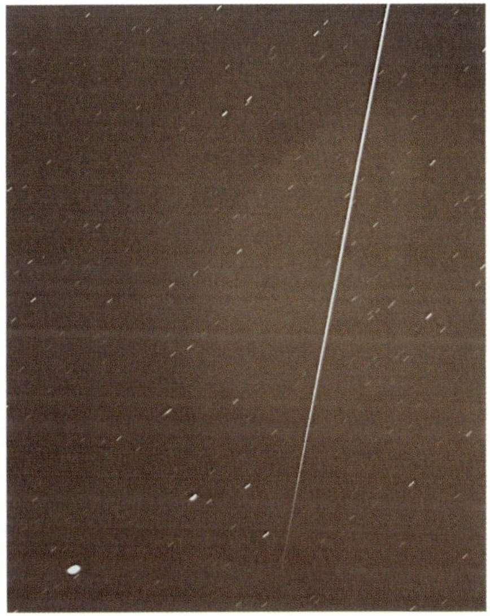

Paul Sutherland

The International Space Station is easy to spot with the naked eye. Here it fades as it flies into the Earth's shadow.

BINOCULARS

A pair of binoculars greatly increases your observational range, since they are basically a compact pair of low-power telescopes offering a wide field of view. This makes them ideal for viewing star clusters and nebulae as well as the brighter comets. Even if you acquire a telescope, binoculars remain an invaluable item of equipment.

Binoculars are generally very reasonably priced. As always, be careful when purchasing: some are little more than toys while others, often advertised in newspapers, offer high, unrealistic magnifications making them almost impossible to use.

Binoculars are usually described in terms of their magnification and the diameter of their lenses in millimeters. So a pair of

10x50s, for example, have twin lenses, each 2in/50mm across, and a magnifying power of 10. A pair of that size will offer an ideal tool for scanning the night sky, producing wide views rich with stars. Another popular and useful size is 8x30. It's best not to pick much greater magnifying power, as they will also magnify shaking hand movements by the same degree.

Pocket binoculars with smaller lenses collect a lot less light and are not recommended, except as a spare traveling pair. At the other end of the scale, are binoculars with 3.9in/100mm or 4.9in/125mm lenses and a magnification of 25-30 times. These expensive instruments are designed to be placed on solid mountings like telescopes and will be heavy and unwieldy without.

A typical view of the moon as seen through a pair of binoculars.

You may find it a strain to hold binoculars for long periods of time, especially while pointing them up at the sky. And, if you cannot hold your binoculars steady, it will be difficult to keep the objects you are observing in view. You can buy simple attachments which allow mounting binoculars on a photographer's tripod. If that is not possible, you may be able to support your elbows by observing from a garden chair or leaning against a wall.

Be careful not to drop your binoculars; heavy impact may dislodge the prisms which help fold the light path into a compact size. This will put the two barrels of the binoculars out of alignment and, even if it's by too slight an amount for you to notice, could cause headaches.

If you buy binoculars at a store, make sure you give them a basic checkover, and ask to look through them outside so that you can view a distant object. You can then at least tell if there is anything seriously wrong with their alignment. You may feel self-conscious doing this, but it's as useful as lying on a bed in a furniture store before purchase.

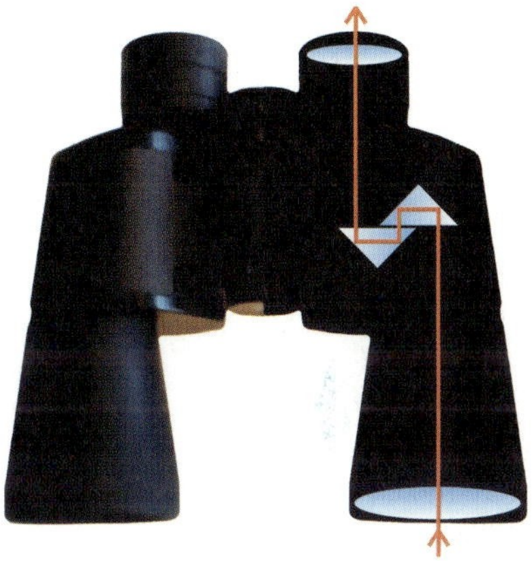

Peter Grego

A cutaway diagram shows how light passes through prisms in popular binoculars.

A recent and expensive development has been image-stabilizing binoculars. These work because they contain a special prism which instantly adjusts its alignment to counter the movements of your hands.

Image-stabilizing binoculars are pricey but can compensate for shaking hands .

TELESCOPES

Telescopes come in many shapes and sizes, but they all perform the same function: collecting radiation from space and magnifying it.

Dave Pearson

A 6in reflector is a useful and portable telescope. Here an observer peers through the finder to line up on a target.

Optical telescopes collect light while other professional telescopes may collect signals from other parts of the rainbow-like electromagnetic spectrum – radio telescopes observe radio waves, for example.

The optical telescopes used by amateur astronomers come in various forms, but all work in the same way: by collecting more light from an object than the eye can manage alone, and focusing it so that it can be viewed.

In a simple refracting telescope, or refractor, the light-collecting part is a large lens called an objective. Its curved surfaces take parallel rays of light from an object and refract them along a tube towards the point where they converge. The distance of this point from the lens determines its focal length.

A second important element of the refractor is the eyepiece: a magnifying lens, or set of lenses, used to magnify the image produced by the main lens. Astronomers normally use

A medium-sized refracting telescope on an equatorial mount is ideal for viewing planets.

a range of eyepieces to observe objects at different levels of magnification.

The second basic type of optical telescope is the Newtonian reflecting telescope, or

Yoji Hirose

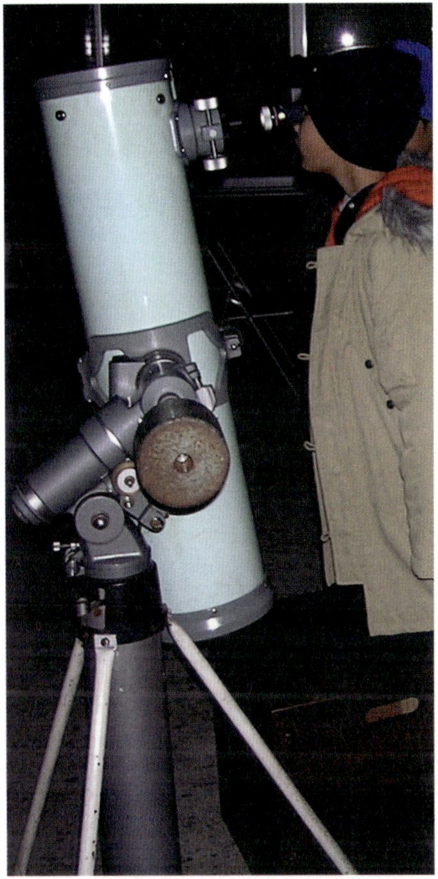

An 8in reflector is a useful size for observing galaxies, clusters and planets. Reflecting telescopes avoid false color problems but can slip out of alignment more easily than refractors.

reflector. Invented by Sir Isaac Newton, this instrument uses a curved mirror called the primary, a sophisticated version of the shaving mirror, which sits at the bottom of a tube and collects the light.

Light rays are directed back up the tube to a much smaller, flat mirror, at a 45 degree angle, called the secondary. This directs the light out through a hole in the side of the tube, where the eyepiece is placed in its focusing mount.

The main mirror's curve is usually parabolic in shape, although smaller, cheaper models may be ground to a simpler spherical form.

With either a refracting telescope or a reflector, the greater the size of your objective or primary mirror, the more light you will receive from the object you are observing and, generally speaking, the more you will be able to magnify it. Dividing the focal length of the telescope by the diameter of the objective or mirror will tell you the telescope's focal ratio. You can combine this with the focal length of the eyepiece to work out the power of magnification needed.

The greater the curve of the lens or mirror, the shorter the focal length and the smaller the focal ratio. Planetary observers look for long focal lengths because it gives them more detail to view on their favored targets. Amateurs who prefer to observe star clusters, galaxies and nebulae often choose the shorter focal lengths, because the instruments let them view wider areas of the sky with brighter stars and other objects. These instruments are often termed Rich-Field Telescopes, or RFTs.

Both these two main types of telescope have their fans. Refractors are especially convenient as smaller, portable telescopes. The smallest useful size is usually considered to have an objective lens 60mm in diameter. Reflectors are cheaper to build when it comes to larger instruments, and some amateurs are today working with mirrors 20in or more in diameter, although 6in-8in is a much more common size.

Refractors suffer an effect where light passing through the objective gets refracted to slightly different points, depending on its color. This is called chromatic aberration and leads to objects being observed showing colorful fringes around them. Telescope manufacturers attempt to counter this failing by using a combination of lenses, rather than one alone, to form the objective. The most successful, and expensive, are called apochromatic refractors, which show little, if any, signs of fringes.

There are other types of optical telescope marrying the two basic forms, and they're becoming increasingly popular with amateur astronomers. Termed catadioptric telescopes, they combine mirrors and lenses to produce a compact instrument with a long focal length. The main mirrors are spherical and so easier to manufacture, and a glass corrector plate at the top of the tube compensates

for any distortions this would normally introduce. The telescope's secondary mirror then sends the light back towards a hole in the center of the main mirror, beyond which the eyepiece is placed.The most common sort of catadioptric telescope is the Schmidt-Cassegrain. Others include the Maksutov and Ritchey-Chrétien. One point which distinguishes an astronomical telescope, and which you will notice at once if you look at Earth-bound objects, is that it turns them upside down. This so-called inverted image is accepted by astronomers. Terrestrial telescopes have another lens attachment added to turn things the right way up, but this extra bit would cut down some of that vital light from the heavens.

Similarly, some catadioptric telescopes, such as in Meade's ETX range, give a mirror image of objects, because their light is reflected three times during its passage through the compact optical arrangement.

Meade's ETX range provides a popular choice of small catadioptric telescopes that are are portable and have built-in computer controls.

Amateur astronomer Martin Lewis at a UK star party with the giant 20in reflecting telescope he built himself. Monster instruments like this offer superb views of galaxies and nebulae although portability is sacrificed.

Paul Sutherland

HOW TO CHOOSE A TELESCOPE

There has probably never been a better time to buy a telescope, since they are less expensive in real terms than they have ever been. Much of this is due to the scale of manufacture as well as construction techniques at the factories, which are often found in the Far East, particularly China. You can pay a reasonable sum, perhaps similar to the cost of a simple digital camera, and obtain an extremely useful instrument.

The important factors are that the optics are of good quality and the telescope sits on a firm mounting, because magnification you apply to an image will also magnify vibrations by a similar amount. Beware of many cheap toy telescopes, such as those found in catalogs, which may have poor lenses and flimsy support. Auction sites on the internet are also home to some rather dubious lesser-known brands.

It's also important to pick a telescope that suits your circumstances. If you live in a city apartment and need to drive out of town stargaze, you will need one which is portable and can be set up and dismantled swiftly and easily. If you have a country home with room for a permanent observatory, you will be able to consider a larger and heavier instrument.

Paul Sutherland

Astronomers with deep pockets pay large sums for top-of-the range refracting telescopes with high-quality optics. This set-up is sheltered in a purpose-designed observing tent.

Seek advice from other, experienced amateurs. If you join a local astronomical group grab the chance to look through other members' telescopes and find the one that suits you best. Many groups organize observing sessions or star parties, where you can check out an array of instruments. Although the entry prices for telescopes is generally reasonable, it is still as true in amateur astronomy, as in other areas of life, that you get what you pay for.

For the highest-quality telescopes with particularly fine optics, metal tubes and other parts, plus a really solid mounting, you will be asked to part with a lot more money.

Another important point with cheaper telescopes is that the manufacturers often save on costs by providing two or three very basic eyepieces. It's generally well worth investing in at least two or three good quality eyepieces straight away. You can buy these without breaking the bank, the improvement in telescope performance will be huge.

EYEPIECES AND OTHER ACCESSORIES

The most important accessory for your telescope is the eyepiece. With your telescope, you may have already received two or three, to give you different powers of magnification.

If you have one of the cheaper telescopes, your eyepieces will probably contain simple lenses. Better quality eyepieces, which you should consider buying, consist of a more sophisticated arrangement of higher grade lenses arranged in a metal tube called a barrel. They are made to standard diameters, with basic models having a barrel diameter of 1.25in, so you can switch from your cheap eyepieces to quality optics without much fuss. Serious amateurs often adapt their telescopes to use eyepieces 2in in diameter.

Eyepieces are available in a number of different forms, depending on their physical design. These include the kellner, the orthoscopic, the ramsden and the erfle. But the industry today seems to have settled on one design, called the plossl, for most telescopes made for amateur astronomers.

Whereas telescopes are usually described by the diameter of their primary lens or mirror, eyepieces get described by their focal lengths – 0.4in/10mm, 0.8in/20mm and so on. These will magnify by different amounts, depending on the telescope.

Divide the focal length of the telescope by the focal length of the eyepiece, making sure you use the same units in each case. So if you have a refractor with a focal length of 19in/480mm and you insert a 0.8in/20mm eyepiece, your magnification will be 24 times. Switch to a 0.35in/9mm eyepiece and the magnification becomes 53 times.

You can find eyepieces with much shorter focal lengths, but there will be practical limits, depending on the size of your telescope and therefore its light-collecting ability, as well as the steadiness of the atmosphere on any particular night. If atmospheric currents are making Jupiter wobble, it will be better to observe with a lower power eyepiece. On rare nights of

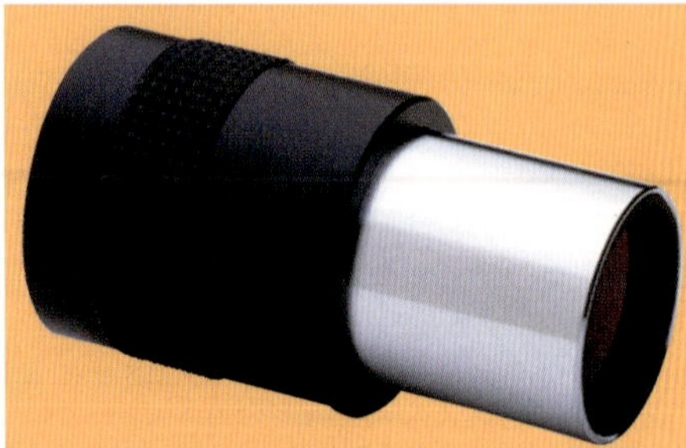

Eyepieces come in many different types, shapes and sizes, and their designs offer different magnifications and apparent fields of view. A barlow lens, like that pictured on the left, can be placed between an eyepiece and telescope to increase the power of magnification.

Invest in a foam-lined aluminium case to protect eyepieces in transit.

still air, when the planet barely ripples, you can switch to higher powers.

The telescope may also arrive with something else resembling an eyepiece, called a barlow lens. This device increases the magnification of any eyepiece that is inserted into it, usually by two times. It can therefore double the capabilities of your entire collection of eyepieces.

A wedge-shaped item in the telescope package is likely to be a star diagonal, into which eyepieces are inserted. This holds a prism directing the light passing through a telescope at a 90 degree angle. It can make observing an object high in the sky much more comfortable when using a refractor, because it saves you having to stoop down and squint up the tube. The barlow lens and star diagonal with cheaper telescopes are likely to be of very basic quality, and you may want to upgrade.

The finderscope or finder is a smaller and simple telescope attached to the side of the main tube which helps line up on a celestial object. These can be tricky to use, and it's wise to ensure that yours is aligned correctly with the telescope by testing on, say, a distant chimney pot or radio mast during daylight. Get that in the center of a high-power eyepiece, clamp the telescope so that it cannot wander, then adjust the finder screws to make sure the object lies in the center of its field of view as well.

An increasing trend is for finderscopes to be replaced by a red dot finder that uses an LED to project a virtual bright dot, which is pointed at the target.

If you are starting out, invest in a special eyepiece and filter kit that comes already cased. The range of eyepieces will suit many observing situations and the filters, though not essential, will help bring out colors or add contrast when you are viewing nebulae or observing detail.

MOUNTINGS

When choosing a telescope, don't neglect the mounting. Its quality is as important as any other part of the instrument.

A small refracting telescope on a simple alt-azimuth mount which would make an appropriate starter instrument for a child.

Superb optics are of little use if they are supported by a rickety mount which vibrates at the slightest touch. Those vibrations will magnify greatly and ruin attempts to observe when you look through the scope.

A shop-bought telescope usually comes with a tripod, which may be made of aluminum or wood. At the top of the tripod is the mount. There are two basic types – the alt-azimuth and the equatorial mounts – although you will find them in various forms.

Alt-azimuth mounts are the simplest and will swivel the telescope in two directions: up and down in altitude – the alt bit – and around parallel to the horizon – the azimuth. This is a perfectly adequate way of using a telescope for terrestrial viewing and for simple star spotting. But after just a few moments of astronomical use, you will discover the limitations.

Earlier in the book, we described the basic geometry of the celestial sphere and how the sky appears to turn as the Earth rotates. From most parts of the globe, any astronomical body will seem to drift in both altitude and azimuth during this process. This means that you will have to keep moving your telescope sideways and up or down simultaneously to keep it in your field of view. The only exceptions are if you live on the Equator, where you will simply have to move the scope vertically, or at the north or south pole, where you will only need to swing it horizontally.

All alt-azimuth mounts, whatever the designs, will perform in the same fashion. You might find one atop a tripod supporting a cheap refractor. A different type turns the popular Dobsonian reflecting telescope, where the rotating parts are close to the ground.

Many modern 'goto' telescopes come with an alt-azimuth mount but the built-in computer adjusts both elevation and azimuth constantly to keep the instrument on target.

Meade's computerized LX200 range of telescopes uses fork mounts which can be set up in alt-azimuth or equatorial mode.

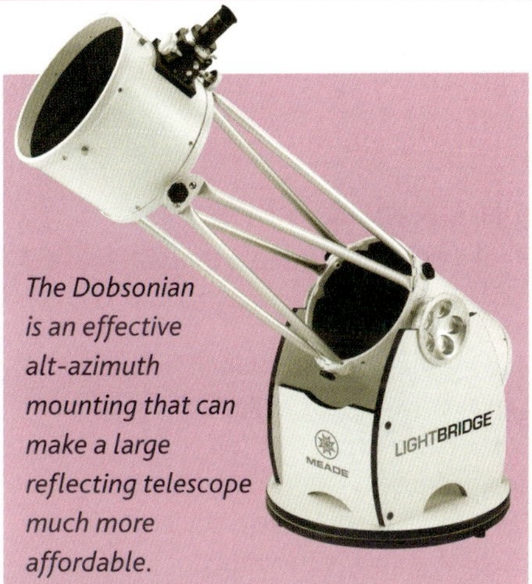

The Dobsonian is an effective alt-azimuth mounting that can make a large reflecting telescope much more affordable.

Equatorial mounts were designed to make astronomers' lives easier, although they can seem a difficult concept to grasp for a beginner. The central shaft, or polar axis, of the mounting is angled to point towards the north or south celestial pole, so that it is aligned with the Earth's own axis. This allows the telescope again to be moved in two directions, but instead of those being horizontally and vertically, they are parallel with the Right Ascension and Declination coordinates of the celestial sphere.

The beauty of the equatorial mount is that, once the telescope is pointed at a star or planet, it will then only have to be turned on one axis to follow that object as the Earth rotates. An electric motor drive may be fitted to turn the telescope automatically, and nowadays this often uses a computerized system.

For the system to work, it is essential that the mount is aligned correctly in the first place.

If you live in the northern hemisphere, you will first need to place your tripod mount so that it stands level and the polar axis is lined up in the direction of north on the horizon. A clamp will allow you to alter the angle at which the shaft points upwards. Make sure that this angle corresponds with the latitude of your own location. In London, for example, the polar axis should be turned to an angle of 51 degrees. In New York, this angle should be 41 degrees.

With the aid of a compass, you should be able to set up your mounting in this way in daylight and it will serve you well for casual viewing. For even more precise orientation, more expensive mounts contain a mini-telescope within the polar axis, so that you can make sure that Polaris, the star that lies close to the north celestial pole, is properly positioned.

In the southern hemisphere, the procedure is very similar except that you should align your mount's polar axis in a southerly direction and then adjust its angle to your own latitude south of the equator. It should be 34 degrees, for example, for an astronomer living in Sydney, Australia.

A popular form of the equatorial mount is the German mounting, on which the telescope tube is held to one side of the polar axis, on the end of the declination axis. This requires a suitable counterweight to be placed on the other side of the declination axis to maintain balance.

Another form of equatorial mount has the optical telescope sitting in a fork-type mounting on top of the polar axis. This is commonly used to mount giant professional telescopes, although Meade's ETX is held in the same way when set up equatorially.

A small, computer-controlled telescope from Celestron, fitted with a solar filter.

GETTING READY

A golden rule when planning an observing session is: make sure you are comfortable. Observing in shirt-sleeves may be possible in some lucky parts of the world, but in many others nights can feel very cold indeed, even after a warm, sunny day.

The most spectacular comet in the sky can seem a lot less appealing if you are wearing just a thin top and the temperature is below zero. Any strong breeze will make it seem colder than usual, due to what weathermen call the wind-chill factor. It may seem obvious, but try to find an observing spot that is sheltered from the wind.

So make sure you are well wrapped up, preferably in several layers to help trap the air, and with a wind-resistant outer coat. A woolly hat is important as considerable body heat is lost from the head. Choose thick socks and good boots to keep your feet warm. It can help if you stand on a mat to help insulate yourself further against the cold ground. You will probably need a pair of warm gloves too, and fingerless mittens can be very useful if you are taking notes or operating fiddly controls on your telescope.

Skiwear is ideal, even if you are not going anywhere near any mountains or snow.

It is important to wear suitable clothes.

Some of the gear that an amateur might use to observe and take notes. Fingerless mittens make them easier to handle.

Mainstream stores now offer outfits at reasonable prices, and often discounts on last year's fashions.

A deckchair will make life easier for binocular users sweeping the heavens for clusters and nebulae, particularly if it has arms on which to rest your elbows. It also makes life a lot more comfortable if you are simply observing with your eyes. Being able to lean back in a relaxed position will also help you to avoid getting a cricked neck. Another option for binocular observers is to place the instrument on a tripod. Remember to take a few snacks and a hot drink with you if you are going to be viewing for long periods of time.

If you are using a telescope, make sure it is positioned so that you can view through it comfortably. You might be able to extend the legs of the tripod, for example, or sit on a stool to look through the eyepiece more comfortably.

But however cold it is, try not to be tempted to take your telescope indoors to observe. If you point your instrument through a window to view your target, the warmth of the house will create air currents that will distort the image and make proper observing impossible, especially at higher magnifications.

Observing is not much fun if you drop something vital, like a screw, and then have to scrabble around to find it in the darkness. One solution is to put down a groundsheet or blanket before setting up your telescope, so that it catches anything that falls.

PROBLEMS THAT OBSERVERS FACE

Astronomy comes with its disappointments. Many a night you will find your observing plans thwarted by bad weather, or an eclipse of the Sun can be obscured by clouds.

The vagaries of the climate are a major problem for astronomers and, to be honest, there's not a lot that one can do about it aside from getting to know how weather patterns work.

Neither can we do much about the fact that the Moon, at its brightest phases, will conspire to drown out many of the fainter and more delicate sights we might want to see.

Even a sparse amount of cloud cover can spoil your view.

The trick is to plan your observing sessions to take account of the best times to see the best sights. Reserve nights around New Moon for hunting out deep sky targets and then use the moonlit nights to study the fascinating features found on our natural satellite.

Another enemy of the astronomer is light pollution. Everyone is keen to be environment-minded these days, but we continue to drown out the wonders of the sky in a luminous fog. Even with improvements in streetlight design, too much wasted light is spread into the heavens. The situation is often exacerbated by the proliferation of domestic security lighting pointing upwards to the skies.

A century ago, people could step outside their homes and stare up at a dark sky studded with stars. Today, in many parts of the world, they will see nothing but an orange haze.

There are organizations battling to reverse or at least control the damage, but we have a long way to go before we can t look out and appreciate our place in the universe.

In many heavily populated regions of the world, we have to travel away from home to enjoy an interest in astronomy. Always be aware of your personal safety and be careful, also, not to trespass.

Paul Sutherland

The lamp on the left will shine light directly downwards, replacing the old lamp that spreads light in all directions.

The long white trail running through the center is a space station that has been captured as it heads towards orbit. Light pollution has made this bright orbiting outpost harder to see.

Observing is not much fun if you find a nice country spot only to be bothered by strange animal noises, a worried farmer, courting couples or a police patrol. There's nothing like headlights on full beam to ruin a session observing faint galaxies.

Astronomy is often a solitary pursuit but you might feel a lot more comfortable sharing a remote observing session with a fellow enthusiast.

Even if the sky is cloud-free, the weather can still affect observation. You will want to make sure you are sheltered if a strong wind is blowing, and certain times of year can bring the curse of the night: humidity.

When telescopes cool in humid air, they quickly collect dew, producing a film of water across the optics and making observing very difficult.

Amateur astronomers counter this in various ways. Extend the length of your telescope's dew cap, or create one, by wrapping a sheet of black paper, plastic or foam into a cylinder around the front end of the tube. How about taking the telescope into a shed or outhouse for a short while now and again, to allow it to warm up?

You can buy special anti-dew heaters which coil around the telescope's objective lens to warm it up and prevent dew from forming. Some people use portable hair-dryers to give the optics a quick blast and clear them every now and again.

Nights that appear to be clear can still provide very different viewing conditions, and what may seem a wonderful frosty night with sparkling stars may be a disappointment through the telescope. On such nights, a planet might seem to jump around and show little detail, because the atmosphere is unstable. On other exceptional nights, all may seem particularly calm with the planets steady and revealing more. Astronomers describe these changing conditions as "the seeing".

Incidentally, you may notice nights when the stars twinkle but planets don't. This is because we see even the closest stars to us as just points of light. The planets are tiny disks, even if they are not obvious to the naked eye, and so the distortion by the atmosphere is less spectacular.

Clouds rolling in as evening approaches can mean disappointment and a wasted night for an astronomer.

SKETCHING AND RECORDING

Don't expect to be able to observe the intricacies of the sky immediately. The eyes are remarkably efficient at adapting to a wide range of brightnesses, but it takes time for them to adapt.

You will have noticed a similar effect when you go from the light into a dark room. You see nothing at first, but as your eyes adjust and pupils grow larger, you are able to make out objects.

When you step out beneath a dark sky, your eyes will take several minutes to be at their most sensitive and become, as astronomers say, "dark adapted". So go for the brighter targets in the sky first, before you attempt to hunt out a faint object such as a nebula. Avoid white lights while you are observing, which might mean closing your eyes or looking away if car headlights suddenly appear.

Fortunately, the eyes are a lot less sensitive to red light, so you can check out star charts or an observing guide by using a torch covered with red film or with red LEDs.

Use a red light so you don't ruin your "dark adapted" vision.

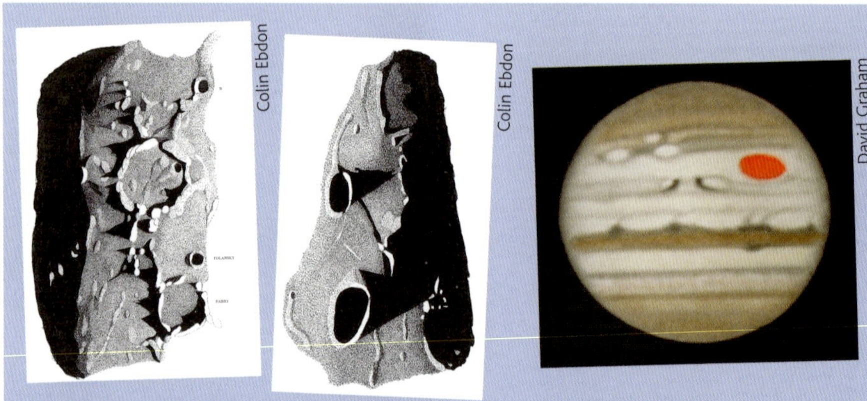

Despite the popularity of imaging equipment, it is still rewarding to make your own sketches, such as those here of lunar craters Guericke, left, Diophantus and Delisle, and planet Jupiter.

When you are at the telescope, even if you are dark adapted and the seeing is ideal, you should not expect to see all there is in an object straight away. A cursory glance at Saturn, for example, will show the ball of the planet and its rings, but it takes time and experience to discern the subtle shadings in the image.

In an age when we expect instant gratification, it can be immensely rewarding to take the time and patience to look at an object carefully. It's doubly rewarding if you keep notes or make sketches of what you are observing. You don't need to be a great artist; just some simple shadings can give an indication of what you saw. The result will be that, in time, you build up a fascinating observing log –

something to enjoy looking through on those cloudy nights years later.

When you have gained experience in drawing the planets, the Moon's craters, or a nebula or galaxy in deep space, you may find that your observations will be welcomed by of the larger astronomical societies collecting records of members' work. Many supply special template forms, called blanks, for you to sketch on. Observers usually make a rough sketch of a planet at the eyepiece and then make a copy on such a form for sending to the society.

It is quite normal, by the way, to sketch, say, a nebula in a negative way, with the brightest areas shown darkest and the dark sky left white. The human brain is able to invert an image in this way.

Similar template forms are provided for written observations of other celestial events, such as meteor showers or variable stars. The work amateurs do in these areas provides a valuable service to professional astronomers researching these phenomena.

If you're observing meteors, amateur organizations are keen that contributors keep watch on nights other than those of predicted maximum activity, and even on nights when there are no known showers and only the sporadics on view. This way we learn more about the level of meteor activity throughout the year.

If you are monitoring variable stars, be careful not to allow bias to affect your work. Be ready for anything, and report what you actually see. Just because a star has been brightening and might be expected to be brighter still when you are looking, does not mean that it really will be. Try to keep an open mind.

The American Association of Amateur Astronomers

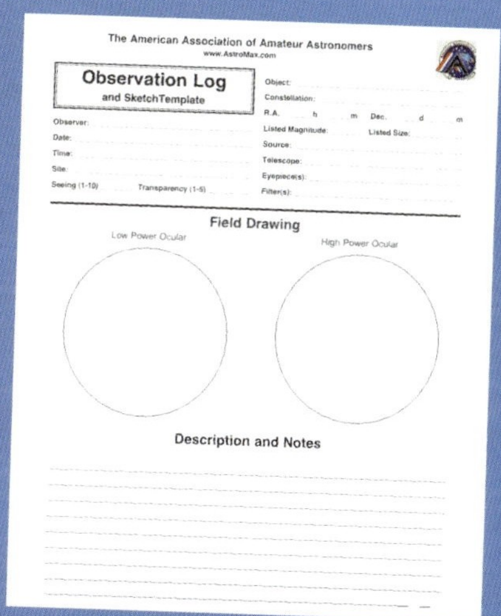

An example of one of the templates provided by larger astronomical societies.

American Association of Variable Star Observers

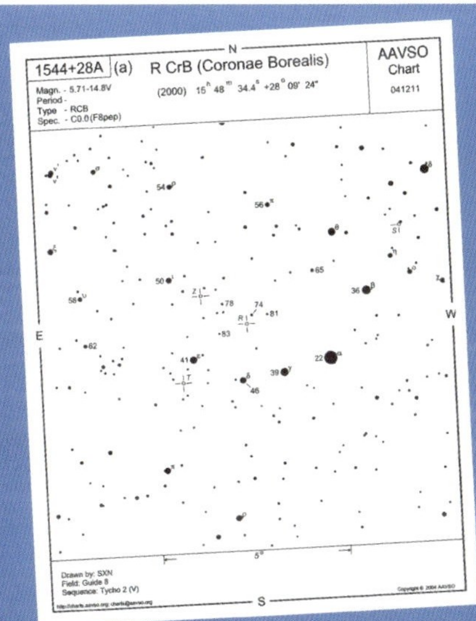

Specialist groups provide charts to help locate and estimate the brightness of variable stars.

PHOTOGRAPHING THE SKY

Photography is an excellent way to record astronomical events. Astrophotography is an increasingly popular method, though we are usually working with much lower levels of light than we have in daytime photography.

You will often want to experiment with different exposures and other settings, if that is possible with your camera, to obtain decent results. The great advantage of modern digital cameras is that you can see straight away whether you have been successful and adjust accordingly.

A time-exposure of a few minutes will be enough for stars to trail in your photograph as the Earth rotates.

If you have a basic camera and have to take a quick snapshot of the night sky, the chances are that little, if anything, will show. You will be limited to twilight landscape shots with perhaps a crescent Moon or Venus in the picture. To record anything more of the stars, your camera will need to be capable of taking time exposures. This ability is built into single lens reflex (SLR) cameras, whether film or digital, where it may be shown as the Bulb, or B, setting.

The Bulb setting enables you to open the shutter and release it after a chosen amount of time has elapsed. Place your camera on a tripod and use a cable release to take the exposure to produce images that do not show camera shake. Better digital SLRs allow you to control the exposure with a cable directly from your computer. Remember to turn off the flash.

Cameras allow you to set an exposure of several seconds. If you have no cable release, use this setting, together with the

shutter delay that is usually intended to allow photographers to become the subjects of their own pictures. This work around will avoid the shake introduced by pressing the shutter button with your finger.

It will only require a very few seconds of exposure before a surprising number of stars record on your image. If you are using a standard lens and your exposure lasts longer than 15 to 20 seconds, you will notice that the stars appear stretched. They are beginning to show trailing, the effect of the rotation of the Earth.

The way to avoid this effect in longer time exposures is to mount your camera on a guided platform that counteracts the Earth's rotation. You could mount it piggyback on a telescope with a motor drive, for example – but it will need to be properly aligned.

You will find practical limits in the exposures that you take, such as the amount of light pollution that will build up in your image, and the electronic "noise" that may build up in a digital camera. But your shots could indicate, for example, how, they stars circle the celestial poles in little arcs, the stars' paths are longer and straighter around the celestial equator. If you are using film, you may find that the stars' colors show clearly in your exposures. Unfortunately, digital cameras seem less capable of recording star color in such shots.

The sensitivity of different types of film to light used to be measured by its ISO rating, such as 100 ISO, 200 ISO, 400 ISO. This determines the speed of the film, the higher numbers being faster. The system is still used following the arrival of digital photography, although everything is handled electronically.

Faster settings are very effective at capturing fainter stars, but the longer the exposure, the greater the risk that light pollution will build up. Digital cameras may suffer the additional problem of electronic noise, which shows itself as bright dots or patches in your pictures. Noise reduction systems are usually built in, with varying degrees of success. It's worth experimenting with different exposure times and ISO speeds to test the results.

Paul Sutherland

This shot of the Moon was taken with a snapshot camera attached to the eyepiece of a small telescope.

Obviously, the major benefit of digital imaging is that you can import your photos directly into a computer for processing and enhancing. For greatest flexibility during processing, take your images at the camera's RAW setting, if it has one, although you need the relevant software that can handle this format.

Long exposures with digital cameras, or electronic film cameras can run down camera batteries, so make sure you carry a spare. They don't last so long in cold conditions. This is an area where the old mechanical SLR cameras come into their own.

If you have a telescope, you could hold the camera to a focused eyepiece and fire a few shots of the Moon. Its surface brightness is comparable to snapping a landscape view on Earth, so your camera may well give you a pleasing result. Some amateurs, just for fun, have even tried such snaps with the cameras built into mobile phones, with recognizable results!

This superb picture of Saturn was taken using a CCD camera, then enhanced

Dave Tyler

The difficulty with using this "afocal" approach is lining up the camera and eyepiece correctly. If the camera is only slightly tilted, the Moon's image will miss the film or chip in the camera. You could mount your camera on a tripod alongside the telescope to help, although you would need to keep moving the set-up as the Moon drifts out of view due to the rotation of the Earth. Another option is to purchase adaptors which allow you to clamp the camera over the eyepiece, or even join the two together.

Camera adaptors (T-mounts)

You may get simple snaps of the brighter planets in this way. Just don't expect much in the way of detail.

The same techniques may be used with video cameras, although attaching any heavy device to the telescope can cause problems balancing the instrument's weight.

If you have an SLR camera, you may be able to remove the lens from your camera and then attach the telescope without its eyepiece, so it effectively becomes a telephoto lens. This is called prime focus photography and usually requires a simple adapter for the telescope, plus a T-mount specific to your camera model.

A lucky gift for astrophotography was the appearance of the webcam in computing.

The device's sensitivity to low light makes it useful for recording images of the Moon and planets through the telescope. It's also light enough to be attached without the balancing problems introduced by normal cameras. You can buy adapters that screw into the front of the webcam and allow it to sit in the eyepiece holder.

More sophisticated CCD cameras are produced specially for astronomy. These contain a charge-coupled device, which is a chip with an array of sensors that are highly receptive to the levels of light involved. The chips are generally cooled to reduce vastly any noise on the image from the electronics.

Images taken with webcams and their more sophisticated (and costly) CCD cousins can be processed with computers, to produce extraordinary results.

Eclipses can be fun to photograph. For solar eclipses, you will need the same sort of filters as you would use for viewing, otherwise you will quickly damage or destroy your camera. Lunar eclipses are a safe target but require a range of different exposures, depending on whether you are bringing out the part of the Moon still in sunlight or the region that is in shadow.

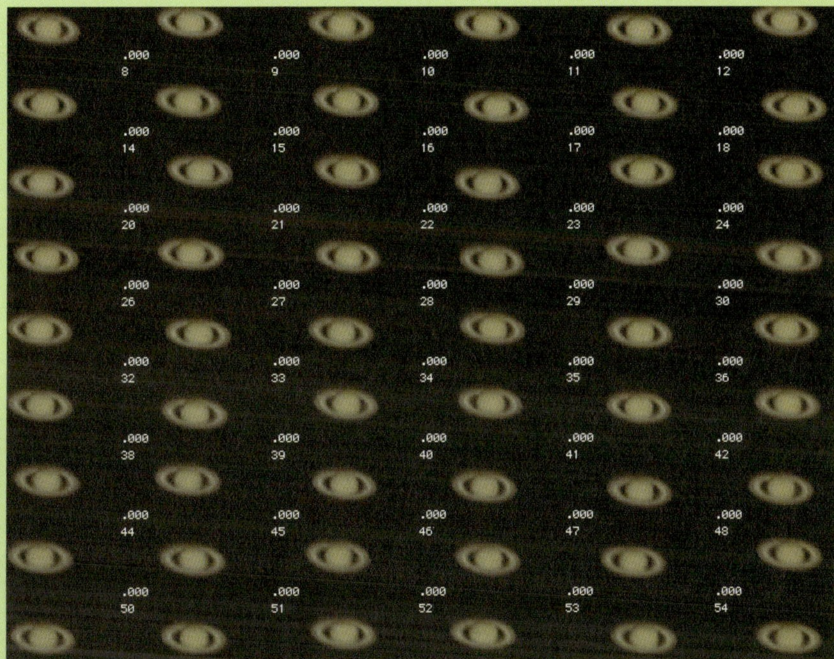

Paul Sutherland

These are individual frames from a web-cam "movie" through a small telescope. Best frames were selected and stacked to form a final image.

Paul Sutherland

A final enhanced webcam image of Saturn.

COMPUTERS

Computers have made a major impact on every walk of life, and astronomy is no exception. Professional scientists use them extensively to process and analyze data, and to control telescopes that may be far away.

Computers ease researchers' work greatly when they are studying such things as how stars or planets form. The most complex space missions to distant planets and their moons are made possible by the power of the processor.

Not to be outdone, amateur astronomers have also taken up the challenge of computing. Their telescopes are now often driven by microprocessors with databases of stellar delights that tell them where to point. But they are also, like the professionals, using their home computers to work with the data that their observations have supplied.

Digital photographs, as described in the previous section, can be transformed into high-quality images thanks to computer techniques. Many amateurs are taking webcam "movies" of planets through their telescopes.

From possibly hundreds of individual frames, the sharpest, caught during moments of excellent seeing, are selected and the rest rejected. Special software then allows the good frames to be combined, or stacked. Finally, the image that is left is enhanced using the tools within photo-editing software. The results from amateurs using such techniques can be little short of stunning.

This is cutting-edge astronomy for dedicated amateurs, but computers are helping stargazing beginners, too, with a variety of programs that allow you to produce a planetarium on your desktop. These can accurately recreate the sky for any date and time and from any location

Stellarium is an amazing piece of free software which creates a realistic view of the sky on your own home computer.

on Earth. The best programs have the capability of showing beginners a realistic view of the night sky yet may be used by advanced amateurs to obtain precise details of astronomical events, and even to control their telescopes.

One of the most realistic planetarium programs is the free and remarkable Stellarium, which is available for PCs and Macs. It was used to help create the star maps in this book.

Of course, the internet has become a valuable resource for professional and amateur scientists alike. From our homes, we have access to all manner of databases and information sources, including those provided by major observatories and space agencies such as NASA. Some services are interactive and will produce anything from a star chart for your location to predictions of times and directions to find satellites such as the International Space Station when it passes over your part of the world. Others will simply provide galleries of images from telescopes and space probes that you can spend happy hours studying.

The internet has also aided communication between astronomers. Such social networking, to use the buzz phrase, ranges from the simple blogs that act like online observing logs to busy discussion forums and chatrooms where stargazers gather to talk about the latest events and seek advice.

The world's leading astronomical societies have extended their operations into cyberspace with useful websites to help keep members informed and assisted. Some astronomical websites offer reviews of telescopes, while others act to support users of particular models.

Or, of course, you can find and buy from dealers online or scour auction sites such as for a bargain. Reference resources such as online encyclopedias can bring you bang up to date on any aspect of science, and you can sign up to email bulletins that will notify you of the latest events in astronomy or space research.

Celestron's SkyScout is a "point and shoot" tool using GPS to identify objects in the sky.

GLOSSARY

ABSOLUTE MAGNITUDE
The brightness at which a star would appear at a distance of ten parsecs (32.6 light years) from the Earth, It allowing stellar brightnesses to be compared.

ACCRETION
The collecting together of dust and debris to form stars and planets.

ALBEDO
A term to describe the reflectivity of a planetary surface.

APHELION
A planet's furthest point from the Sun in its orbit. Earth reaches this in July.

APOGEE
The furthest point in the orbit of the Moon or a satellite around the Earth.

ARC MINUTE
An angular measure of separation between two points in the sky; one sixtieth of a degree. An arc second is one sixtieth of an arc minute.

ASTERISM
A small but distinct pattern of stars within a constellation.

ASTRONOMICAL UNIT
The average distance between the Earth and the Sun: equivalent to 93 million miles/149,597,870 km..

BINARY STAR
A pair of stars revolving around a common center of mass.

BLACK HOLE
An object with a gravitational field so powerful that no light or radiation within it can escape. Anything inside the black hole's event horizon is effectively cut off from the rest of the universe.

CELESTIAL EQUATOR
An imaginary line running around the celestial sphere directly above the Earth's equator.

CHROMATIC ABERRATION
False coloring seen in cheap refracting telescopes, due to simple lenses bringing different parts of the spectrum to focus at different points.

CHROMOSPHERE
The region of the Sun between the visible surface, or photosphere, and its corona.

CONJUNCTION
A close encounter in the sky between two bodies such as planets. It also describes the point when the outer planets pass on the far side of the Sun.

CONSTELLATION
Imaginary patterns of stars in the sky, originally created by ancient man. Today there are 88 official groupings, each with defined borders.

CORONA
The outer layer of the solar atmosphere, and its hottest part.

CULMINATION
The moment when a star or other object reaches its highest point in the sky during the daily turning of the heavens.

DECLINATION
A co-ordinate on the celestial sphere corresponding to latitude on the Earth. It is used along with Right Ascension to describe an object's position in the sky.

ECCENTRICITY
A description of how much an elliptical orbit is stretched from circular.

A black hole.

ECLIPSE
The term correctly applies when a body such as a moon or satellite moves into the shadow of another body. However, it is also used to describe the passage of the Moon in front of the Sun.

ECLIPTIC
The path that the Sun appears to take against the celestial sphere as the Earth orbits it each year.

ELONGATION
The apparent distance of an astronomical object from the Sun in the sky. Greatest elongation is used to describe the point when Mercury and Venus appear furthest from the Sun.

EQUATORIAL MOUNT
A telescope mount that allows the instrument to rotate in alignment with the celestial sphere. It counters the Earth's rotation and makes it easier to follow objects as they move across the sky.

EQUINOX
The date in March or September when the Earth's orbit makes the Sun appear to cross the Celestial Equator.

GALAXY
Vast 'cosmic cities' of many billions of stars held together by gravitational force.

GLOBULAR CLUSTER
A roughly spherical collection of older stars. They are often found in haloes around galaxies.

GRANULATION
The crystallized appearance of the visible surface of the Sun, caused by convection currents.

INCLINATION
The amount by which the plane of a planet or comet's orbit is tilted to the ecliptic.

INFERIOR PLANETS
Planets that lie inside the orbit of the Earth and are therefore closer to the Sun. They are Mercury and Venus.

KUIPER BELT
The region beyond Neptune where many thousands of icy, comet-like bodies are believed to lurk. Pluto is now thought to be part of this belt.

LIGHT YEAR
The distance that light travels in a year. The speed of light in a vacuum is 983,571,056ft/299,792,458m per second.

LUNATION
The length of time between one New Moon and the next.

MAGNETOSPHERE
A natural magnetic force field around a planet such as Earth that protects it from the solar wind.

MAGNITUDE
The scale by which stars' brightnesses are measured: the bigger the number, the fainter the star. Apparent magnitude describes how bright the stars appear. Bright stars such as Capella and Vega are zero magnitude. The faintest stars visible with the unaided eye in ideal conditions are around magnitude six. Absolute magnitude is the brightness they would show if all were placed at the same distance.

Stars in the filaments of a nebula.

A spiral galaxy.

METEOR
The streak of light seen in the sky as a particle of debris vaporizes in the atmosphere. The particle itself, usually no bigger than a grain of sand, is called a meteoroid. Larger rocks that reach the ground are called meteorites.

NEBULA
A cloud of gas and dust. A nebula may shine by reflecting starlight or by being excited by stars within it, or it may be dark and reveal itself by blotting out stars further away.

NOCTILUCENT CLOUDS
Shimmering midnight clouds high in the atmosphere, seen particularly in summer months. Also known as mesospheric clouds.

OCCULTATION
The passage of one celestial body in front of another, such as the Moon in front of a star or planet. An eclipse of the Sun should properly be termed an occultation.

OPEN CLUSTER
A related collection of stars, randomly scattered.

OPPOSITION
The point when one of the outer planets is opposite the Sun in the sky.

ORBIT
The path one body, such as a planet or moon, takes around another with which it is gravitationally linked.

PARALLAX
The angular shift against the starry background that a closer object shows when viewed from two widely separated points, for example, opposite sides of the Earth's orbit.

PARSEC
A unit of measurement, equal to 3.2616 light years, used to describe huge distances in space.

PENUMBRA
The lighter outer shadow through which the Moon travels during a lunar eclipse. The term also describes the lighter surroundings of a dark sunspot.

PERIGEE
The closest point in the Moon's or a satellite's orbit around the Earth.

PERIHELION
The point at which an orbiting planet or comet is closest to the Sun. The Earth is at perihelion in January.

PHOTOSPHERE
The Sun's visible surface on which sunspots are often seen.

PLANETARY NEBULA
A shell of gas ejected by a dying red giant star. It has nothing to do with planets and was so called because its shape resembled a planetary disk.

PRECESSION
A slow circular wobble of the Earth's axis over a period of 27,700 years. It means that Polaris, which roughly marks the position of the north celestial pole, is only temporarily the "pole star".

PROMINENCE
An ejection of hot gas into the Sun's corona. Special solar telescopes show them leaping from the edge of the Sun into space.

PULSAR
A rapidly spinning, collapsed neutron star left by a supernova. Pulsars can rotate hundreds of times a second, emitting radio signals so regular that it was briefly thought they might be from aliens when they first were discovered in 1967.

A bright aurora.

QUASAR
A highly luminous object at a vast distance, thought to be the active nucleus of a galaxy around a supermassive black hole. Short for Quasi-stellar radio source.

RADIANT
The point in the sky from which meteors in a meteor shower appear to come. It is purely an effect of perspective because the meteoroids are traveling in parallel paths. Meteor showers are usually named after the constellation in which the radiant lies.

RED SHIFT
An effect that causes the signature lines marking the elements in a spectrum to shift towards the red in light from an object moving away from the observer at great speed.

RIGHT ASCENSION (RA)
The co-ordinates on the celestial sphere that correspond to lines of longitude on the Earth. The 24 hours of RA equate to 360 degrees. RA, together with an object's Declination, will pinpoint an object's position against the sky.

SIDEREAL TIME
Time measured by the stars rather than the Sun. The Sidereal Day is 23h 56m long.

SOLAR CYCLE
An 11-year variation in activity on the Sun.

SOLSTICE
The points in June and December when the Sun reaches its most northerly or southerly position in the sky.

SUPERNOVA
A star that destroys itself in a catastrophic explosion.

TERMINATOR
The boundary between the day side and night side of a planet or moon.

UMBRA
The main dark shadow in a lunar eclipse or the central region of a sunspot.

VARIABLE STAR
A star whose brightness changes over time.

ZENITH
The point in the sky that lies directly overhead.

ZODIAC
Loved by astrologers, this is the band of sky through which the Sun and planets appear to travel.